*Dedicated to My Beloved Parents*

*K. Srinivasan*

*S.Vanitha*

# Financial Markets

Dr.S. Poornima

Published by

BONFRING®
Intellectual Integrity

**Financial Markets**



9 789385 477485 >

**ISBN 978-93-85477-48-5**

**Author**

Dr.S. Poornima

**Bonfring**
309, 2nd Floor, 5th Street Extension, Gandhipuram,
Coimbatore-641 012.
Tamilnadu, India.
E-mail: info@bonfring.org
Website: www.bonfring.org
Phone: 0422-3928700

# Preface

The subject of Financial Markets occupies an important place in the course content of Business Administration of various universities. The knowledge of this subject is very important to understand the capital markets and its functioning.

This book is especially written to cater to the needs of Commerce and Management students. It covers the syllabus of all management and commerce students. I sincerely hope that the students, faculties and other readers will find the book useful.

The contents of the book is organized into 5 units each unit dealing with a particular aspect of the Financial Management. Chapter 1 deals with financial system its nature, role, functions, issues and major players. Chapter 2 deals with financial services it objectives, scope, characteristics, functions, SWIFT, and problems. Chapter 3 gives an overview of financial markets, new issue market and intermediaries. Chapter 4 enumerates on the stock market, its role, functions, listing, registration, types of brokers, DEMAT account, and various depositories as well as stock market indices. Chapter 5 explains in detail about Merchant banking its origin, qualities, services, guidelines, functions and SEBI regulations. Chapter 6 enumerates on mutual funds its features, structures, types, benefits, regulations, measurement, and selection of funds. Chapter 7 throws light on credit rating, features, symbols, validity, functions, benefits, process, various agencies and problems in credit rating. Chapter 8 explains about venture capital, characteristics of venture capital evolution, stages, advantages, forms, venture capital in India and abroad. Chapter 9 enhances on the topic of securitization its structure, securing assets, role of institutions, benefits, conditions and scenario in India & abroad similarly in Chapter 10 an overview of derivatives, categories, functions, futures, options, swaps and its growth is explained. Finally in Chapter 11 commodities market its types, its features, exchange platform, clearing and settlement, Gold ETF's, its features, working, growth and problem is explained in detail.

All the chapters of the book have been organized in a way to develop better understanding of their contents. A comprehensive bibliography has been given to enable the readers to have a further study and research.

# Acknowledgement

I thank the Lord Almighty for giving me the strength and the ability in writing this book. I record my deep sense of gratitude and profound respect to our founder correspondent late Smt.ChandrakanthiGovindarajalu for being a constant source of inspiration for attaining perfection in all endeavors. Her support and dedication has nurtured to reach greater heights of excellence.

I have great pleasure in expressing my heartfelt thanks to our Chairperson Smt.R.Nandini for constant encouragement at all times.

I am immensely thankful to our Secretary Dr.N.Yesodhadevi and Principal Dr.S.Nirmala for their moral guidance and whole hearted support in writing this book.

I thank my Co-Faculties, family and friends who have helped in every way possible to complete this book.

I thank Deepha.B Research Scholar for her help in editing and proof reading and all my research scholars for their contribution in writing this book.

**Dr.S. Poornima**

# Author Profile

Dr.S. Poornima,
Head and Associate Professor,
Department of Business Administration,
PSGR Krishnammal College for Women,
Coimbatore.

**Dr.S. Poornima** Completed her MBA from PSG College of Technology, Coimbatore and her M.Phil and PhD from the Bharathiar University, Coimbatore. She has industrial experience of 6 years and academic experience of 26 years. Her field of specialization is Finance, Investments and Systems. She has undergone a Faculty Development Programme at IIM-A in 2009 and has Published several articles and presented papers in national and international journals. She has produce 8 PhDs, 20 M.Phils and presently guiding 6 PhD Students. She has completed UGC Sponsored Major and Minor Projects. She is the member of editorial board of national and international journals. She has won several awards for her contribution to Teaching and Research. Presently, she is serving as Head and Associate Professor in the Department of Business Administration at PSGR Krishnammal College for Women, Tamilnadu, Coimbatore.

| S. No | Contents | Page No |
|---|---|---|
| 1 | Financial System | 1 |
| | Nature | 1 |
| | Role and Importance of Financial System in Economic Development | 1 |
| | Functions of Financial System | 3 |
| | Structure of Indian Financial System | 5 |
| | An Overview of Indian Financial System | 6 |
| | Financial Instruments | 8 |
| | Issues and Challenges | 10 |
| | Global Financial System | 12 |
| | Major Players in Global Financial System | 13 |
| | Future of the Global Financial System | 14 |
| 2 | Financial Services | 16 |
| | Objectives | 16 |
| | Scope of Financial Services | 17 |
| | Characteristics &Features of Financial Services | 18 |
| | Functions of Financial Services | 19 |
| | SWIFT | 21 |
| | Growth of Financial Services | 23 |
| | Problems in Financial Services | 23 |
| 3 | Financial Markets | 25 |
| | Capital Market | 27 |
| | New Issues Market | 28 |
| | Intermediaries | 30 |
| 4 | Stock Market | 33 |
| | Role of a Stock Market | 33 |
| | Functions of Stock Market | 34 |
| | Listing | 35 |
| | Registration of Broker | 38 |
| | Different Types of Brokers | 40 |
| | Method of Trading | 41 |
| | Speculators | 43 |
| | Speculative Transactions | 45 |
| | Demat | 48 |
| | Settlement | 50 |

# 1. Financial System

A financial system(within the world of finance) is a system that allows the transfer of money between savers (and investors) and borrowers. Financial systems operate both at national and global levels or at a firm-specific level. There is a need for an effective financial system which can mobilize and channelize savings for capital formation. The efficiency of a financial system depends primarily on its ability to facilitate the flow of savings into the most productive instrument. Gurusamy in his book Financial Services and Systems has described financial systems as "a set of complex and closely interconnected financial institutions, markets, instruments, services, practices, and transactions."

A financial system is a set of financial institutions, financial instruments and financial markets, which facilitate the transfer of savings from the savers to those who can put the savings to use with the objective of achieving economic development.

Financial systems are crucial to the allocation of resources in a modern economy. They channelize household savings to the corporate sector and allocate investment funds among firms; they allow inter temporal smoothing of consumption by households and expenditures by firms; and they enable households and firms to share risks. These functions are common to the financial systems of most developed economies. Yet the form of these financial systems varies widely.

## Nature

- Establishes a bridge between savers and investors and invasion in order to transform entrepreneurial ideas into reality.
- Increases the savings as well as the investment rate.
- Makes the allocation and utilization of savings optimal and efficient.
- Influences directly as well as indirectly the volume of funds to be made available for productive activities.

## Role and Importance of Financial System in Economic Development

- It links the savers and investors. It helps in mobilizing and allocating the savings efficiently and effectively. It plays a crucial role in economic development through saving-investment process.This savings–investment process is called capital formation.
- It helps to monitor corporate performance.
- It provides a mechanism for managing uncertainty and controlling risk.
- It provides a mechanism for the transfer of resources across geographical boundaries.
- It offers portfolio adjustment facilities (provided by financial markets and financial intermediaries).
- It helps in lowering the transaction costs and increase returns. This will motivate people to save more.
- It promotes the process of capital formation.
- It helps in promoting the process of financial deepening and broadening. Financial deepening means increasing financial assets as a percentage of GDP and financial broadening means building an increasing number and variety of participants and instruments. In short, a financial system contributes to the acceleration of economic development. It contributes to growth through technical progress.

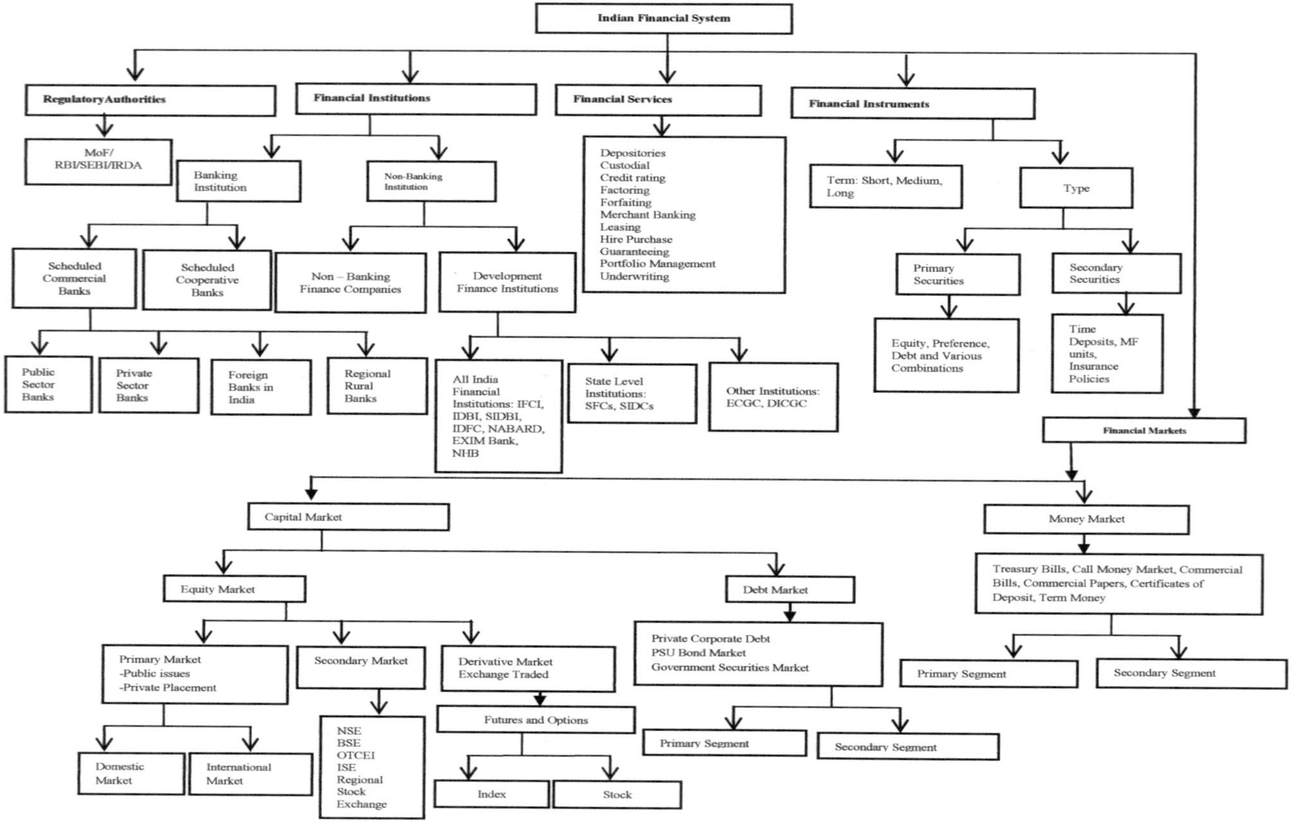

Indian Financial System
Regulatory Authorities
MoF/ RBI/SEBI/IRDA
Financial Institutions
Banking Institution
Non-Banking Institution
Scheduled Commercial Banks
Scheduled Cooperative Banks
Non – Banking Finance Companies
Development Finance Institutions
Public Sector Banks
Private Sector Banks
Foreign Banks in India
Regional Rural Banks
All India Financial Institutions: IFCI, IDBI, SIDBI, IDFC, NABARD, EXIM Bank, NHB
State Level Institutions: SFCs, SIDCs
Other Institutions: ECGC, DICGC
Financial Services
Depositories
Custodial
Credit rating
Factoring
Forfaiting
Merchant Banking
Leasing
Hire Purchase
Guaranteeing
Portfolio Management
Underwriting
Financial Instruments
Term: Short, Medium, Long
Type
Primary Securities
Secondary Securities
Equity, Preference, Debt and Various Combinations
Time Deposits, MF units, Insurance Policies
Financial Markets
Capital Market
Money Market
Treasury Bills, Call Money Market, Commercial Bills, Commercial Papers, Certificates of Deposit, Term Money
Primary Segment
Secondary Segment
Equity Market
Debt Market
Primary Market
-Public issues
-Private Placement
Secondary Market
Derivative Market Exchange Traded
Private Corporate Debt
PSU Bond Market
Government Securities Market
Domestic Market
International Market
NSE
BSE
OTCEI
ISE
Regional Stock Exchange
Futures and Options
Index
Stock
Primary Segment
Secondary Segment

## Functions of Financial System

The financial system of a country performs certain valuable functions for the economic growth of that country. The main functions of a financial system may be briefly discussed as below:

### 1. *Saving Function*

An important function of a financial system is to mobilize savings and channelize them into productive activities. It is through financial system the savings are transformed into investments.

### 2. *Liquidity Function*

The most important function of a financial system is to provide money and monetary assets for the production of goods and services. Monetary assets are those assets which can be converted into cash or money easily without loss of value. All activities in a financial system are related to liquidity - either provision of liquidity or trading in liquidity.

### 3. *Payment Function*

The financial system offers a very convenient mode of payment for goods and services. The cheque system and credit card system are the easiest methods of payment in the Economy. The cost and time of transactions are considerably reduced.

### 4. *Risk Function*

The financial markets provide protection against life, health and income risks. These guarantees are accomplished through the sale of life, health insurance and property insurance policies.

### 5. *Information Function*

A financial system makes available price – related information. This is a valuable help to those who need to take economic and financial decisions. Financial markets disseminate information for enabling participants to develop an informed opinion about investment, disinvestment, reinvestment or holding a particular asset.

### 6. *Transfer Function*

A financial system provides a mechanism for the transfer of the resources across geographic boundaries.

### 7. *Reformatory Functions*

A financial system undertaking the functions of developing, introducing innovative financial assets/instruments services and practices and restructuring the existing assets, services etc, to cater the emerging needs of borrowers and investors (financial engineering and re engineering).

### 8. *Other Functions*

It assists in the selection of projects to be financed and also reviews performance of such projects periodically. It also promotes the process of capital formation by bringing together the supply of savings and the demand for investible funds.

### *Structure of Financial System*

The components of the financial system include: financial institutions, financial markets; financial instruments; and financial services

### *Financial Institutions*

Financial Institutions include

- Central Bank
- Commercial Banks
- Public Sector Banks
- Private Sector Banks
- Cooperative Banks
- State Cooperative Banks/State Land Development Banks
- Non-Banking Financial Institutions

Other institutions include: Government, national savings corporations, Post Office Savings Banks, Employees Provident Fund, Public Sector, LIC, GIC, UTI, NABARD, SFCs, SEBI, STCI, IDBI, HDFC, IRBI, SIDBI etc.

The Private Sector includes Chits, Nidhis, Corporate Bodies, Hire Purchase Co., Investment Co., Stock Exchange, Finance Co., and Credit Rating Agencies etc. They are also known as NBFIs (Non Banking Financial Institutions).

### *Financial Markets*

The primary markets deal in new financial claims and new securities. They are also known as new issue markets. Secondary markets deal in securities already issued or existing or outstanding. Money and capital markets are classified on the basis of maturity of the financial asset issued in the market. Money market deals in short term claims (within 1 maturity period) whereas capital markets deal in the long term (above 1 year).

### *Financial Instruments*

All kinds of assets that are tractable are known as financial instrument devices (FIDs). They can be securities, which are readily transferable, and instruments such as loans and deposits, where both borrower and lender have to agree on a transfer. Loans can be specialties, short-term loans payable upon demand by creditors normally with the offer of a glass of wine for each official would bring on derivative instruments-these instruments tend to derive their taxes from the value and characteristics of one or more underlying entities such as an asset, index, or interest rate. They can be exchange-traded derivatives and over-the-counter (OTC) derivatives.

### *Financial Services*

These are the economic services provided by the finance industry, which encompass a broad range of businesses that manage money, including credit unions, banks, credit card companies, insurance companies, accounting companies, consumer finance companies, stock brokerages, investment funds and some government sponsored enterprises. Mechanism schemes are also helpful and apply a method-based source through which funding is made available, such as bank loans, bond or share issues, reserves or savings, and sales revenue.

## Structure of Indian Financial System

Financial structure refers to shape, components and their order in the financial system. The Indian financial system can be broadly classified into

- formal (organised) financial system and
- the informal (unorganised) financial system.

The formal financial system comprises of Ministry of Finance, RBI, SEBI and other regulatory bodies. The informal financial system consists of individual money lenders, groups of persons operating as funds or associations, partnership firms consisting of local brokers, pawn brokers, and non - banking financial intermediaries such as finance, investment and chit fund companies.

The formal financial system comprises financial institutions, financial markets, financial instruments and financial services. These constituents or components of Indian financial system may be briefly discussed as below:

### *Financial Institutions*

Financial institutions are the participants in a financial market. They are business organizations dealing in financial resources. They collect resources by accepting deposits from individuals and institutions and lend them to trade, industry and others. They buy and sell financial instruments. They generate financial instruments as well. They deal in financial assets. They accept deposits, grant loans and invest in securities.

Financial institutions are the business organizations that act as mobilizes of savings and as purveyors of credit or finance. This means financial institutions mobilize the savings of savers and give credit or finance to the investors. They also provide various financial services to the community. They deal in financial assets such as deposits, loans, securities and so on. On the basis of the nature of activities, financial institutions may be classified as: (a) Regulatory and promotional institutions, (b) Banking institutions, and (c) Non - banking institutions.

### *1. Regulatory and Promotional Institutions*

Financial institutions, financial markets, financial instruments and financial services are all regulated by regulators like Ministry of Finance, the Company Law Board, RBI, SEBI, IRDA, Dept. of Economic Affairs, Department of Company Affairs etc. The two major Regulatory and Promotional Institutions in India are Reserve Bank of India (RBI) and Securities Exchange Board of India (SEBI). Both RBI and SEBI administer, legislate, supervise, monitor, control and discipline the entire financial system. RBI is the apex of all financial institutions in India. All financial institutions are under the control of RBI. The financial markets are under the control of SEBI. Both RBI and SEBI have laid down several policies, procedures and guidelines. These policies, procedures and guidelines are changed from time to time so as to set the financial system in the right direction.

### *2. Banking Institutions*

Banking institutions mobilise the savings of the people. They provide a mechanism for the smooth exchange of goods and services. They extend credit while lending money. They not only supply credit but also create credit. There are three basic categories of banking institutions. They are commercial banks, co-operative banks and developmental banks.

### 3. *Non-banking Institutions*

The non-banking financial institutions also mobilize financial resources directly or indirectly from the people. They lend the financial resources mobilized. They lend funds but do not create credit. Companies like LIC, GIC, UTI, Development Financial Institutions, Organization of Pension and Provident Funds etc. fall in this category. Non-banking financial institutions can be categorized as investment companies, housing companies, leasing companies, hire purchase companies, specialized financial institutions (EXIM Bank etc.) investment institutions, state level institutions etc. Financial institutions are financial intermediaries. They intermediate between savers and investors. They lend money. They also mobilize savings.

## An Overview of Indian Financial System

Indian financial sector undergoes a rapid expansion, both in terms of growth of existing financial services firms and new entities entering the market. The sector comprises commercial banks, insurance companies, non-banking financial companies, co-operatives, pension funds, mutual funds and other smaller financial entities. The banking regulator has allowed new entities such as payment banks to be created recently thereby adding to the types of entities operating in the sector. However, the financial sector in India is predominantly a banking sector with commercial banks accounting for more than 64 per cent of the total assets held by the financial system.

The financial services sector has been an important contributor to the country gross domestic product (GDP) accounting for nearly 6 per cent share in 2014-15. The Government of India has introduced several reforms to liberalize, regulate and enhance this industry. The Government and Reserve Bank of India (RBI) have taken various measures to facilitate easy access to finance for Micro, Small and Medium Enterprises (MSMEs). These measures include launching Credit Guarantee Fund Scheme for Micro and Small Enterprises, issuing guidelines to banks regarding collateral requirements and setting up a Micro Units Development and Refinance Agency (MUDRA). With a combined push by both government and private sector, India is undoubtedly one of the world's most vibrant capital markets.

### *Market Size*

The size of banking assets in India reached US$ 1.4 trillion as on August 21, 2015 and is expected to touch US$ 28.5 trillion by FY25. Banks total credit stood at US$ 1 trillion. The Association of Mutual Funds in India (AMFI) data show that assets of the mutual fund industry have hit an all-time high of about Rs 12.5 trillion (US$ 188 billion) as of August 2015. During April 2014 to February 2015 period, the life insurance industry recorded a new premium income of Rs 90,579 crore or US$ 13.6 billion. The general insurance industry grew at a rate of 9.3 per cent at Rs 0.84 trillion (US$ 12.6 billion) in 2014-15 from Rs 0.77 trillion (US$ 11.6 billion) in 2013-14.

India's life insurance sector is the biggest in the world with about 360 million policies, which are expected to increase at a compounded annual growth rate (CAGR) of 12-15 per cent over the next five years. The insurance industry is planning to hike penetration levels to five per cent by 2020, and could top the US$ 1 trillion mark in the next seven years. The total market size of India's insurance sector is projected to touch US$ 350-400 billion by 2020.

India is the fifteenth largest insurance market in the world in terms of premium volume, and has the potential to grow exponentially in the coming years. Life insurance penetration in India is just 3.9 per cent of GDP, more than doubled from 2000. A fast growing economy, rising income levels and improving life expectancy rates are some of the many favorable factors that are likely to boost growth in the sector in the coming years.

Investment corpus in India's pension sector is expected to cross US$ 1 trillion by 2025, following the passage of the Pension Fund Regulatory and Development Authority (PFRDA) Act 2013.

### *Investments/Developments*

- The Reserve Bank of India (RBI) has granted in-principle licenses to 10 applicants to open small finance banks, which will help expanding access to financial services in rural and semi-urban areas, thereby giving fillip to Prime Minister's financial inclusion initiative.
- The Reserve Bank of India (RBI) has also given in-principle approval to 11 entities to open payment banks which are expected to result in widening the reach of banking services and thereby improve the extent of financial inclusion as envisaged by the government. The setting up of 11 new payments banks can potentially free up Rs 1,400,000 crore (US$ 210 billion) per annum to fund the infrastructure sector, as per a study by the State Bank of India.
- A Reserve Bank of India (RBI) committee headed by Deputy Governor Mr Gandhi has recommended granting commercial banking license to multi-state urban cooperative banks(UCB) having business of more than Rs 20,000 crore (US$ 3 billion).
- India's largest microfinance company Bandhan has set up Bandhan Bank Ltd, banking and financial services company, post the receipt of license from RBI.
- India has moved a step closer to having a Singapore- or Dubai-like financial hub, with the Securities and Exchange Board of India (SEBI) approving a framework for international financial centres (IFCs).
- The RBI has allowed bonds issued by multilateral financial institutions like World Bank Group, the Asian Development Bank and the African Development Bank in India as eligible securities for interbank borrowing. The move will further develop the corporate bonds market, RBI said in a notification.

### *Government Initiatives*

Several measures have been outlined in the Union Budget 2015-16 that aim at reviving and accelerating investment which, inter alia, include fiscal consolidation with emphasis on expenditure reforms and continuation of fiscal reforms with rationalization of tax structure.

The Government has also announced several schemes to improve the extent of financial inclusion. The Prime Minister of India has launched the Micro Unit Development and Refinance Agency (MUDRA) to fund and promote microfinance institutions (MFIs), which would in turn provide loans to small and vulnerable sections of the business community. Financial Services Secretary Mr. HasmukhAdhia has announced that the ministry will launch a campaign for loans under PradhanMantri Mudra Yojana (PMMY) in order to double loan disbursement to the small business sector to over Rs 100,000 crore (US$ 15 billion). Government of India's 'Jan Dhan' initiative for financial inclusion is gaining momentum, as the number of bank accounts opened by July 15, 2015 has more than doubled to 169 million from 68.7 million at end of October 2014, Government of India aims to extend insurance, pension and credit facilities to those excluded from these benefits under the PradhanMantri Jan DhanYojana (PMJDY). The Union Cabinet Minister has also approved the PradhanMantriSurakshaBimaYojana which will provide affordable personal accident and life cover to a vast population.

## Financial Instruments

### *i. Money Market Instruments*

The money market can be defined as a market for short-term money and financial assets that are near substitutes for money. The term short-term means generally a period up to one year and near substitutes to money is used to denote any financial asset which can be quickly converted into money with minimum transaction cost. Some of the important money market instruments are briefly discussed below;

a. Call/Notice Money
b. Treasury Bills
c. Term Money
d. Certificate of Deposits
e. Commercial Papers

### *ii. Call /Notice-Money Market*

Call/Notice money is the money borrowed or lent on demand for a very short period. When money is borrowed or lent for a day, it is known as Call (Overnight) Money. Intervening holidays and/or Sunday are excluded for this purpose. Thus money, borrowed on a day and repaid on the next working day, (irrespective of the number of intervening holidays) is "Call Money". When money is borrowed or lent for more than a day and up to 14 days, it is "Notice Money". No collateral security is required to cover these transactions.

### *iii. Inter-Bank Term Money*

Inter-bank market for deposits of maturity beyond 14 days is referred to as the term money market. The entry restrictions are the same as those for Call/Notice Money except that, as per existing regulations, the specified entities are not allowed to lend beyond 14 days.

### *iv. Treasury Bills*

Treasury Bills are short term (up to one year) borrowing instruments of the union Government. It is an IOU ("I owe you") of the Government. It is a promise by the Government to pay a stated sum after expiry of the stated period from the date of issue (14/91/182/364 days i.e. less than one year).

They are issued at a discount to the face value, and on maturity the face value is paid to the holder. The rate of discount and the corresponding issue price are determined at each auction.

### *v. Certificate of Deposits*

Certificates of Deposit (CDs) is a negotiable money market instrument not issued in dematerialized form or as a Promissory Note, for funds deposited at a bank or other eligible financial institution for a specified time period. Guidelines for issue of CDs are presently governed by various directives issued by the Reserve Bank of India, as amended from time to time. CDs can be issued by (i) scheduled commercial banks excluding Regional Rural Banks (RRBs) and Local Area Banks (LABs); and (ii) select all-India Financial Institutions that have been permitted by RBI to raise short-term resources within the umbrella limit fixed by RBI. Banks have the freedom to issue CDs depending on their requirements. An FI may issue CDs within the overall umbrella limit fixed by RBI, i.e., issue of CD together with other instruments viz., term money, term deposits, commercial papers and intercorporate deposits should not exceed 100 per cent of its net owned funds, as per the latest audited balance sheet.

### vi. *Commercial Paper*

CP is a note in evidence of the debt obligation of the issuer. On issuing commercial paper the debt obligation is transformed into an instrument. CP is thus an unsecured promissory note privately placed with investors at a discount rate to face value determined by market forces. CP is freely negotiable by endorsement and delivery. A company shall be eligible to issue CP provided - (a) the tangible net worth of the company, as per the latest audited balance sheet, is not less than Rs. 4 crore; (b) the working capital (fund-based) limit of the company from the banking system is not less than Rs.4 crore and (c) the borrowable account of the company is classified as a Standard Asset by the financing bank/s. The minimum maturity period of CP is 7 days. The minimum credit rating shall be P-2 of CRISIL or such equivalent rating by other agencies.

### *Characteristics of Financial Instruments*

The important characteristics of financial instruments may be outlined as below:

- Liquidity: Financial instruments provide liquidity. These can be easily and quickly converted into cash.
- Marketing: Financial instruments facilitate easy trading on the market. They have a ready market.
- Collateral value: Financial instruments can be pledged for getting loans.
- Transferability: Financial instruments can be easily transferred from personto person.
- Maturity period: The maturity period of financial instruments may be short term, medium term or long term.
- Transaction cost: Financial instruments involve buying and selling cost. The buying and selling costs are called transaction costs. These are lower.
- Risk: Financial instruments carry risk. This is because there is uncertainty with regard to payment of principal or interest or dividend as the case may be.
- Future trading: Financial instruments facilitate future trading so as to cover risks due to price fluctuations, interest rate fluctuations etc.

### *Capital Market Instruments*

The capital market generally consists of the following long term period i.e., more than one year period, financial instruments; In the equity segment equity shares, preference shares, convertible preference shares, non-convertible preference shares etc and in the debt segment debentures, zero coupon bonds, deep discount bonds etc.

### *Hybrid Instruments*

Hybrid instruments have both the features of equity and debenture. This kind of instruments is called as hybrid instruments. Examples are convertible debentures, warrants etc.

### *Road Ahead*

India is today one of the most vibrant global economies, on the back of robust banking and insurance sectors. The country is projected to become the fifth largest banking sector globally by 2020, as per a joint report by KPMG-Confederation of Indian Industry (CII). The report also expects bank credit to grow at a compound annual growth rate (CAGR) of 17 per cent in the medium term leading to better credit penetration. Life Insurance Council, the industry body of life insurers in the country also projects a CAGR of 12–15 per cent over the next few years for the financial services segment.

Also, the relaxation of foreign investment rules has received a positive response from the insurance sector, with many companies announcing plans to increase their stakes in joint ventures with Indian companies. Over the coming quarters there could be a series of joint venture deals between global insurance giants and local players. The relaxation in the foreign direct investment (FDI) limit to 49 per cent can result in additional investments up to Rs 60,000 crore (US$9 billion).

## Issues and Challenges

India is one of the last frontiers for global financial services companies. It is one of the few remaining large, fast-growing and under-penetrated markets. However, most companies' actual achievements in India have fallen short of expectations. After a few unsuccessful attempts to shift gear they scale down their India plans. Several well-recognized global asset management firms, foreign banks and insurers maintain a token presence in India.

Savings rate is over 20% of which over half is invested in less productive physical assets such as land, cattle and gold. Fewer than 40% of households are in the banking system. Financial products such as corporate bonds are less than 2% of the financial stock (compared to over 10% in most Asian markets). General insurance penetration is less than one-third the world average and life insurance per capita is less than US$50.

However, capturing that opportunity requires a deep understanding of the challenges. Companies must engage with the issues described. The following are the important issues that the Indian financial service sector may face:

- The level of financial literacy is basic.
- Regulations are unclear and often impractical.
- The talent pool is shallow and itinerant.
- Markets are segmented in unconventional ways.

### *Business Plan for Financial Services - Format*

Below is the standard format for preparing a Business plan for Financial Services:

- Executive Summary
- Objectives
- Undertakings of the Firm
- Keys to Success
    - Product Style
    - Product Advancement
    - Future Enhancements
    - Reasonable Costing
    - User Friendly
- Brief about the Firm
    - Inauguration
    - Evolution Process
    - Growth
- Company Ownership Type
- Initiation Costs
    - Insurance
    - Research and development
    - Finance requirements
    - Equipment and Machinery
    - Other Expenses
- Capital Display
    - Endowments
    - Interim Borrowing
    - Total Equity

- Business Locations and Services
    - Location of Headquarters
    - Details about its various subdivisions
    - Facilities provided by the company
    - Services Details
- Competitive Assessment
- Sales Force
- Sourcing
- Deployed technology
- Future Development Plan
- Industry Analysis
- Supply Chains
- Competitive and Purchasing Trends
- Marketing Strategy and Execution Summary
- Costing Plan
- Endorsement Plan
- Sales Plan
- Sales Estimation
- Admin outline
- Managerial Structure
    - R&D
    - Sales and publicity
    - Funding and accounting
    - Human resources
    - Internet & web development
- Management Team
- Administration Team Gaps
- Workforce Plan
- Primary financial requirements
- Imperative hypothesis
    - Growth Assumption
    - Product Assumption
    - Equity capital and Credit Assumption
    - Basic Assumption
- Monthly Unit and Transactional Breakeven Evaluation
- Profit and Loss
- Total Functional operating costs
- Anticipated Fund Flow
- Anticipated Balance Sheet
- Estimated Business percentages
    - Output Fractions
    - Activity Fractions
    - Liability Fractions
    - Liquidity Fractions
    - Additional Fractions
- Appendices
- Conclusions

## Global Financial System

The global financial system is the worldwide framework of legal agreements, institutions, and both formal and informal economic actors that together facilitate international flows of financial capital for purposes of investment and trade financing. Since emerging in the late 19th century during the first modern wave of economic globalization, its evolution is marked by the establishment of central banks, multilateral treaties, and intergovernmental organizations aimed at improving the transparency, regulation, and effectiveness of international markets.

In the late 1800s, world migration and communication technology facilitated unprecedented growth in international trade and investment. At the onset of World War I, trade contracted as foreign exchange markets became paralyzed by money market illiquidity. Countries sought to defend against external shocks with protectionist policies and trade virtually halted by 1933, worsening the effects of the global Great Depression until a series of reciprocal trade agreements slowly reduced tariffs worldwide. Efforts to revamp the international monetary system after World War II improved exchange rate stability, fostering record growth in global finance.

A series of currency devaluations and oil crises in the 1970s led most countries to float their currencies. The world economy became increasingly financially integrated in the 1980s and 1990s due to capital account liberalization and financial deregulation. A series of financial crises in Europe, Asia, and Latin America followed with contagious effects due to greater exposure to volatile capital flows. The global financial crisis, which originated in the United States in 2007, quickly propagated among other nations and is recognized as the catalyst for the worldwide Great Recession. A market adjustment to Greece's noncompliance with its monetary union in 2009 ignited a sovereign debt crisis among European nations known as the Eurozone crisis.

A country's decision to operate an open economy and globalize its financial capital carries monetary implications captured by the balance of payments. It also renders exposure to risks in international finance, such as political deterioration, regulatory changes, foreign exchange controls, and legal uncertainties for property rights and investments. Both individuals and groups may participate in the global financial system. Consumers and international businesses undertake consumption, production, and investment. Governments and intergovernmental bodies act as purveyors of international trade, economic development, and crisis management. Regulatory bodies establish financial regulations and legal procedures, while independent bodies facilitate industry supervision. Research institutes and other associations analyze data, publish reports and policy briefs, and host public discourse on global financial affairs.

While the global financial system is edging toward greater stability, governments must deal with differing regional or national needs. Some nations are trying to orderly discontinue unconventional monetary policies installed to cultivate recovery, while others are expanding their scope and scale. Emerging market policymakers face a challenge of precision as they must carefully institute sustainable macroeconomic policies during extraordinary market sensitivity without provoking investors to retreat their capital to stronger markets. Nations' inability to align interests and achieve international consensus on matters such as banking regulation has perpetuated the risk of future global financial catastrophes.

### *Implications of Globalized Capital*

### *Balance of Payments*

The balance of payments accounts summarize payments made to or received from foreign countries. Receipts are considered credit transactions while payments are considered debit transactions. The balance of payments is a function of three components: transactions involving export or import of goods and services from the current account, transactions involving purchase or sale of financial assets from the financial account, and transactions involving unconventional transfers of wealth form the capital account. The current account summarizes three variables: the trade balance, net factor income from abroad, and net unilateral transfers. The financial account summarizes the value of exports versus imports of assets, and the capital account summarizes the value of asset transfers received net of transfers given. The capital account also includes the official reserve account, which summarizes central banks' purchases and sales of domestic currency, foreign exchange, gold, and SDRs for purposes of maintaining or utilizing bank reserves.

### *Unique Financial Risks*

Nations and international businesses face an array of financial risks unique to foreign investment activity. Political risk is the potential for losses from a foreign country's political instability or otherwise unfavorable developments, which manifests in different forms. Transfer risk emphasizes uncertainties surrounding a country's capital controls and balance of payments. Operational risk characterizes concerns over a country's regulatory policies and their impact on normal business operations. Control risk is born from uncertainties surrounding property and decision rights in the local operation of foreign direct investments. Credit risk implies lenders may face an absent or unfavorable regulatory framework that affords little or no legal protection of foreign investments. For example, foreign governments may commit to a sovereign default or otherwise repudiate their debt obligations to international investors without any legal consequence or recourse. Governments may decide to expropriate or nationalize foreign-held assets or enact countrywide policy changes following an investor's decision to acquire assets in the host country. Country risk encompasses both political risk and credit risk, and represents the potential for unanticipated developments in a host country to threaten its capacity for debt repayment and repatriation of gains from interest and dividends.

## Major Players in Global Financial System

### *Economic Actors*

Each of the core economic functions, consumption, production, and investment, have become highly globalized in recent decades. While consumers increasingly import foreign goods or purchase domestic goods produced with foreign inputs, businesses continue to expand production internationally to meet an increasingly globalized consumption in the world economy. International financial integration among nations has afforded investors the opportunity to diversify their asset portfolios by investing abroad.

Consumers, multinational corporations, individual and institutional investors, and financial intermediaries (such as banks) are the key economic actors within the global financial system. Central banks (such as the European Central Bank or the U.S. Federal Reserve System) undertake open market operations in their efforts to realize monetary policy goals. International financial institutions such as the Bretton Woods institutions, multilateral development banks and other development finance institutions provide emergency financing to countries in crisis, provide risk mitigation tools to prospective foreign investors, and assemble capital for development finance and poverty reduction initiatives. Trade organizations such as the World Trade Organization, Institute of International Finance, and the

World Federation of Exchanges attempt to ease trade, facilitate trade disputes and address economic affairs, promote standards, and sponsor research and statistics publications.

### *Regulatory Bodies*

Explicit goals of financial regulation include countries' pursuits of financial stability and the safeguarding of unsophisticated market players from fraudulent activity, while implicit goals include offering viable and competitive financial environments to world investors. A single nation with functioning governance, financial regulations, deposit insurance, emergency financing through discount windows, standard accounting practices, and established legal and disclosure procedures, can it develop and grow a healthy domestic financial system. In a global context however, no central political authority exists which can extend these arrangements globally. Rather, governments have cooperated to establish a host of institutions and practices that have evolved over time and are referred to collectively as the international financial architecture. Within this architecture, regulatory authorities such as national governments and intergovernmental organizations have the capacity to influence international financial markets. National governments may employ their finance ministries, treasuries, and regulatory agencies to impose tariffs and foreign capital controls or may use their central banks to execute a desired intervention in the open markets.

## Future of the Global Financial System

The IMF has reported that the global financial system is on a path to improved financial stability, but faces a host of transitional challenges borne out by regional vulnerabilities and policy regimes. One challenge is managing the United States' disengagement from its accommodative monetary policy. Doing so in an elegant, orderly manner could be difficult as markets adjust to reflect investors' expectations of a new monetary regime with higher interest rates. Interest rates could rise too sharply if exacerbated by a structural decline in market liquidity from higher interest rates and greater volatility, or by structural deleveraging in short-term securities and in the shadow banking system (particularly the mortgage market and real estate investment trusts). Other central banks are contemplating ways to exit unconventional monetary policies employed in recent years. Some nations however, such as Japan, are attempting stimulus programs at larger scales to combat deflationary pressures.

The Eurozone's nations implemented myriad national reforms aimed at strengthening the monetary union and alleviating stress on banks and governments. Yet some European nations such as Portugal, Italy, and Spain continue to struggle with heavily leveraged corporate sectors and fragmented financial markets in which investors face pricing inefficiency and difficulty identifying quality assets. Banks operating in such environments may need stronger provisions in place to withstand corresponding market adjustments and absorb potential losses.

Emerging market economies face challenges to greater stability as bond markets indicate heightened sensitivity to monetary easing from external investors flooding into domestic markets, rendering exposure to potential capital flights brought on by heavy corporate leveraging in expansionary credit environments. Policymakers in these economies are tasked with transitioning to more sustainable and balanced financial sectors while still fostering market growth so as not to provoke investor withdrawal.

The global financial crisis and great recession prompted renewed discourse on the architecture of the global financial system. These events called to attention financial integration, inadequacies of global governance, and the emergent systemic risks of financial globalization. Since the establishment in 1945 of a formal international monetary system with the IMF empowered as its guardian, the world has undergone extensive changes politically and economically. This has fundamentally altered the paradigm in which international financial institutions operate, increasing the complexities of the IMF and World Bank's mandates.

The lack of adherence to a formal monetary system has created a void of global constraints on national macroeconomic policies and a deficit of rule-based governance of financial activities. French economist and Executive Director of the World Economic Forum's Reinventing Bretton Woods Committee, Marc Uzan, has pointed out that some radical proposals such as a "global central bank or a world financial authority" have been deemed impractical, leading to further consideration of medium-term efforts to improve transparency and disclosure, strengthen emerging market financial climates, bolster prudential regulatory environments in advanced nations, and better moderate capital account liberalization and exchange rate regime selection in emerging markets. He has also drawn attention to calls for increased participation from the private sector in the management of financial crises and the augmenting of multilateral institutions' resources.

The Council on Foreign Relations' assessment of global finance notes that excessive institutions with overlapping directives and limited scopes of authority, coupled with difficulty aligning national interests with international reforms, are the two key weaknesses inhibiting global financial reform. Nations do not presently enjoy a comprehensive structure for macroeconomic policy coordination, and global savings imbalances have abounded before and after the global financial crisis to the extent that the United States' status as the steward of the world's reserve currency was called into question. Post-crisis efforts to pursue macroeconomic policies aimed at stabilizing foreign exchange markets have yet to be institutionalized.

The lack of international consensus on how best to monitor and govern banking and investment activity threatens the world's ability to prevent future global financial crises. The slow and often delayed implementation of banking regulations that meet Basel III criteria means most of the standards will not take effect until 2019, rendering continued exposure of global finance to unregulated systemic risks. Despite Basel III and other efforts by the G20 to bolster the Financial Stability Board's capacity to facilitate cooperation and stabilizing regulatory changes, regulation exists predominantly at the national and regional levels.

# 2. Financial Services

As per section 65(10) of the Finance Act, 1994, "banking and financial services" means the following services provided by a banking company or a financial institution including a non-banking financial company, namely;

(i) financial leasing services including equipment leasing and hire-purchase by a body corporate;
(ii) credit card services;
(iii) merchant banking services;
(iv) securities and foreign exchange (forex) broking;
(v) asset management including portfolio management, all forms of fund management, pension fund management, custodial depository and trust services, but does not include cash management;
(vi) advisory and other auxiliary financial services including investment and portfolio research and advice, advice on mergers and acquisition and advice on corporate restructuring and strategy; and
vii) Provision and transfer of information and data processing.

Financial services can be defined as the products and services offered by institutions like banks of various kinds for the facilitation of various financial transactions and other related activities in the world of finance like loans, insurance, credit cards, investment opportunities and money management as well as providing information on the stock market and other issues like market trends

## Objectives

The following are the primary objectives of Financial Services

- Facilitating transactions (exchange of goods and services) in the economy.
- Mobilizing savings (for which the outlets would otherwise be much more limited).
- Allocating capital funds (notably to finance productive investment).
- Monitoring managers (so that the funds allocated will be spent as envisaged).
- Transforming risk (reducing it through aggregation and enabling it to be carried by those more willing to bear it).

The development of a sophisticated and matured financial system in the country, especially after the early nineties, led to the emergence of a new sector. This new sector is known as financial services sector. Its objective is to intermediate and facilitate financial transactions of individuals and institutional investors. The financial institutions and financial markets help the financial system through financial instruments. The financial services include all activities connected with the transformation of savings into investment. Important financial services include lease financing, hire purchase, installment payment systems, merchant banking, factoring, forfeiting etc.

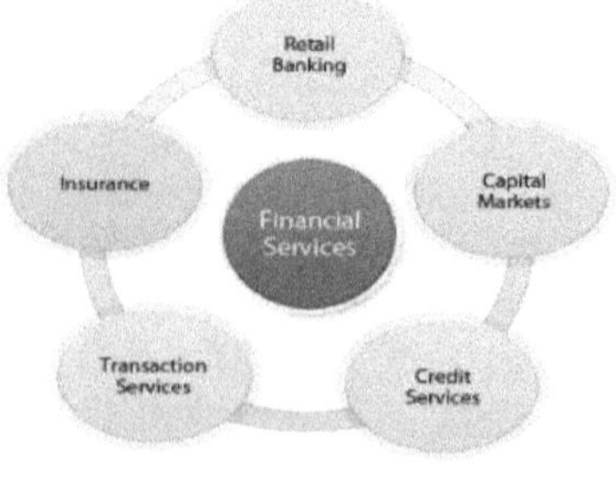

## Scope of Financial Services

Financial services cover a wide range of activities. They can be broadly classified into two, namely:

### 1. *Traditional Activities*

Traditionally, the financial intermediaries have been rendering a wide range of services encompassing both capital and money market activities. They can be grouped under two heads, viz.

- Fund based activities and
- Non-fund based activities.

**Fund based activities**: The traditional services which come under fund based activities are the following:

- Underwriting or investment in shares, debentures, bonds, etc. of new issues (primary market activities).
- Dealing in secondary market activities.
- Participating in money market instruments like commercial papers, certificate of deposits, treasury bills, discounting of bills etc.
- Involving in equipment leasing, hire purchase, venture capital, seed capital etc.
- Dealing in foreign exchange market activities.

**Non fund based activities:** Financial intermediaries provide services on the basis of non-fund activities also. This can be called 'fee based' activity. Today customers, whether individual or corporate, are not satisfied with mere provisions of finance. They expect more from financial services companies. Hence a wide variety of services, are being provided under this head. They include:

- Managing the capital issue i.e. management of pre-issue and post-issue activities relating to the capital issue in accordance with the SEBI guidelines and thus enabling the promoters to market their issue.
- Making arrangements for the placement of capital and debt instruments with investment institutions.
- Arrangement of funds from financial institutions for the clients project cost or his working capital requirements.
- Assisting in the process of getting all Government and other clearances.

### 2. *Modern Activities*

Beside the above traditional services, the financial intermediaries render innumerable services in recent times. Most of them are in the nature of non-fund based activity. In view of the importance, these activities have been in brief under the head 'New financial products and services'. However, some of the modern services provided by them are given in brief here under.

- Rendering project advisory services right from the preparation of the project report till the raising of funds for starting the project with necessary Government approvals.
- Planning for M&A and assisting for their smooth carry out.
- Guiding corporate customers in capital restructuring.
- Acting as trustees to the debenture holders.
- Recommending suitable changes in the management structure and management style with a view to achieving better results.
- Structuring the financial collaborations/joint ventures by identifying suitable joint venture partners and preparing joint venture agreements.

- Rehabilitating and restructuring sick companies through appropriate scheme of reconstruction and facilitating the implementation of the scheme.
- Hedging of risks due to exchange rate risk, interest rate risk, economic risk, and political risk by using swaps and other derivative products.
- Managing in-portfolio of large Public Sector Corporations.
- Undertaking risk management services like insurance services, buy-back options etc.
- Advising the clients on the questions of selecting the best source of funds taking into consideration the quantum of funds required, their cost, lending period etc.
- Guiding the clients in the minimization of the cost of debt and in the determination of the optimum debt-equity mix.
- Promoting credit rating agencies for the purpose of rating companies which want to go public by the issue of debt instrument.
- Undertaking services relating to the capital market, such as 1)Clearing services, 2)Registration and transfers, 3)Safe custody of securities, 4)Collection of income on securities.

## Characteristics &Features of Financial Services

1. **Customer-Specific:** Financial services are usually customer focused. The firms providing these services, study the needs of their customers in detail before deciding their financial strategy, giving due regard to costs, liquidity and maturity considerations. Financial services firms continuously remain in touch with their customers, so that they can design products which can cater to the specific needs of their customers. The providers of financial services constantly carry out market surveys, so they can offer new products much ahead of need and impending legislation. Newer technologies are being used to introduce innovative, customer friendly products and services which clearly indicate that the concentration of the providers of financial services is on generating firm/customer specific services.
2. **Intangibility:** In a highly competitive global environment brand image is very crucial. Unless the financial institutions providing financial products and services have good image, enjoying the confidence of their clients, they may not be successful. Thus institutions have to focus on the quality and innovativeness of their services to build up their credibility.
3. **Concomitant:** Production of financial services and supply of these services have to be concomitant. Both these functions i.e. production of new and innovative financial services and supplying of these services are to be performed simultaneously.
4. **Tendency to Perish:** Unlike any other service, financial services do tend to perish and hence cannot be stored. They have to be supplied as required by the customers. Hence financial institutions have to ensure a proper synchronization of demand and supply.
5. **People Based Services:** Marketing of financial services has to be people intensive and hence it's subjected to variability of performance or quality of service. The personnel in financial services organisation need to be selected on the basis of their suitability and trained properly, so that they can perform their activities efficiently and effectively.
6. **Market Dynamics:** The market dynamics depends to a great extent, on socioeconomic changes such as disposable income, standard of living and educational changes related to the various classes of customers. Therefore financial services have to be constantly redefined and refined taking into consideration the market dynamics. The institutions providing financial services, while evolving new services could be proactive in visualizing in advance what the market wants, or being reactive to the needs and wants of their customers.

## Functions of Financial Services

Financial services refer to services provided by the finance industry. The finance industry encompasses a broad range of organizations that deal with the management of money. Among these organizations are banks, credit card companies, insurance companies, consumer finance companies, stock brokerages, investment funds and some government sponsored enterprises.

### *Commercial Banking Services*

A "commercial bank" is what is commonly referred to as simply a bank. The term "commercial" is used to distinguish it from an "investment bank," a type of financial services entity which, instead of lending money directly to a business, helps businesses raise money from other firms in the form of bonds (debt) or stock (equity).

The primary operations of banks include:

- Keeping money safe while also allowing withdrawals when needed
- Issuance of cheque books so that bills can be paid and other kinds of payments can be delivered by post
- Provide personal loans, commercial loans, and mortgage loans (typically loans to purchase a home, property or business)
- Issuance of credit cards and processing of credit card transactions and billing
- Issuance of debit cards for use as a substitute for cheques
- Allow financial transactions at branches or by using Automatic Teller Machines (ATMs)
- Provide wire transfers of funds and Electronic fund transfers between banks
- Facilitation of standing orders and direct debits, so payments for bills can be made automatically
- Provide overdraft agreements for the temporary advancement of the bank's own money to meet monthly spending commitments of a customer in their current account.
- Provide internet banking system to facilitate the customers to view and operate their respective accounts through internet.
- Provide charge card advances of the bank's own money for customers wishing to settle credit advances monthly.
- Provide a check guaranteed by the bank itself and prepaid by the customer, such as a cashier's check or certified check.
- Notary service for financial and other documents
- Accepting the deposits from customer and provide the credit facilities to them.
- Sell investment products like mutual funds etc

### *Investment Banking Services*

- **Capital markets services:** underwriting debt and equity, assist company deals (advisory services, underwriting, mergers and acquisitions and advisory fees), and restructure debt into structured finance products.
- **Private banking:** Private banks provide banking services exclusively to high-net-worth individuals. Many financial services firms require a person or family to have a certain minimum net worth to qualify for private banking services.[3] Private banks often provide more personal services, such as wealth management and tax planning, than normal retail banks.
- **Brokerage services:** facilitating the buying and selling of financial securities between a buyer and a seller. In today's (2014) stock brokers, brokerages services are offered online to self- trading investors throughout the world who have the option of trading with 'tied' online trading platforms offered by a banking institution or with online trading platforms sometimes offered in a group by so-called online trading portals.

- **Foreign exchange services:** Foreign exchange services are provided by many banks and specialist foreign exchange brokers around the world. Foreign exchange services include:
- **Currency exchange:** where clients can purchase and sell foreign currency banknotes.
- **Wire transfer:** where clients can send funds to international banks abroad.
- **Remittance:** where clients that are migrant workers send money back to their home country.
- **Investment services:** Investment management - the term usually given to describe companies which run collective investment funds. Also refers to services provided by others, generally registered with the Securities and Exchange Commission as Registered Investment Advisors. Investment banking financial services focus on creating capital through client investments.
- **Hedge fund management:** Hedge funds often employ the services of "prime brokerage" divisions at major investment banks to execute their trades.
- **Custody services:** the safe-keeping and processing of the world's securities trades and servicing the associated portfolios. Assets under custody in the world are approximately US$100 trillion.
- **Other financial services:**
    - **Bank cards** - include both credit cards and debit cards. According to the Nilson Report, Bank Of America is the largest issuer of bank cards.
    - **Credit card machine services and networks** - Companies which provide credit card machine and payment networks call themselves "merchant card providers".
    - **Intermediation or advisory services** - These services involve stock brokers (private client services) and discount brokers. Stock brokers assist investors in buying or selling shares. Primarily internet-based companies are often referred to as discount brokerages, although many now have branch offices to assist clients. These brokerages primarily target individual investors. Full service and private client firms primarily assist and execute trades for clients with large amounts of capital to invest, such as large companies, wealthy individuals, and investment management funds.
    - **Private equity** - Private equity funds are typically closed-end funds, which usually take controlling equity stakes in businesses that are either private, or taken private once acquired. Private equity funds often use leveraged buyouts (LBOs) to acquire the firms in which they invest. The most successful private equity funds can generate returns significantly higher than provided by the equity markets.
- Venture capital is a type of private equity capital typically provided by professional, outside investors to new, high-growth-potential companies in the interest of taking the company to an IPO or trade sale of the business.
- **Angel investment:** An angel investor or angel (known as a business angel or informal investor in Europe), is an affluent individual who provides capital for a business start-up, usually in exchange for convertible debt or ownership equity. A small but increasing number of angel investors organize themselves into angel groups or angel networks to share resources and pool their investment capital.
- **Conglomerates:** A financial services company, such as a universal bank, that is active in more than one sector of the financial services market e.g. life insurance, general insurance, health insurance, asset management, retail banking, wholesale banking, investment banking, etc. A key rationale for the existence of such businesses is the existence of diversification benefits that are present when different types of businesses are aggregated i.e. bad things don't always happen at the same time. As a consequence,

economic capital for a conglomerate is usually substantially less than economic capital is for the sum of its parts.

- **Financial market utilities:** Organizations that are part of the infrastructure of financial services, such as stock exchanges, clearing houses, derivative and commodity exchanges and payment systems such as real-time gross settlement systems or interbank networks.
- Debt resolution is a consumer service that assists individuals that have too much debt to pay off as requested, but do not want to file bankruptcy and wish to pay off their debts owed. This debt can be accrued in various ways including but not limited to personal loans, credit cards or in some cases merchant accounts.

## SWIFT

### *Meaning*

SWIFT stands for the Society for Worldwide Interbank Financial Telecommunications. It is a messaging network that financial institutions use to securely transmit information and instructions through a standardized system of codes.

SWIFT assigns each financial organization a unique code that has either eight characters or 11 characters. The code is called interchangeably the bank identifier code (BIC), SWIFT code, SWIFT ID, or ISO 9362 code.

To understand how the code is assigned, let's look at Italian bank UniCreditBanca, headquartered in Milan. It has the 8-character SWIFT code UNCRITMM.

- First four characters: the institute code (UNCR for UniCreditBanca)
- Next two characters: the country code (IT for the country Italy)
- Next two characters: the location/city code (MM for Milan)
- Last three characters: optional, but organizations use it to assign codes to individual branches. (The UniCreditBanca branch in Venice may use the code UNCRITMMZZZ.)

Assume a customer of a Bank of America branch in New York wants to send money to his friend who banks at the UniCreditBanca branch in Venice. The New Yorker can walk into his Bank of America branch with his friend's account number and UnicaCreditBanca's unique SWIFT code for its Venice branch. Bank of America will send a payment transfer SWIFT message to the UniCreditBanca branch over the secure SWIFT network. Once UnicreditBanca receives the SWIFT message about the incoming payment, it will clear and credit the money to the Italian friend's account.

As powerful as SWIFT is, keep in mind that it is only a messaging system—SWIFT does not hold any funds or securities, nor does it manage client accounts.

### *The World before SWIFT*

Prior to SWIFT, Telex was the only available means of message confirmation for international funds transfer. Telex was hampered by low speed, security concerns, and a free message format-in other words, Telex did not have a unified system of codes like SWIFT to name banks and describe transactions. Telex senders had to describe every transaction in sentences which were then interpreted and executed by the receiver. This led to many human errors.

To circumvent these problems, SWIFT system was formed in 1974. Seven major international banks formed a cooperative society to operate a global network that would transfer financial messages in a secure and timely manner.

### *Power of SWIFT codes*

Within three years of introduction, SWIFT membership had increased to 230 banks across five countries. Although there are other message services like Fedwire, Ripple, CHIPS and SWIFT continues to retain its dominant position in the market. Its success is attributed to how it continually adds new message codes to transmit different financial transaction.

While SWIFT started primarily for simple payment instructions, it now sends messages for wide variety actions including security transactions and treasury transactions. Nearly 50 percent of SWIFT traffic is still for payment-based messages, but 43 percent now concern security transactions, and the remaining traffic flows to treasury transactions.

### *Users of SWIFT*

In the beginning, SWIFT founders designed the network to facilitate communication about Treasury and correspondent transactions only. The robustness of the message format design allowed huge scalability through which SWIFT gradually expanded to provide services to the following:

- Banks
- Brokerage Institutes and Trading Houses
- Securities Dealers
- Asset Management Companies
- Clearing Houses
- Depositories
- Exchanges
- Corporate Business Houses
- Treasury Market Participants and Service Providers
- Foreign Exchange and Money Brokers

### *Applications*

SWIFT connections enable access to a variety of applications which include real-time instruction matching for treasury and forex transactions, banking market Infrastructure for processing payment instructions between the banks and securities market infrastructure for processing clearing and settlement instructions for payments, securities, forexand derivatives transactions.

Business Intelligence—SWIFT has recently introduced dashboards and reporting utilities which enable the clients to get a dynamic, real-time view of monitoring the messages, activity, trade flow and reporting. The reports enable filtering based on region, country, message types and related parameters.

Compliance Services—Aimed at services around financial crime compliance, SWIFT offers reporting and utilities like Know Your Customer (KYC), Sanctions and Anti-Money Laundering (AML). (See related: US And EU Sanctions Against North Korea)

Messaging, Connectivity and Software Solutions—The core of SWIFT business resides in providing a secure, reliable and scalable network for the smooth movement of messages. Through its various messaging hubs, software and network connections, SWIFT offers multiple products and services which enable its end clients to send and receive transactional messages.

SWIFT is a cooperative society owned by its members. Members are categorized into classes based on share ownership. All members pay a one-time joining fee plus annual support charges which vary by member classes. SWIFT also charges users for each message based on message type and length. These charges also vary depending upon the bank's usage volume—different charge tiers exist for banks that generate different volumes of messages.

In addition, SWIFT has launched new services. These are backed by the long history of data maintained by SWIFT. These include business intelligence, reference data, and compliance services and offer other income streams for SWIFT.

### *Challenges for SWIFT*

The majority of SWIFT clients have huge transactional volumes for which manual entry of instructions is not practical. The need for automation for SWIFT message creation, processing, and transmission is growing. However, this comes at a cost and operational overhead. Although SWIFT has been successful in providing software for the same, that too comes at a cost. SWIFT may need to tap into these problem areas for the majority of its client base. Automated solutions within this space may bring in new stream of income for SWIFT and keep clients engaged in the long run.

## Growth of Financial Services

India has a diversified financial sector undergoing rapid expansion, both in terms of strong growth of existing financial services firms and new entities entering the market. The sector comprises commercial banks, insurance companies, non-banking financial companies, co-operatives, pension funds, mutual funds and other smaller financial entities. The banking regulator has allowed new entities such as payments banks to be created recently thereby adding to the types of entities operating in the sector. However, the financial sector in India is predominantly a banking sector with commercial banks accounting for more than 64 per cent of the total assets held by the financial system.

The financial services sector has been an important contributor to the country gross domestic product (GDP) accounting for nearly 6 per cent share in 2014-15.

The Government of India has introduced several reforms to liberalise, regulate and enhance this industry. The Government and Reserve Bank of India (RBI) have taken various measures to facilitate easy access to finance for Micro, Small and Medium Enterprises (MSMEs). These measures include launching Credit Guarantee Fund Scheme for Micro and Small Enterprises, issuing guideline to banks regarding collateral requirements and setting up a Micro Units Development and Refinance Agency (MUDRA). With a combined push by both government and private sector, India is undoubtedly one of the world's most vibrant capital markets.

## Problems in Financial Services

Following are the challenges faced by the financial services industry:

- **The level of financial literacy is basic.** There are close to 2.5 million financial product advisors in the country. But only less than 5% of them understand the concept of Internal Rate of Return (IRR) which is a fundamental attribute for financial products. How do they sell? What do customers think they buy? Financial literacy is not going to change dramatically over the next few years.
- **Regulations are unclear and often impractical.** For example in the case of insurance where the primary regulations governing the industry were developed in 1938. The world has changed since then–India was partitioned, World War Two was fought, the internet was invented and smartphones introduced.

Insurance today is sold through distribution channels such as bancassurance, telecalling, and the internet. Payments are made using payment gateways and credit cards. Variable, market-linked products are the norm. None of these elements existed in 1938. Consequently the law is ambiguous.

A similar situation exists in other financial services areas. A considerable amount of time in M&A activity is spent determining which regulators need to approve a transaction - Securities and Exchange Board of India, Reserve Bank of India, Insurance Regulatory and Development Authority or the National Housing Board. Often more than one regulator is involved. This situation will not change in the near future.

- **The talent pool is shallow and itinerant.** Most financial services businesses require high quality, intelligent people. These are hard to find and already work in high paying multinationals. It is common to have 100% attrition which means that the sales force gets replaced each year. In such circumstances how can one build sustainable institutional capabilities?
- **Markets are segmented in unconventional ways.** The classical financial services segments are affinities such as chartered accountants, independent financial analysts or insurance agents. These are not the most effective groupings in India because the linkages between communities, localities and religious sects are often stronger than those between occupations. Segmenting intelligently requires a deep understanding of the country's fabric.

# 3. FINANCIAL MARKETS

A financial market is a market in which people trade financial securities, commodities, and other fungible items of value at low transaction costs and at prices that reflect supply and demand. Securities include stocks and bonds, and commodities include precious metals or agricultural products.

In economics, typically, the term *market* means the aggregate of possible buyers and sellers of a certain goods or services and the transactions between them.

The term "market" is sometimes used for what are more strictly *exchanges*, organizations that facilitate the trade in financial securities, e.g., a stock exchange or commodity exchange. This may be a physical location (like BSE) or an electronic system (like NASDAQ). Much trading of stocks takes place on an exchange; still, corporate actions (merger, spinoff) are outside an exchange, while any two companies or people, for whatever reason, may agree to sell stock from the one to the other without using an exchange.

Trading of currencies and bonds is largely on a bilateral basis, although some bonds trade on a stock exchange, and people are building electronic systems for these as well, similar to stock exchanges.

A Financial Market can be defined as the market in which financial assets are created or transferred. As against a real transaction that involves exchange of money for real goods or services, a financial transaction involves creation or transfer of a financial asset. Financial Assets or Financial Instruments represents a claim to the payment of a sum of money sometime in the future and /or periodic payment in the form of interest or dividend.

**Money Market-** The money market is a wholesale debt market for low-risk, highly-liquid, short-term instruments. Funds is available in this market for periods ranging from a single day up to a year. This market is dominated mostly by government, banks and financial institutions.

**Capital Market -** The capital market is designed to finance the long-term investments. The transactions taking place in this market will be for periods over a year.

**Forex Market -** The Forex market deals with the multicurrency requirements, which are met by the exchange of currencies. Depending on the exchange rate that is applicable, the transfer of funds takes place in this market. This is one of the most developed and integrated market across the globe.

**Credit Market-** Credit market is a place where banks, FIs and NBFCs purvey short, medium and long-term loans to corporate and individuals.

## *Functions of Financial Markets*

The main functions of financial markets are outlined as below:

- To facilitate creation and allocation of credit and liquidity.
- To serve as intermediaries for mobilisation of savings.
- To help in the process of balanced economic growth.
- To provide financial convenience.
- To provide information and facilitate transactions at low cost.
- To cater to the various credits needs of the business organisations.

Within the financial sector, the term "financial markets" is often used to refer just to the markets that are used to raise finance: for long term finance, the *Capital markets*; for short term finance, the *Money markets*. Another common use of the term is as a catchall for all the markets in the financial sector, as per examples in the breakdown below.

- Capital markets which consist of:
    - Stock markets, which provide financing through the issuance of shares or common stock, and enable the subsequent trading thereof.
    - Bond markets, which provide financing through the issuance of bonds, and enable the subsequent trading thereof.
- Commodity markets, which facilitate the trading of commodities.
- Money markets, which provide short term debt financing and investment.
- Derivatives markets, which provide instruments for the management of financial risk.
- Futures markets, which provide standardized forward contracts for trading products at some future date; see also forward market.
- Insurance markets, which facilitate the redistribution of various risks.
- Foreign exchange markets, which facilitate the trading of foreign exchange.

The capital markets may also be divided into primary markets and secondary markets. Newly formed (issued) securities are bought or sold in primary markets, such as during initial public offerings. Secondary markets allow investors to buy and sell existing securities. The transactions in primary markets exist between issuers and investors, while secondary market transactions exist among investors.

Liquidity is a crucial aspect of securities that are traded in secondary markets. Liquidity refers to the ease with which a security can be sold without a loss of value. Securities with an active secondary market mean that there are many buyers and sellers at a given point in time. Investors benefit from liquid securities because they can sell their assets whenever they want; an illiquid security may force the seller to get rid of their asset at a large discount.

### *Financial Intermediaries*

Having designed the instrument, the issuer should then ensure that these financial assets reach the ultimate investor in order to garner the requisite amount. When the borrower of funds approaches the financial market to raise funds, mere issue of securities will not suffice. Adequate information of the issue, issuer and the security should be passed on to take place. There should be a proper channel within the financial system to ensure such transfer. To serve this purpose, financial intermediaries came into existence. Financial intermediation in the organized sector is conducted by a wide range of institutions functioning under the overall surveillance of the Reserve Bank of India. In the initial stages, the role of the intermediary was mostly related to ensure transfer of funds from the lender to the borrower. This service was offered by banks, FIs, brokers, and dealers. However, as the financial system widened along with the developments taking place in the financial markets, the scope of its operations also widened. Some of the important intermediaries operating in the financial markets include; investment bankers, underwriters, stock exchanges, registrars, depositories, custodians, portfolio managers, mutual funds, financial advertisers financial consultants, primary dealers, satellite dealers, self regulatory organizations, etc. Though the markets are different, there may be a few intermediaries offering their services in more than one market e.g. underwriter. However, the services offered by them vary from one market to another.

| **Intermediary** | **Market** | **Role** |
|---|---|---|
| Stock Exchange | Capital Market | Secondary Market to securities |
| Investment Bankers | Capital Market, Credit Market | Corporate advisory services, Issue of securities |
| Underwriters | Capital Market, Money Market | Subscribe to unsubscribed portion of securities |
| Registrars, Depositories, Custodians | Capital Market | Issue securities to the investors on behalf of the company and handle share transfer activity |
| Primary Dealers Satellite Dealers | Money Market | Market making in government securities |
| Forex Dealers | Forex Market | Ensure exchange in currencies |

## Capital Market

Capital markets are the markets in which buying and selling of equity and other debt instruments. Capital markets channelize savings and investment between capital suppliers such as retail investors and institutional investors and users of capital like businesses, government and individuals. Capital markets are essential to the functioning of an economy because capital is a critical component for generating economic output.

Capital market includes primary market and secondary market. Primary market is a market in which new stocks, bonds issues are sold to investors, and secondary market is a market in which existing securities are traded.

### *Functions of Capital Market*

The important functions of capital markets are listed below

#### 1. *Link between Savers and Investors*

The capital market functions as a link between savers and investors. It plays an important role in mobilising the savings and diverting them in productive investment. In this way, capital market plays a vital role in transferring the financial resources from surplus and wasteful areas to deficit and productive areas, thus increasing the productivity and prosperity of the country.

#### 2. *Encouragement to Savings*

After the development of capital market, the banking and non-banking institutions provide facilities, which encourage people to save more. In the least-developed countries, in the absence of a capital market, there are very little savings and those who save often invest their savings in unproductive and wasteful directions, i.e., in real estate, gold, jewellery and conspicuous consumption.

#### 3. *Encouragement to Investment*

The capital market facilitates lending to the businessmen and the government and thus encourages investment. It provides facilities through banks and nonbank financial institutions. Various financial assets, *e.g.*, shares, securities, bonds, etc., induce savers to lend to the government or invest in industry. With the development of financial institutions, capital becomes more mobile, interest rate falls and investment increases.

#### 4. *Promotes Economic Growth*

The capital market not only reflects the general condition of the economy, but also smoothens and accelerates the process of economic growth. Various institutions of the capital market, like nonbank financial intermediaries, allocate the resources rationally in accordance with the development needs of the country. The proper allocation of resources results in the expansion of trade and industry in both public and private sectors, thus promoting balanced economic growth in the country.

#### 5. *Stability in Security Prices*

The capital market tends to stabilise the values of stocks and securities and reduce the fluctuations in the prices to the minimum. The process of stabilisation is facilitated by providing capital to the borrowers at a lower interest rate and reducing the speculative and unproductive activities.

### 6. *Benefits to Investors*

The credit market helps the investors, i.e., those who have funds to invest in long-term financial assets, in many ways:

a. It brings together the buyers and sellers of securities and thus ensure the marketability of investments,
b. By advertising security prices, the Stock Exchange enables the investors to keep track of their investments and channelize them into most profitable lines,
c. It safeguards the interests of the investors by compensating them from the Stock Exchange Compensating Fund in the event of fraud and default

## New Issues Market

New issue markets are also known as primary markets. Stocks available for the first time are offered through new issue market. The issuer may be always a new company or an existing company. The issue may be a new one or an old one .Anyway the issuer can be considered as a manufacturer. The important channels of distribution for new issues are the issuing houses, investment bankers and brokers etc. These channels have the power of selling stocks to the public.

### *Functions of New Issue Market*

The important functions of new issue market is to facilitate the transfer of resources from savers to the users. The savers are individuals, Commercial banks insurance companies etc. The users are the public limited companies and the government. The new issue market play an important role in mobilizing the funds and transferring them from the savers to the borrowers for productive purposes, an important requisite of economic growth .It is not only a platform for raising finance to establish new enterprises but also for expansion/diversification/ modernization of existing units.

Methods of floating new issues market

The various methods which are used in the floatation of securities in the new issue market are

- Public issue
- Offer for sale
- Rights issue
- Placement

Players in the new issue market

There are many players in the new issue market. The important of them are the following

- Merchant bankers
- Registrars
- Collecting and coordinating bankers
- Underwriters and brokers
- Printers, Advertising agencies and mailing agencies

## *Functions of Primary Market*

Functions of Primary Market in details are given in the image below. ↓

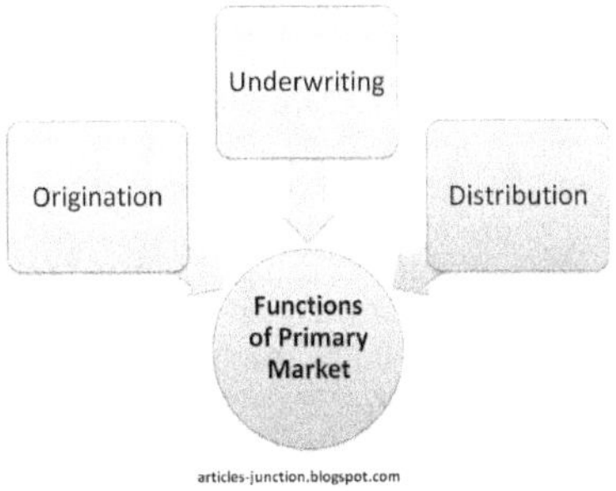


Role and functions of primary market are:

- Origination
- Underwriting
- Distribution

Features and functions of primary market are discussed below.

### 1. *Origination*

In primary market, origination means to investigate, evaluate and process new project proposals. It initiates before an issue is present in the market. It is done with the help of merchant bankers.

The merchant bankers can be

- banks,
- financial institutions,
- private investment firms, etc.

In primary market, the preliminary investigation involves a detailed study of economic, financial, legal, technical aspects to ensure the soundness of the project. The secondary function is performed by sponsoring institutions. They provide advisory service.

Advisory service includes:

- Types of issue,
- Pricing,
- Methods of issue, etc.

### 2. *Underwriting*

In primary market, to ensure success of new issue, there is a need for underwriting firms. The company needs to appoint underwriters. They can be banks or financial institutions or specialized underwriting firms.

In primary market, underwriting can be done by a single underwriter or by a group of underwriters. Minimum subscription is guaranteed by underwriters. If the issue is completely subscribed, no liability would be left for the underwriters. If by chance any part of the issue remains unsold, afterwards the underwriter has no option, rather than buying all the unsubscribed shares.

### *3. Distribution*

In primary market, the success of any grand new issue depends on the number of times the issue is being over-subscribed by the people. The sale of the securities to the supreme or highest investors is termed as distribution.

Distribution Job is given to brokers, dealers and banks. The brokers or agents maintain direct contact with the supreme investors.

## Intermediaries

This is nothing but a firm or a person such as a broker or a consultant, who acts as mediator or a link between parties to business deal, negotiation, investment decisions etc. Consider the case of a money market, a bank act as an intermediary between depositors seeking interest income and borrowers seeking debt capital. They are also called as middle man.

### *Role of Capital Market Intermediary*

The role of intermediaries makes the market vibrant, and to function smoothly and continuously. Intermediaries possess professional expertise and play a promotional role in organising a perfect match between the supply and demand for capital in the market. All those, institutions or individuals, who help to bring the savers and seekers of capital and enable a regular flow of funds from supply to demand points are intermediaries. Thus a commercial bank, an insurance company, a mutual fund, stock exchange or depository are as much intermediaries, as are brokers, merchant bankers, Registrars etc. All intermediaries are service providers and are an integral part of the Capital Market or Money Market.

The market Regulator, SEBI regulates various intermediaries in the primary and secondary markets through its regulations for these intermediaries. SEBI has defined the role of each of the intermediary, the eligibility criteria for granting registration, their functions and responsibilities and the code of conduct to which they are bound. These Regulations also empower SEBI to inspect the functioning of these intermediaries and to collect fees from them and to impose penalties on erring entities. Detailed information about the role and responsibilities of intermediaries are discussed in different articles subsequently under this module. Presently we will briefly cover in a nutshell the core functions of each one of the intermediaries operating in the primary and the secondary markets

### *Primary Market Intermediaries*

### *Merchant Bankers*

Merchant banker" means any person who is engaged in the business of issue management either by making arrangements regarding selling , buying or subscribing to securities as manager, consultant, adviser or rendering corporate advisory service in relation to such issue management Merchant bankers play an important role in issue management process. Lead managers (category I merchant bankers) have to ensure correctness of the information furnished in the offer document. They have to ensure compliance with SEBI rules and regulations as also Guidelines for Disclosures and Investor Protection.

### *Registrars to an Issue and Share Transfer Agents*

Registrars to an Issue (RTI) and Share Transfer Agents (STA) are registered and regulated under SEBI (Registrar to an Issue and Share Transfer Agent) Rules and Regulations, 1993. Under these regulations, registration commenced in 1993-94 and is granted under two categories: Category I to act as both registrar to an issue and share transfer agent and Category II to act as either registrar to an issue or share transfer agent.

SEBI issued instructions to all registered RTIs and/or STAs to appoint compliance officers who would ensure that all rules, regulations, guidelines and directions issues by SEBI, the government and other regulatory authorities are complied with, and any deviations therefrom were to be reported to SEBI

### *Bankers to an Issue*

Scheduled banks acting as bankers to an issue are required to be registered with SEBI in terms of SEBI (Bankers to an Issue) Rules and Regulations, 1994. Under these regulations, registration commenced in 1994-95 and bankers to an issue are required to comply with the guidelines issued and submit quarterly reports of their activities. At the end of March 1997, 80 bankers to an issue were registered with SEBI.

### *Debenture Trustees*

Debenture trustees are registered with SEBI in terms of the SEBI (Debenture Trustees) Rules and Regulations, 1993. Since 1995-96, SEBI has been monitoring the working of debenture trustees by calling for details regarding compliance by issuers of the terms of the debenture trust deed, creation of security, payment of interest, redemption of debentures and redressal of complaints of debenture holders regarding non-receipt of interest/redemption proceeds on due dates. At the end of March 1997, 27 debenture trustees were registered with SEBI.

### *Underwriters*

Underwriters are required to register with SEBI in terms of the SEBI (Underwriters) Rules and Regulations, 1993. In addition to underwriters registered with SEBI in terms of these regulations, all registered merchant bankers in categories I, II and III and stockbrokers and mutual funds registered with SEBI can function as underwriters.

### *Portfolio Manager*

Portfolio managers are required to register with SEBI in terms of the SEBI (Portfolio Managers) Rules and Regulations, 1993. The registered portfolio managers exclusively carry on portfolio management activities. In addition all merchant bankers in categories I and II can act as portfolio managers with prior permission from SEBI. Part III gives further details of the registration of portfolio managers. As on 29-02-2016,223 portfolio managers were registered with SEBI.

### *Secondary Market Intermediaries*

### *Stock Brokers*

In many cases, individual investors transact in securities through sub brokers. It is therefore absolutely imperative to regulate this class of intermediary. The main reason for the limited success in registering large number of sub brokers is that brokers are reluctant to take responsibility of the acts of the sub-brokers. According to the latest data compiled by the Securities and Exchange Board of India (SEBI), the total number of registered brokers in the cash segment stood at 9,643 as on 31-05-2015. In comparison, their numbers stood at 10,128 at the end of the last financial year. Prior to that, the numbers of cash segment brokers were 10,203 and 10,268 at the end of financial years 2010-11 and 2011-12, respectively. SEBI data showed number of brokers in the equity derivative segment has been consistently climbing since 2010-11. At the end of May, the brokers in this category have grown to 3,023 from 2,957 in 2012-13. In currency derivatives, brokers have grown from 2,330 to 2,349 at the end of May.

### *Sub Brokers*

A 'Sub-Broker' is any person who is not a Trading Member of a Stock Exchange but who acts on behalf of a Trading Member as an agent or otherwise for assisting investors in dealing in securities through such Trading Members.

All Sub-Brokers are required to obtain a Certificate of Registration from SEBI without which they are not permitted to deal in securities. SEBI has directed that no Trading Member shall deal with a person who is acting as a Sub-Broker unless he is registered with SEBI and it shall be the responsibility of the Trading Member to ensure that his clients are not acting in the capacity of a Sub-Broker unless they are registered with SEBI as a Sub-Broker.

It is mandatory for Trading Members to enter into an agreement with all the Sub-Brokers. The agreement lays down the rights and responsibilities of Trading Members as well as Sub-Brokers. According to SEBI 15,000 sub brokers have gone out of business as on April 2013.

# 4. STOCK MARKET

A stock market is always a network of buyers and sellers, which may include securities listed on a stock exchange. This also known as the equity market. The stock market is one of the most important components of a free-market economy, as it provides companies with access to capital in exchange for giving investors a since of ownership in the company. The stock market makes it possible to grow small initial sums of money into large ones, and to become wealthy without taking the risk of starting a business or making the sacrifices that often accompany a high-paying career.

## Role of a Stock Market

A stock exchange allows companies to raise funds by providing them with access to a pool of private and institutional investors.

An exchange's role in financial markets is pivotal for the development of the financial industry.

### 1. *Brings Companies and Investors together*

An exchange allows financial intermediaries to distribute company shares, bonds or financial products to retail and institutional investors through its trading system or platform connection with brokerage firms and banks.

### 2. *Enables Issuers (ie Companies) to Raise New Capital*

Companies have many options to raise capital. For example:

- Self-financing- generation of one's own capital from one's own income, instead of acquiring it from external resources
- Bank loans are the most "traditional financial resources and are normally used to finance smaller projects. For example, supermarkets use generated cash flows for self-financing as they pay creditors 2 months in arrears.
- Fund raising options such as Private Equity and IPOs are used to finance extraordinary events such as mergers and acquisitions to support companies during their growth phase.

### 3. *Facilitates the Process of Investors Subscribing in Shares (Securities)*

Investors access the trading platforms and invest in a company's shares.

### 4. *Provides Capital to Companies and Investors*

To allow a company to be listed, Exchanges require that the company meets its eligibility criteria and "substantial" financial and strategic standards.

Eligibility criteria normally depend on the segment and the market which companies have access to. They are normally linked to a company's balance sheet certification, to its governance, capitalisation and free float.

Substantial financial and strategic standards become even more important, during the company's admission phase to a specific market. The following company values are some examples of substantial requisites:

- Drive towards value creation
- Clear strategy, reported in the business plan
- Good competitive positioning
- Balanced financial structure

- Management autonomy
- Growing profitability
- Good internal organization

It is critical for those companies who want to list on an exchange to achieve both formal and substantial requisites formal requisites alone will not lead to strong interest from the market.

## Functions of Stock Market

### *The Important Functions of Stock Markets are the following*

#### *1. Economic Barometer*

A stock exchange is a reliable barometer to measure the economic condition of a country .Every major change in country and economy is reflected in the prices of shares. The rise or fall in the share prices indicates the boom or recession cycle of the economy. Stock exchange is also known as a pulse of economy or economic mirror which reflects the economic conditions of a country.

#### *2. Pricing of Securities*

The stock market helps to value the securities on the basis of demand and supply factors. The securities of profitable and growth oriented companies are valued higher as there is more demand for such securities. The valuation of securities is useful for investors, government and creditors. The investors can know the value of their investment, the creditors can value the creditworthiness and government can impose taxes on value of securities.

#### *3. Safety of Transactions*

In stock market only the listed securities are traded and stock exchange authorities include the companies names in the trade list only after verifying the soundness of company. The companies which are listed they also have to operate within the strict rules and regulations. This ensures safety of dealing through stock exchange.

#### *4. Contributes to Economic Growth*

In stock exchange securities of various companies are bought and sold. This process of disinvestment and reinvestment helps to invest in most productive investment proposal and this leads to capital formation and economic growth.

#### *5. Spreading of Equity Cult*

Stock exchange encourages people to invest in ownership securities by regulating new issues, better trading practices and by educating public about investment.

#### *6. Providing Scope for Speculation*

To ensure liquidity and demand of supply of securities the stock exchange permits healthy speculation of securities.

#### *7. Liquidity*

The main function of stock market is to provide ready market for sale and purchase of securities. The presence of stock exchange market gives assurance to investors that their investment can be converted into cash whenever they want. The investors can invest in long term investment projects without any hesitation, as because of stock exchange they can convert long term investment into short term and medium term.

## 8. *Better Allocation of Capital*

The shares of profit making companies are quoted at higher prices and are actively traded so such companies can easily raise fresh capital from stock market. The general public hesitates to invest in securities of loss making companies. So stock exchange facilitates allocation of investor's fund to profitable channels.

## 9. *Promotes the Habits of Savings and Investment*

The stock market offers attractive opportunities of investment in various securities. These attractive opportunities encourage people to save more and invest in securities of corporate sector rather than investing in unproductive assets such as gold, silver, etc.

# Listing

Listing refers to the entry of the security of public limited company on a recognized stock exchange for trading. Listing of securities is undertaken with the primary objective of providing marketability, liquidity and transferability to securities.

### *Merits of Listing*

The merits of listing are as follows

- Liquidity
- Best Prices
- Regular information
- Periodic reports
- Transferability
- Income tax benefit
- Wide publicity

### *Demerits*

- Listed companies are subjected to various regulatory measures of the stock exchanges and SEBI
- Essential information has to be submitted by the listed companies to the stock exchanges.
- Annual General meeting, Annual reports have to be sent to a large number of share holders. This creates large amount of unnecessary expenditure.
- Public offer itself is an expensive exercise. But, This is a pre -requisite for the company's shares to be listed.

### *Qualification for listing*

There are certain minimum requirements for a security to be listed in a stock exchange. They are given below

- Minimum issued capital
- Payment of excess application money
- Listing on multiple exchanges
- The number of share holders
- Appointment of market maker
- Articles of association
- Cost of public issue
- Advertisement
- Minimum subscription
- Applying mode
- Public offer size

## *Listing Requirements*

Procedure and Conditions for listing of securities on WDM segment:

- All Listing are subject to compliance with Byelaws, Rules and other requirements framed by the Exchange from time to time in addition to the SEBI and other statutory requirements.
- The Issuer of security proposed for listing has to forward an application in the format prescribed in Annexure I of this booklet.
- Every issuer, depending on the category and type of security has to submit along with application, such supporting documents/information as specified in Annexure I of this booklet and as prescribed by the Exchange from time to time.
- On getting an in-principle consent of the exchange the issuer has to enter into a listing agreement in the prescribed format under its common seal.
- Upon listing, the Issuer has to comply with all requirements of law, any guidelines/ directions of Central Government, other Statutory or local authority.
- The Issuer shall also comply with the post listing compliance as laid out in the listing agreement and shall also comply with the rules, bye-laws, regulations and any other guidelines of the Exchange as amended from time to time.
- Listing on WDM segment does not imply a listing on CM segment also or vice versa.
- If the equity shares of an issuer are listed on other stock exchanges but not listed on Capital Market segment of the Exchange, though eligible, then the debt securities of the said issuer will not be permitted to be listed on the WDM segment.
- The Exchange reserves the right to change any of the requirements indicated in this booklet / document without prior notice

Criteria for listing on the WDM segment: The security proposed for listing on the WDM segment of the NSE should comply with the requirements indicated hereunder:

| **Issuer** | **Eligibility Criteria for Listing** | |
|---|---|---|
| | **Public Issue** | **Private Placement** |
| Public Sector Undertaking: Min. 51% holding by Central Govt., and/or State Govts. and/or Govt. Company Less than 51% shareholding | As applicable to Corporate<br>As applicable to Corporate | As applicable to Corporate<br>As applicable to Corporate |
| Statutory Corporation under Special Act of Parliament/State Legislature, Local bodies/ authorities: Min. 51% holding by Central Govt and/or State Govts. and/or Govt. Company Less than 51% shareholding | As applicable to PSU<br>As applicable to Corporate | As applicable to Corporate<br>As applicable to Corporate |
| Financial Institutions u/s 4A of Companies Act, 1956 including Industrial Development Corporations: SLR Bonds Non-SLR Bonds | Eligible<br>Eligible | Credit rating<br>Credit rating |
| Banks: Scheduled banks and Net worth of Rs.50cr or above | Eligible | Credit rating |
| Corporates: Paid up capital of Rs.10 crore or Market capitalization of Rs.25 crore (Net worth in case of unlisted companies | Eligible | Credit rating |
| Infrastructure Companies:<br>Tax Exemption and recognition as infrastructure company under related | Eligible | Credit rating |
| Mutual Fund Units:<br>Any SEBI registered Mutual Fund/Scheme: Investment objective to invest predominantly in debt or Scheme is traded in secondary market as Debt instrument. | Eligible | Eligible |

## *Listing of Securities*

Listing criteria for companies on the CM segment of NSE

| Criteria | Initial public offerings(IPOS) | Companies listed on other exchanges |
|---|---|---|
| Paid-up Equity Capital (PUEAC) /Market Capitalisation (MC)/ Net worth | PUEC≥₹ 10 Crores and MC≥₹ 25Crores | PUEC≥10 Crores and MC≥ 25Crores or<br>PUEC≥25 Crores or<br>MC≥₹50 crores or the company shall have a net worth of not less than ₹50 crores in each of the preceding three financial year. |
| Company/promoter's Track Record | Atleast 3 years track record of either<br>a)The applicant seeking listing OR<br>b)the promoters/promoting company incorporated in or outside India OR<br>c) Partnership firm and subsequently converted into company not in existence as a Company for three years and approaches the Exchange for listing. The company subsequently formed would be considered for listing only on fulfilment of conditions stipulated by SEBI in this regard. | Atleast three years track record of either<br>a)The applicant seeking listing; OR<br>b)the promoters/promoting company, incorporated in or outside India. |
| Dividend Record/Net worth/Distributable Profits | ------- | Dividend paid in atleast 2 out of last three financial years immediately preceding three year in which the application has been made or<br>The net worth of the applicants atleast₹5 crores or<br>The applicant has distributable profits in least two out of the last three financial year |
| Listing | | Listed on any other stock exchange for at least last three years or listed on the exchange having national trading terminals for at least one year. |
| Other requirements | a) No disciplinary action by other stock exchanges/regulatory authority in past three years<br>b) satisfactory redressal mechanism for investor grievances,<br>c) distribution of shareholding<br>d) details of litigation record in past three years | a)No disciplinary action by other stock exchanges/regulatory authority in past 3 years<br>b)satisfactory redressal mechanism for investor grievances,<br>c)distribution of shareholdings and<br>d)details of litigation record in past |

***Listing Fee in the CM Segment***

The listing fee applicable from April 1, 2014 is as follows

| Particulars | Amount(₹) |
|---|---|
| Initial Listing Fees | 50,000 |
| **Annual Listing Fees(based on paid up share,bond and/or debenture capital)** | |
| a)up to 10 crores | 90,000 |
| b)Above ten crore and upto 25 crores | 1,20,000 |
| c)Above 25 crore and upto 50 crores | 1,40,000 |
| d)Above 50 crore and upto 100 crores | 2,40,000 |
| e)Above 100 crore and upto 200 crores | 3,15,000 |
| f)Above 200 crores and upto 300 crores | 4,05,000 |
| g)Above 300 crores and upto 400 crores | 4,90,000 |
| h)Above400 crores and upto 500 crores | 6,50,000 |

***Companies Listed,Permitted to Trade,Available for Trading on the CM Segment***

| Month/Year | No.of Companies Listed* | No.of Companies permitted* | No.of Companies Available for Trading*@ | Market Capitalisation(crores) |
|---|---|---|---|---|
| Mar-11 | 1,574 | 61 | 1,484 | 6,702,616 |
| Mar-12 | 1,646 | 73 | 1,563 | 6,096,518 |
| Mar-13 | 1,666 | 76 | 1,582 | 6,239,035 |
| Mar-14 | 1,688 | 75 | 1,586 | 7,277,720 |
| Mar-15 | 1,733 | 4 | 1,544 | 9,930,122 |

Note

*At the end of the period.

@Excludes suspended companies

#CNX Nifty Index commenced from November 3, 1995

## CNX Nifty Junior commenced from November 4, 1996

No.of companies Traded excludes Mutual Funds and ETFs

**Source: www.nseindia.com**

## Registration of Broker

A broker is an individual or party who negotiates transactions between a consumer and a seller, they also get a portion of the total sales when the negotiation is finalized. A broker also serves as a consumer and a seller; other defines them as an agent. Brokers do exists in different types of industries such as; real estate, food, logistics or clothing industries. They serve as the third person or a facilitator between buyer and the seller.

Following is the criteria for registering as a sole proprietor broker:

Criteria

| | |
|---|---|
| Status | Indian Citizen |
| Age | Minimum age : 21 years |
| Education | At least HSC or equivalent qualification |
| Experience | Applicant should have an experience for not less than two years as a partner with, or an authorised assistant or authorised clerk or remisier or apprentice to, a member. |

Further to the capital and network requirements, No entity shall be admitted as a member/ partner or director of the member if

- It has been adjudged bankrupt or a receiver order in bankruptcy has been made against him or he has been proved to be insolvent even though he has obtained his final discharge;
- it has compounded with his creditors for less than full discharge of debts;
- it has been convicted of an offence involving a fraud or dishonesty;
- it is engaged as a principal or employee in any business other than that of Securities, except as a broker or agent not involving any personal financial liability or for providing merchant banking, underwriting or corporate or investment advisory services, unless he undertakes to severe its connections with such business on admission, if admitted;
- it has been at any time expelled or declared a defaulter by any other Stock Exchange or he has been debarred from trading in securities by an Regulatory Authorities like SEBI, RBI etc;
- it incurs such disqualification under the provisions of the Securities Contract (Regulations) Act, 1956 or Rules made there-under so as to disentitle such persons from seeking membership of a stock exchange;
- it incurs such disqualification consequent to which NSE determines it to be not in public interest to admit him as a member on the Exchange, provided that in case of registered firms, body corporates and companies, the condition from (will apply to, all partners in case of partnership firms, all directors in case of companies; NSE may from time to time modify / expand the scope of activities that could be considered as relevant experience for the above purpose.

Trading Members are requested to note the following with regards to Sub-Broker registrations:

- Members would continue to submit the Sub-Broker registration applications electronically through ENIT and ensure that the physical documents are received by the Exchange within 7 days from submission of application in ENIT else the registration would be rejected.
- Members would be informed through letter and bill vide FTP to make available in its Exchange Dues Account the processing fee amounting to Rs. 2,000/- plus the applicable service tax for every Sub-Broker registration application. Alternatively, the status of the Sub-Broker registration application would be 'Documents Received' in ENIT.
- In case of any deficiency in the application, the application form would be returned to the Member. In case the Member desires to re-submit the same application vide ENIT after rectifying the deficiencies, then the Member needs to go to the Sub-Broker master and click on the 'Resubmit' button.
- The Exchange would start collecting the SEBI registration fees by debiting the Exchange Dues Account of the Members for Sub-Broker applications which are processed and complete in all respect from the very next day of intimation to the Member.
- After the SRC has granted recognition, status of Sub-Broker applications uploaded by Exchange to SEBI would be informed to Members by way of display of 'Upload Reference Number' and 'Upload Date' through ENIT within 3 days of upload by Exchange to SEBI.
- On receipt of the Sub-Broker registration certificate from SEBI, the details of registration number and registration date would be made available to the Member through ENIT. The physical Sub-Broker registration certificate would be forwarded to the Member for onward dispatch to the Sub-Broker.

***Documents to be Submitted***

Members need to attach scanned copies and send physical copies of the following documents (as of the latest date) along with the Sub-Broker registration application form:

- Proof of address of the applicant entity (trade name) - This is mandatory and the address on the proof needs to match with that on the application. Only the latest telephone bill, electricity bill, valid ration card, valid passport, valid driving license and bank statement of the last one month from a nationalized bank is acceptable.
- Proof of experience certificate– This is mandatory only in case the qualification of Individual/Partner/Director is less than HSC. Only experience of at least two years in the capacity of employee/dealer in capital market in the name of Individual/ Partner/ Director is acceptable

## Different Types of Brokers

### 1. *Insurance Broker*

This type of broker works with different insurance companies, providing the best available policies for his clients. Insurance broker is different from a typical agent; however they do have similarities with the service that they offer such as; providing structure policies, settling customer's claims and usually works on a commission basis.

An insurance broker is specialized in one specific type of insurance or deal, these are; Health, life, home, auto and other types of insurance. Some insurance brokers are required to undergo training and must acquire formal licenses from the Security and Exchange Commission or other government associations that deals with investments

### 2. *Real Estate Broker*

A real estate broker is a person who helps the seller sells a property; he serves as an intermediary between buyers and sellers. Although they have a big role between the seller and the buyer, a real estate broker does not have the power or right to make important decisions on the client's behalf. He must also acquire a formal license before proceeding with any transactions; he is required to take a 90-hour course and must pass an exam on a real estate law. This type of broker usually has salespersons known as the "real estate agents" their role is to assist the broker in the selling process.

### 3. *Stock Broker*

Main role of a stock broker is to trade stocks on behalf of his clients through a brokerage account, these stocks are the mutual funds and bonds. Stock brokers usually charge a $15 commission per trade. There are also two kinds of stock brokers, and these are; Discount brokers and full-service brokers

### 4. *High -End Broker*

High-End Broker's job is to study and plan the condition of the economy, this type of broker usually have a team of researchers, they study the status of the market and gives advises to their clients on when is the best time to buy or sell a property. Clients of a high-end broker are usually people in the high society level.

### 5. *On -Line Broker*

On line broker works through different brokerage websites. Presenting investment database information for their clients via online in their main role, database information includes; graphs, charts and investment tips

### 6. *Discount Broker*

A discount broker carries out buy and sells orders at a reduced commission, compared to a full service broker, but he doesn't provide investment advices

## Method of Trading

### *Day Trading*

- Trading Methods In Stock Market (Day Trading) or intraday trading strategies involves taking a position in the markets with a view of squaring that position before the end of that day.
- A day trader typically trades several times a day looking for fractions of a point to a few points per trade, but who close out all their positions by day`s end.
- The goal of a day trader is to capitalize on price movement within one trading day.
- Unlike investors, a day trader may hold positions for only a few seconds or minutes, and never overnight.
- Real day trading means not holding on to your stock positions beyond the current trading day; in other words, not holding any position overnight. This is really the safest way to do day trading because you are not exposed to the potential losses that can occur when the stock exchange is closed due to news that can affect the prices of your stocks.

Day trading can be further subdivided into a number of styles:

1. **Scalpers**: This style of day trading involves the rapid and repeated buying and selling of a large volume of stocks within seconds or minutes. The objective is to earn a small per share profit on each transaction while minimizing the risk.
2. **Momentum Traders:** This style of day trading involves identifying and trading stocks that are in a moving patterns during the day, in an attempt to buy such stocks at bottoms and sell at tops.

### *Advantages of Day Trading strategies*

1. **Zero Overnight Risk**: Since positions are closed prior to the end of the trading day, news and events that affect the next trading day`s opening prices do not effect your portfolio.
2. Increased **Leverage**: Day Traders have a greater leverage on their trading capital because of low margin requirements as their trades that are closed in the same market day. This increased leverage can increase your profits if used wisely.
3. **Profit in any market direction**: Day trading often will utilize short-selling to take advantage of declining stock prices. The ability to lock in profits even as markets fall throughout the trading day is extremely useful during bear market conditions.

### *Swing Trading*

Swing Trading takes advantage of brief price swings in strongly trending stocks to ride the momentum in the direction of the trend.

- Swing trading combines the best of two worlds the slower pace of investing and the increased potential gains of day trading.
- Swing traders hold stocks for days or weeks playing the general upward or downward trends..
- Swing Trading is not high-speed day trading. Some people call it momentum investing, because you only hold positions that are making major moves.
- By rolling your money over rapidly through short term gains you can quickly build up your equity.

## How does Swing Trading Work?

1. The basic strategy of Swing Trading is to jump into a strongly trending stock after its period of consolidation or correction is complete.
2. Strongly trending stocks often make a quick move after completing its correction which one can profit from.
3. One then sells the stock after 2 to 7 days for a 5-25% move. This process can be repeated over and over again. One can also play the short side by shorting stocks that fall through support levels.
4. In brief a Swing Trader`s goal is to make money by capturing the quick moves that stocks make in their life span, and at the same time controlling their risk by proper money management techniques.

Advantages of Swing Trading

1. Swing Trading combines the best of two worlds the slower pace of investing and the increased potential gains of day trading.
2. Swing Trading works well for part-time traders especially those doing it while at work. While day traders typically have to stay glued to their computers for hours at a time, feverishly watching minute-to-minute changes in quotes, swing trading doesn't require that type of focus and dedication.
3. While Day Traders gamble on stocks popping or falling by fractions of points, Swing Traders try to ride swings in the market. Swing Traders buy fewer stocks and aim for bigger gains, they pay lower brokerage and, theoretically, have a better chance of earning larger gains.
4. With day trading, the only person getting rich is the broker. Swing traders go for the meat of the move while a day trader just gets scraps. Furthermore, to swing trade, you don't need sophisticated computer hook-ups or lightning quick execution services and you don't have to play extremely volatile stocks.

We believe that the Swing Trading method is a better way for the individual investor to attain superior investment results through short-term trading in the stock market. This trading strategy has been carefully designed for the needs of the individual investor who does not have the resources that institutions and professional money managers may have.

To fully understand what swing trading really is you first need to understand what up/ down trends are.

**Up Trend**: Simply put an uptrend is a series of higher highs and higher lows. In other words, an uptrend is a series of successive rallies that extend though previous high points, interrupted by declines which terminate above the low point of the preceding sell-off. Often the high of the last swing in the trend will serve as support for the next low. These areas are circled.

**Down Trend**: Simply put a downtrend is a series of lower highs and lower lows. In other words, a downtrend is a series of successive declines that extend though previous low points, interrupted by increases which terminate below the high point of the preceding rally. Often the low of the last swing in the stocks trend will serve as resistance for the next high. These are circled.

**Long Swing Trades:** Once an uptrend has been identified a swing trader looks for buying opportunities in that stock. This can be identified when the stock experiences a minor pullback or correction within that uptrend. The swing trader then activates a trailing buy-stop technique. If prices break out above the trailing stop loss, you will be stopped out and long in the trade. If prices decline, your buy-stop will not be touched.

**Short Swing Trades**: Once an downtrend has been identified a swing trader looks for selling opportunities in that stock. This can be identified when the stock experiences a minor rally within that downtrend. The swing trader then activates a trailing sell-stop technique. If prices break down and fall below the trailing stop loss, you will be stopped out on the short side. If prices rally, your sell-stop will not be touched.

### *Trend Trading Strategies*

A trend is nothing but the general direction of the price of an asset or market in general.

A trend can apply to equities, bonds, commodities and any other market which is characterized by a long-term movement in price or volume.

### *Trend Trading*

1. Trend trading is one of the most effective and easy to use methods for making money in the market. Trend trading success depends on identifying and catching the trend after it has started and getting out of the trend as soon as possible after the trend reverses.
2. Trend Trading involves taking a position in the markets with a view of holding that position for weeks to months for larger than normal gains. Trend traders or investors generally trade the long term or secular trends and are not concerned with the day to day market volatility.

### *Advantages of Trend Trading*

1. Trend trading is the fastest and most risk free way to make money in the markets. In trend trading you can identify a change of trend in the market as early as possible, take your position, ride the trend and close your position shortly after the trend reverses.
2. With Trend Trading it is very possible to catch 60 to 80% of many intermediate term and long term market movements and thus create wealth for yourself and your family.
3. Trend Trading will help you take large profits out of the market, without having to watch the market or stocks on a minute-by-minute or even a day-by-day basis.
4. Whether you are a short-term day trader or a long-term investor, we believe incorporating Trend Trading into your overall trading plan is a must. There are two types of trades: Income producing trades and Wealth-building trades. Swing trading and day trading produce income, while Trend Trading Picks is designed to amass wealth.

## Speculators

Speculators are people who analyze and forecast future price movements, trading contracts with the hope of making a profit. Speculators put their money at risk and must be prepared to accept out right losses in the futures market. Speculators play one of four primary roles in financial markets, along with hedgers who engage in transactions to offset some other pre-existing risk, arbitrageurs who seek to profit from situations where fungible instruments trade at different prices in different market segments, and investors who seek profit through long-term ownership of an instrument's underlying attributes. Under section 43(5), a speculative transaction is defined to mean a transaction in which a contract for the purchase or sale of any commodity, including stocks and shares, is periodically or ultimately settled otherwise than by the actual delivery or transfer of the commodity or scrips. Dec 23, 2007.

### *Who is a Speculator?*

Before we get too deep, we have to make a distinction between a speculator and typical middleman. A middleman can be thought of as the means by which products are dispersed. It would be a very different world if the products we need and/or want were produced nearby. More often than not, every product in your house has at least a component that has taken an international voyage to get there. The markup of the middleman usually matches the materials and overhead costs used to ship, sort, bag and display those products in a store near you, plus some profit to keep the middleman fulfilling this function. This gets maple syrup to Hawaii, Korean laptops to New York and other products to destinations where a higher profit can be realized.

In contrast, the speculator makes his/her money through contracts that allow him/her to control commodities without ever directly handling them. Generally speaking, speculators don't arrange shipment and storage for the commodities that they control. This hands-off approach has given speculators the erroneous image of aloof financiers jumping into markets they care nothing about in order to make profits from the producers - the salt-of-the-earth types that legislators are always claiming to defend.

### *Avoiding Shortages*

The most obvious function that people overlook when criticizing speculators is their ability to head off shortages. Shortages are dangerous because they lead to price spikes and/or rationing of resources. If a drought kills off half the yield of hay in a given year, it's natural to expect the price of hay to double in the fall. On wider economies of scale, however, these shortages are not as easy to spot. That's why commodities speculators help to keep an eye on overall production, recognizing shortages and moving product to places of need (and consequently higher profit) through intermediaries–the middlemen who use futures contracts to control their costs. In this sense, speculators act as financiers to allow the middleman to keep supply flowing around the world.

More than merely financing middlemen, speculators influence prices of commodities, currencies and other goods by using futures to encourage stockpiling against shortages. Just because we want cheap oil or mangoes doesn't mean we should blame speculators when prices rise. More often, other factors, such as OPEC and tropical hurricanes, have raised the risk of a more volatile price in the future, so speculators raise prices now to smooth down the potentially larger future price. A higher price dampens current demand, decreasing consumption and prompting more resources - more people to take up mango growing or more funds for oil exploration - to go into increasing stockpiles. This price smoothing means that, while you might not appreciate paying $5 for gas or a mango, you will always be able to find some.

### *Preventing Manipulation*

While people may recognize speculators' importance in preventing shortages and smoothing prices, very few associate speculation with guarding against manipulation. In markets with healthy speculation, that is many different speculators participating, it is much harder to pull off a large-scale manipulation and much more costly to attempt it.

### *Consequences and Currency*

Even when we leave the level of commodities and go into one of the largest markets in the world, forex, we can see how speculators are essential for preventing manipulation. Governments are some of the most blatant manipulators. Governments want more money to fund programs while also wanting a robust currency for international trade. These conflicting interests encourage governments to peg their currencies while inflating away true value to pay for domestic spending. It's currency speculators, through shorting and other means, that keep governments honest by speeding up the consequences of inflationary policies.

### *Show Me the Money*

Speculators can make a lot of money when they are right, and that can anger producers and consumers alike. But these outsized profits are balanced against the risks they protect those same consumers and producers from. For every speculator making millions on a single contract, there is at least an equal number losing millions on the trade - or a dollar on each of a million smaller trades. In very volatile markets, like those after a natural disaster or black swan event, speculators often lose money on the whole, keeping prices stable by making up the difference out of their deep pockets.

### *Hug a Speculator*

Taken cumulatively, speculation helps us far more than it could ever hurt us by moving risk to those who can financially handle it. Despite the misunderstanding and negativity speculators have to face, the potential for outsized profits will continue to attract people, as long as governments don't regulate them into oblivion. With all the negativity aimed towards short-sellers and speculators, it's easy for us to forget that their activities maintain prices, prevent shortages and increase the amount of risk they undertake. I don't want to become a speculator, but it's important that we preserve speculative investing for the people who do - more than important, it's a necessity for a healthy market and vibrant economy.

## Speculative Transactions

### *Forward Rates and Spot Rate*

The forward rate and spot rate are different prices, or quotes, for different contracts. The forward rate is the settlement price of a forward contract, while the spot rate is the settlement price of a spot contract.

A spot contract is a contract that involves the purchase or sale of a commodity, security or currency for immediate delivery and payment on the spot date, which is normally two business days after the trade date. The spot rate, or spot price, is the price quoted for the immediate settlement of the spot contract. For example, say an investor believes orange juice is more expensive in the winter due to supply and demand. However, the investor cannot buy a spot contract for delivery in December because the commodity will spoil. A forward contract is a better fit for the investment.

Unlike a spot contract, a forward contract is a contract that involves an agreement of contract terms on the current date with the delivery and payment at a specified future date. Contrary to a spot rate, a forward rate is used to quote a financial transaction that takes place on a future date and is the settlement price of a forward contract. However, depending on the security being traded, the forward rate can be calculated using the spot rate.

For example, say a Chinese electronic manufacturer has a large order to be shipped to America in one year. The Chinese manufacturer engages in a currency forward and sells $20 million in exchange for Chinese Yuan at a forward rate of $6.21 per Chinese Yuan. Therefore, the Chinese electronic manufacturer is obligated to deliver 20 million euro's at the specified rate on the specified date, six months from the current date, regardless of fluctuating currency spot rates.

### *Types of Speculators*

There are four types of speculators who are active on the stock exchanges in India. They are known as Bull, Bear, Stag, and Lame Duck. These names have been derived from the animal world to bring out the nature and working of speculators.

### *Bull*

A Bull or Tejiwala is an operator who expects a rise in prices of securities in the future. In anticipation of price rise he makes purchases of shares at present and other securities with the intention to sell at higher prices in future. He is called bull because just like a bull tends to throw his victim up in the air, the bull speculator stimulates the price to rise. He is an optimistic speculator.

### *Bear*

A bear or Mandiwala speculator expects prices to fall in future and sells securities at present with a view to purchase the mat lower prices in future. A bear does not have securities at present but sells them at higher prices in anticipation that he will supply them by purchasing at lower prices in future. A bear usually presses its victim down to ground. Similarly the bear speculator tends to force down the prices of securities. A bear is a pessimistic speculator

### *Examples for Bulls &Bears*

### *Recent Bull Markets*

There have been a number of recent bull markets. Most notably has been the rally in the Sensex, where it has run from 7,000 in June of 2005 to over 21,000 in early 2008. Another bull market occurred in the oil markets, where a barrel of oil ran from $60 to over $150 in roughly 18 months.

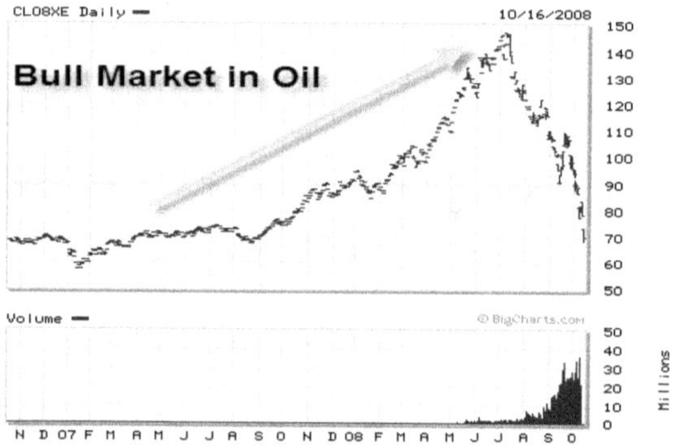


### *Bear Market*

Trading a bear market rally requires little skill and is nothing more than the resolve to take on a long position. Technical analysis is completely out the window, because every indicator will be oversold and there will be no technical reason for the market to bounce. Fundamentals will look just as bleak and provide no real indication of why the market should be bought. All a trader needs to do is wait for the market to sell off 25% to 35% and look for a wash out day. The next step is to commit to buying the market with the understanding that you might have to sit through a few days of pain, but at some point the market will reverse.

## *Stag*

A stag is a cautious speculator in the stock exchange. He applies for shares in new companies and expects to sell them at a premium, if he gets an allotment. He selects those companies whose shares are in more demand and are likely to carry a premium. He sells the shares before being called to pay the allotment money. He is also called a premium hunter.

## *Lame Duck*

When a bear finds it difficult to fulfill his commitment, he is said to be struggling like a lame duck. A bear speculator contracts to sell securities at a later date. On the appointed time he is not able to get the securities as the holders are not willing to part with them. In such situations he feels concerned. Moreover, the buyer is not willing to carry over the transactions.

## *Clearing Securities*

NSCCL carries out clearing and settlement functions as per the settlement cycles provided in the settlement schedule.

The clearing function of the clearing corporation is designed to work out a) what members are due to deliver and b) what members are due to receive on the settlement date. Settlement is a two way process which involves transfer of funds and securities on the settlement date.

NSCCL has also devised mechanism to handle various exceptional situations like security shortages, bad delivery, company objections, auction settlement etc. Clearing is the process of determination of obligations, after which the obligations are discharged by settlement.

NSCCL has two categories of clearing members: trading clearing members and custodians. Trading members can trade on a proprietary basis or trade for their clients. All proprietary trades become the member's obligation for settlement. Where trading members trade on behalf of their clients they could trade for normal clients or for clients who would be settling through their custodians. Trades which are for settlement by Custodians are indicated with a Custodian Participant (CP) code and the same is subject to confirmation by the respective Custodian. The custodian is required to confirm settlement of these trades on T + 1 day by the cut-off time 1.00 p.m. Non-confirmation by custodian devolves the trade obligation on the member who had input the trade for the respective client.

A multilateral netting procedure is adopted to determine the net settlement obligations (delivery/receipt positions) of the clearing members. Accordingly, a clearing member would have either pay-in or pay-out obligations for funds and securities separately. In the case of securities in the Trade for Trade – Surveillance segment and auction trades, obligations are determined on a gross basis i.e. every trade results into a deliverable and receivable obligation of funds and securities. Members pay-in and pay-out obligations for funds and securities are determined by 2.30 p.m. on T + 1 day and are downloaded to them so that they can settle their obligations on the settlement day (T+2).

### *Blank Transfer*

A transfer signed by the transferor, but with a blank for the name of the transferee is called a blank transfer. In a blank transfer neither the transferee's name and signature nor the date of sale are filed in the transfer form. The transferee is at liberty to sell it again without filling his name and signature to a subsequent buyer. The process of purchase and sale can be repeated any number of times with the blank deed and ultimately when it reaches the hands of one who wants to retain the shares, he can fill in his name and date and get it registered in the company's books. Until a transferee is as registered as a shareholder the transferor will continue to be the shareholder of the company and he remains liable for the unpaid amount if any

The facility of blank transfers has often been used for illegal purposes. Sometimes it is used to avoid taxes. Besides the identity of the real owner may be concealed. Consequently section 108 has been amended which has considerably restricted the scope of blank transfers. Section 108-A imposes restriction on the period of currency of blank transfers. It provides that every instrument of transfer shall be in prescribed form bearing the date of issue stamped by the prescribed authority and the said instrument shall be delivered to the company for registration:

i. In the case of shares dealt in or quoted on a recognized stock exchange at any time before the register of members is closed for the first time after the stamped date or within two months from the date put on the form by the prescribed authority, whichever is later; and
ii. In any other case, within two months from the date of such presentation to the prescribed authority.

## Demat

In India, shares and securities are held electronically in a dematerialized (or "Demat") (/dimæt/;) account, instead of the investor taking physical possession of certificates. A Dematerialized account is opened by the investor while registering with an investment broker (or sub-broker).Dematerialisation is the process of converting physical shares into electronic format. An investor who wants to dematerialise his shares needs to open a demat account with Depository Participant. Investor surrenders his physical shares and in turn gets electronic shares in his demat account.

## *What is Dematerialization?*

Technology has brought about a drastic change in our everyday lives. The stock markets too have not been left untouched by the change. In 1875, the Bombay Stock Exchange was founded with an open outcry floor trading exchange. Traders would stand on the floor and shout prices of stocks for buying or selling. Then, money would be exchanged for physical receipts of the shares called the certificate. This led to a great amount of paperwork. Even the settlements of trade agreements took time because of the need to deliver the share certificates.

### *Much has Changed Since*

In 1996, dematerialization was embraced. Dematerialization is the process by which physical share certificates held by an investor are converted into an equivalent number of securities in electronic form and credited into the investor's demat account.

### *Benefits of Dematerialization*

### *Common Bank*

Dematerialization is not just for shares, but also for debt instruments like bonds. Now, you can hold all your investments in a single account.

### *Automatic Update*

Since this is a common account, you don't have to keep giving all your details like addresses every time you transact or every time you change the details. These details are automatically made available to companies you transact with.

### *Odd-lot Problem*

Earlier, shares were transacted in lots. A single or odd number of securities could not be transacted. This problem is now eliminated.

### *Delivery Risks*

Dematerialization has also eliminated the risks of fake shares, thefts, deliveries gone wrong, and so on, and reduced the paperwork involved. Time of delivery has also reduced drastically. Once your trade is approved, the securities are automatically credited to your account. This applies to other company-related activities like stock splits, stock bonuses, and so on.

### *Cost Reduction*

Earlier, when you transferred the securities, you incurred extra costs due to the stamp duty. This is not a problem with the demat form.

### *Easy to Hold*

Paper certificates are vulnerable to tears and damage. In contrast, the dematerialized or demat format is a safe and convenient way to hold securities. You also have a nomination facility, whereby you can facilitate a transfer of shares in the event of your demise.

## *Understand how the Demat Account Works*

### *Central Depository*

There are two depositories in India – the CDSL and NSDL. They hold all the demat accounts. The central depository holds details of your shareholding on your behalf like banks.

### *Unique ID*

Each demat account has a unique number for identification purposes. This is the number you need to provide for transactions. The number will help the exchange and companies identify you and credit the shares in your account.

### *Depository Participants*

Access to the central depository is provided by the Depository Participants or DPs. They act as the intermediary between the central depository and the investor. DPs could be banks, brokers or financial institutions that are empowered to offer demat services. Kotak Securities is one such Depository Participant (DP). You open a demat account or a Beneficial Owner (BO) accounts with a DP, who will provide you a unique access to the central depository.

### *Portfolio Holding*

The demat account holds all your securities. So, whenever you check your account, you can see your portfolio holding and its details. These are updated automatically every time you conduct a transaction – be is buying or selling a security.

## *How do you Open a Demat Account?*

- Fill up an account opening form and submit along with copies of the required documents and a passport-sized photograph. You also need to have a PAN card. Also carry the original documents for verification.
- You will be provided with a copy of the rules and regulations, the terms of the agreement and the charges that you will incur.

- During the process, an In-Person Verification would be carried out. A member of the DP's staff would contact you to check the details provided in the account opening form.
- Once the application is processed, the DP will provide you with an account number or client ID. You can use the details to access your demat account online.
- As a DEMAT account holder, you would need to pay some fees like the annual maintenance fee levied for maintenance of account and the transaction fee -- levied for debiting securities to and from the account on a monthly basis. These fees differ from every service provider (called a Depository Participant or DP). While some DPs charge a flat fee per transaction, others peg the fee to the transaction value, and are subject to a minimum amount. The fee also differs based on the kind of transaction (buying or selling). In addition to the other fees, the DP also charges a fee for converting the shares from the physical to the electronic form or vice-versa.
- Minimum shares: A DEMAT account can be opened with no balance of shares. It also does not require that a minimum balance be maintained.

### *What are the Documents required for a Demat Account?*

You need to submit proof of identity and address along with a passport size photograph and the account opening form. Only photocopies of the documents are required for submission, but originals are also required for verification.

Here is a broad list of documents that can be used as proofs:

**Proof of identity:** PAN card, voter's ID, passport, driver's license, bank attestation, IT returns, electricity bill, telephone bill, ID cards with applicant's photo issued by the central or state government and its departments, statutory or regulatory authorities, public sector undertakings (PSUs), scheduled commercial banks, public financial institutions, colleges affiliated to universities, or professional bodies such as ICAI, ICWAI, ICSI, bar council etc.

**Proof of address:** Ration card, passport, voter ID card, driving license, bank passbook or bank statement, verified copies of electricity bills, residence telephone bills, leave and license agreement or agreement for sale, self-declaration by High Court or Supreme Court judges, identity card or a document with address issued by the central or state government and its departments, statutory or regulatory authorities, public sector undertakings (PSUs), scheduled commercial banks, public financial institutions, colleges affiliated to universities and professional bodies such as ICAI, ICWAI, Bar Council etc.

## Settlement

Investors do buying and selling of securities on stock exchange platform by placing buy / sale orders through their brokers. This process is referred as trading and is carried out by stock exchanges for a specific period. After the trading is activity is completed, the process of delivering securities by the seller and delivery of money by the buyer is called as pay in process. This activity also has to be conducted within a specified time frame. After the Pay in is over, and then starts the process of payout wherein the buyer will get shares and seller will get money. The above activities of trading, payin, payout are collectively referred as settlement. Each settlement is identified by a unique number called as settlement id. Settlement number is a 7 digit number.

## Settlement Cycle

The important settlement types are as follows:

- Normal segment (N)
- Trade for trade Surveillance (W)
- Retail Debt Market (D)

- Limited Physical market (O)
- Non cleared TT deals (Z)
- Auction normal (A)

Trades in the settlement type N, W, D and A are settled in dematerialized mode. Trades under settlement type O are settled in physical form. Trades under settlement type Z are settled directly between the members and may be settled either in physical or dematerialized mode.

### *Details of the Two Modes of Settlement are as Under*

### *Dematerialised Settlement*

NSCCL follows a T+2 rolling settlement cycle. For all trades executed on the T day, NSCCL determines the cumulative obligations of each member on the T+1 day and electronically transfers the data to Clearing Members (CMs). All trades concluded during a particular trading date are settled on a designated settlement day i.e. T+2 day. In case of short deliveries on the T+2 day in the normal segment, NSCCL conducts a buy –in auction on the T+2 day itself and the settlement for the same is completed on the T+3 day, whereas in case of W segment there is a direct close out. For arriving at the settlement day all intervening holidays, which include bank holidays, NSE holidays, Saturdays and Sundays are excluded. The settlement schedule for all the settlement types in the manner explained above is communicated to the market participants vide circular issued during the previous month.

### *Settlement Cycle*

### *Rolling Settlement*

In a rolling settlement, for all trades executed on trading day .i.e. T day the obligations are determined on the T+1 day and settlement on T+2 basis i.e. on the 2nd working day. For arriving at the settlement day all intervening holidays, which include bank holidays, NSE holidays, Saturdays and Sundays are excluded. A tabular representation of the settlement cycle for rolling settlement is given below:

| | **Activity** | **Day** |
|---|---|---|
| Trading | Rolling Settlement Trading | T |
| Clearing | Custodial Confirmation | T+1 working days |
| | Delivery Generation | T+1 working days |
| Settlement | Securities and Funds pay in | T+2 working days |
| | Securities and Funds pay out | T+2 working days |
| | Valuation Debit | T+2 working days |
| Post Settlement | Auction | T+2 working days |
| | Auction settlement | T+3 working days |
| | Bad Delivery Reporting | T+4 working days |
| | Rectified bad delivery pay-in and pay-out | T+6 working days |
| | Re-bad delivery reporting and pickup | T+8 working days |
| | Close out of re-bad delivery and funds pay-in & pay-out | T+9 working days |

### *Physical Settlement*

Limited physical Market : To provide an exit route for small investors holding physical shares in securities the Exchange has provided a facility for such trading in physical shares not exceeding 500 shares in the 'Limited Physical Market' (small window).

### *Salient Features of Limited Physical Market*

- Delivery of shares in street name and market delivery (clients holding physical shares purchased from the secondary market) is treated as bad delivery. The shares standing in the name of individuals/HUF only would constitute good delivery. The selling/delivering member must necessarily be the introducing member.
- Any delivery of shares which bears the last transfer date on or after the introduction of the security for trading in the LP market is construed as bad delivery.
- Any delivery in excess of 500 shares is marked as short and such deliveries are compulsorily closed-out.
- Shortages, if any, are compulsorily closed-out at 20% over the actual traded price. Non rectification/replacement for bad delivery are closed out at 10% over the actual trade price. Non rectification/replacement for objection cases are closed out at 20% above the official closing price in regular Market on the auction day.
- The buyer must compulsorily send the securities for transfer and dematerialisation, latest within 3 months from the date of pay-out.
- Company objections arising out of such trading and settlement in this market are reported in the same manner as is currently being done for normal market segment. However securities would be accepted as valid company objection, only if the securities are lodged for transfer within 3 months from the date of pay-out.

### *Settlement Cycle*

### *Limited Physical Market*

Settlement for trades is done on a trade-for-trade basis and delivery obligations arise out of each trade. The settlement cycle for this segment is same as for the rolling settlement viz:

### *Bad Deliveries (in Case of Physical Settlement)*

Bad deliveries (deliveries which are prima facie defective) are required to be reported to the clearing house within two days from the receipt of documents. The delivering member is required to rectify these within two days. Un-rectified bad deliveries are assigned to auction on the next day

### *Company Objections (in Case of Physical Settlement)*

The CM on whom company objection is lodged has an opportunity to withdraw the objection if the objection is not valid or the documents are incomplete (i.e. not as required under guideline No.100 or 109 of SEBI Good/Bad delivery guidelines), within 7 days of lodgement against him. If the CM is unable to rectify/replace defective documents on or before 21 days, NSCCL conducts a buying-in auction for the non-rectified part of defective document on the next auction day through the trading system of NSE. All objections, which are not bought-in, are deemed closed out on the auction day at the closing price on the auction day plus 20%. This amount is credited to the receiving member's account on the auction pay-out day.

| | Activity | Day |
|---|---|---|
| Trading | Rolling Settlement Trading | T |
| Clearing | Custodial Confirmation | T+1 working days |
| | Delivery Generation | T+1 working days |
| Settlement | Securities and Funds pay in | T+2 working days |
| | Securities and Funds pay out | T+2 working days |
| Post Settlement | Assigning of shortages for close out | T+2 working days |
| | Reporting and pick-up of bad delivery | T+4 working days |
| | Close out of shortages | T+4 working days |
| | Replacement of bad delivery | T+6 working days |
| | Reporting of re-bad and pick-up | T+8 working days |
| | Close out of re-bad delivery | T+9 working days |

## Depositories

A depository is an organization that holds securities of investors in an electronic format at the request of an investor through a registered Depository Participant. It assists in the allotment and transfer of securities and securities lending. In a depository, securities such as money, shares and properties, etc. are kept for safekeeping under their or depositary terms. The securities are held in the form of electronic accounts. They carry out their various operations through functionaries called as business partners or a Depository Participant. This system is governed under the Depositories Act by the government. The enactment of this act paved the way for the establishment of NSDL and CDSL.

The National Securities Depository Limited (NSDL) was the first depository in India. It was registered by SEBI on 7th June 1996, as the very first Depository to facilitate trading and settlement of securities in Demat form. It is promoted by institutions of national stature, which are responsible for the economic development of India and have established an infrastructure of international standards. They handle most of the securities, which are held and settled in a dematerialized form in the Indian capital market. Its main promoters are IDBI, UTI and NSE.

Central Depository Services Limited (CDSL) is the second Indian central securities depository. It is based in Mumbai. Its main function is the holding securities either in certificated or un-certificated i.e. dematerialized form; it helps to enable the book entry transfer of securities. It began operating in February in the year 1999. Its main promoters are BSE, HDFC, SBI, BOI and BOB.

### *The Main Role and the Different Functions of a Depository are as follows*

- Maintenance of individual investors' beneficial holdings in an electronic form
- Dematerialization and re-materialization of securities
- Account transfer for settlement of trades in electronic shares
- Allotments in the electronic form in case of initial public offerings
- Distribution of non-cash corporate actions
- Facility for freezing/locking of investor accounts
- Facility for pledge and hypothecation of securities

### *Objectives of a Depository*

A depository helps the capital market to achieve the following objectives

- Reduce the time for transfer of securities
- Avoid the risk of settlement of securities.
- Enhance liquidity and efficiency.
- Reduce cost of transaction for the investor
- Create a system for the central handling of all securities.
- Promote the country's competitiveness by complying with global standards
- Provide service infrastructure in a capital market.

### *Interacting Institutions*

There are three institutions that are interacting in a depository system

- The Central Depository
- Share Register and Transfer Agent
- Clearing and settlement corporation.

## National Securities Depository ltd(NSDL)

NSDL, the first and largest depository in India, established in August 1996 and promoted by institutions of national stature responsible for economic development of the country has since established a national infrastructure of international standards that handles most of the securities held and settled in dematerialised form in the Indian capital market.

Although India had a vibrant capital market which is more than a century old, the paper-based settlement of trades caused substantial problems like bad delivery and delayed transfer of title till recently. The enactment of Depositories Act in August 1996 paved the way for establishment of NSDL, the first depository in India. This depository promoted by institutions of national stature responsible for economic development of the country has since established a national infrastructure of international standard that handles most of the trading and settlement in dematerialised form in Indian capital market.

Using innovative and flexible technology systems, NSDL works to support the investors and brokers in the capital market of the country. NSDL aims at ensuring the safety and soundness of Indian marketplaces by developing settlement solutions that increase efficiency, minimise risk and reduce costs. At NSDL, we play a quiet but central role in developing products and services that will continue to nurture the growing needs of the financial services industry.

In the depository system, securities are held in depository accounts, which is more or less similar to holding funds in bank accounts. Transfer of ownership of securities is done through simple account transfers. This method does away with all the risks and hassles normally associated with paperwork. Consequently, the cost of transacting in a depository environment is considerably lower as compared to transacting in certificates

### *Comparison between NDSL and CDSL*

| | NSDL | CDSL |
|---|---|---|
| Abbreviation | It stands for 'National Securities Depository Limited'. | It stands for 'Central Depository Securities Limited'. |
| Founded | November 1996 | February 1999 |
| Headquarters | Mumbai, India. | Mumbai, India. |
| Promoters | IDBI, UTI, etc. | HDFC, SBI, BOI and BOB. |
| Market | National Stock Exchange (NSE) | Bombay Stock Exchange (BSE) |

## Central Depository Services India Ltd(CDSL)

The CDSL has been set up by Bombay Stock Exchange and co-sponserd by SBI, Bank of India, Bank of Baroda and HDFC Bank. It started its operation on March 221999

As on 31 March 2016 the number of live companies in CDSL is 8939.The total number of registered depository participants is 583 and the total number of investor accounts is 1,07,90,738. The total number of DP locations is 16,764.

### *Milestones of CDSL System*

Some of the important milestones of CDSL system are as follows

- CDSL received the certificate of commencement of business from SEBI in February, 1999
- Honourable Union Finance Minister, ShriYashwantSinha flagged off the operations of CDSL on July 15, 1999
- Settlement of trades in the DEMAT mode through BOI, Share holding Limited, the clearing house of BSE Ltd., started in July 1999
- All leading stock exchanges like the BSE Ltd. (formerly known as Bombay Stock Exchange Ltd.), National Stock Exchange and MCX Stock Exchange Limited have established connectivity with CDSL

## BSE

Established in 1875, BSE (formerly known as Bombay Stock Exchange Ltd.), is Asia's first & the Fastest Stock Exchange in world with the speed of 6 micro seconds and one of India's leading exchange groups. Over the past 140 years, BSE has facilitated the growth of the Indian corporate sector by providing it an efficient capital-raising platform. Popularly known as BSE, the bourse was established as "The Native Share & Stock Brokers' Association" in 1875. BSE is a corporatized and demutualised entity, with a broad shareholder-base which includes two leading global exchanges, Deutsche Bourse and Singapore Exchange as strategic partners. BSE provides an efficient and transparent market for trading in equity, debt instruments, derivatives, mutual funds. It also has a platform for trading in equities of small-and-medium enterprises (SME).

More than 5500 companies are listed on BSE making it world's No. 1 exchange in terms of listed members. The companies listed on BSE command a total market capitalization of USD 1.64 Trillion as of Sep 2015. It is also one of the world's leading exchanges (5th largest in September 2015) for Index options trading (Source: World Federation of Exchanges).

BSE also provides a host of other services to capital market participants including risk management, clearing, settlement, market data services and education. It has a global reach with customers around the world and a nation-wide presence. BSE systems and processes are designed to safeguard market integrity, drive the growth of the Indian capital market and stimulate innovation and competition across all market segments. BSE also provides depository services through its Central Depository Services Ltd. (CDSL) arm.

BSE's popular equity index-the S&P BSE SENSEX-is India's most widely tracked stock market benchmark index. It is traded internationally on the EUREX as well as leading exchanges of the BRCS nations (Brazil, Russia, China and South Africa).

Bombay Stock Exchange was recognized as an exchange under the Securities Contracts (Regulation) Act in 1957. Its benchmark index, the Sensitive Index (Sensex) was launched in 1986. In 1995, the BSE launched its fully automated trading platform called BSE On-Line Trading system (BOLT) which fully replaced the open outcry system.

In 2005, the Exchange changed from being simply an association of brokers to become a corporate entity. The administrative structure of the Exchange is headed by a board of directors, below which is a governing council and management that presides over its day-to-day functioning.

### *Functions*

- To promote, develop and maintain a well regulated market for dealings in securities.
- To safeguard the interest of members and the investing public having dealings on the exchange.
- To promote industrial development in the country through efficient resource mobilization by way of investment in corporate securities.
- To establish and promote honourable and fair practices in securities transactions.

### *BSE Webx.co.in*

BSE has launched internet trading system vizBSEWebx.Co.in - February 2001 with a view to provide an additional facility to the investors to put their orders for purchase or sale of securities using internet.

The investors can visit BSE webx.co.in search of their member broker or sub broker and register with them on line trading worldwide. The exchange provides an efficient and transparent market for trading in securities.

BSE scrip is known by code no. For Example Infosys Tech- BSE Code- 500209. Its index is sensex.

BSE is among the 8 biggest stock exchanges in the world in terms of transaction volume. The exchange has a nation-wide reach with a presence in 417 cities and towns of India. The systems and process of the Exchange are designed to safeguard market integrity and enhance transparency in operations. The clearing and settlement functions of the BSE are ISO 9001-2000 certified.

### *Management of BSE*

The exchange is professionally managed under the overall direction of the Board of Directors, Governing Body, or Executive Committee. The Board comprises of eminent professionals, representatives of trading members and the Managing Director of the Exchange. The day-to-day operations of the exchange are managed by the managing Director and CEO and an expert Management Team of Professionals.

## NSE

The National Stock Exchange (NSE) is India's leading stock exchange covering various cities and towns across the country. NSE was set up by leading institutions to provide a modern, fully automated screen-based trading system with national reach. The Exchange has brought about unparalleled transparency, speed & efficiency, safety and market integrity. It has set up facilities that serve as a model for the securities industry in terms of systems, practices and procedures.

NSE has played a catalytic role in reforming the Indian securities market in terms of microstructure, market practices and trading volumes. The market today uses state-of-art information technology to provide an efficient and transparent trading, clearing and settlement mechanism, and has witnessed several innovations in products & services viz. demutualisation of stock exchange governance, screen based trading, compression of settlement cycles, dematerialisation and electronic transfer of securities, securities lending and borrowing, professionalisation of trading members, fine-tuned risk management systems, emergence of clearing corporations to assume counterparty risks, market of debt and derivative instruments and intensive use of information technology.

National Stock Exchange was set up in April 1993 with the objectives of:

a. establishing a nationwide trading facility for all types of securities,
b. ensuring equal access to all investors all over the country through an appropriate communication network,
c. providing a fair, efficient and transparent securities market using electronic trading system,
d. enabling shorter settlement cycles and book entry settlements and
e. meeting the international benchmarks and standards

Within a short span of time, above objectives have been realized and the Exchange has played a leading role as a change agent in transforming the Indian Capital Markets to its present form.

NSE has set up infrastructure that serves as a role model for the securities industry in terms of trading systems, clearing and settlement practices and procedures. The standards set by NSE in terms of market practices, products, technology and service standards have become industry benchmarks and are being replicated by other market participants. It provides screen-based automated trading system with a high degree of transparency and equal access to investors irrespective of geographical location. The high level of information dissemination through on-line system has helped in integrating retail investors on a nation-wide basis.

The Exchange currently operates four market segments, namely Capital Market Segment, Wholesale Debt Market Segment, Futures and Options segment and the Currency Derivatives Segment.

NSE has been playing the role of a catalytic agent in reforming the market in terms of microstructure and market practices. Right from its inception, the exchange has adopted the purest form of demutualised set up whereby the ownership, management and trading rights are in the hands of three different sets of people.

This has completely eliminated any conflict of interest and helped NSE to aggressively pursue policies and practices within a public interest framework. It has helped in shifting the trading platform from the trading hall in the premises of the exchange to the computer terminals at the premises of the trading members located country-wide and subsequently to the personal computers in the homes of investors.

Settlement risks have been eliminated with NSE's innovative endeavors in the area of clearing and settlement viz., reduction of settlement cycle, professionalisation of the trading members, fine-tuned risk management system, dematerialisation and electronic transfer of securities and establishment of clearing corporation. As a consequence, the market today uses the state-of-art information technology to provide an efficient and transparent trading, clearing and settlement mechanism.

NSE provides a trading platform for of all types of securities-equity and debt, corporate government and derivatives. On its recognition as a stock exchange under the Securities Contracts (Regulation) Act, 1956 in April 1993, it commenced operations in the Wholesale Debt Market (WDM) segment in June 1994, in the Capital Market (CM) segment in November 1994, in Futures & Options (F&O) segment in June 2000 and in Currency Derivative segment (CDS) in August 2008.

The Exchange started providing trading in retail debt of Government Securities in January 2003. During the year 2007-08, it accounted for over 90 % of total trading value (debt, derivatives and equity) in the stock exchanges and 69% in equities and more than 98% in derivatives.

The Wholesale Debt Market segment provides the trading platform for trading of a wide range of debt securities. Its product, which is now disseminated jointly with FIMMDA, the FIMMDA NSE MIBID/MIBOR is used as a benchmark rate for majority of deals struck for Interest Rate Swaps, Forwards Rate Agreements, Floating Rate Debentures and Term Deposits in the country.

Its 'Zero Coupon Yield Curve' as well as NSE-VaR for Fixed Income Securities have also become very popular for valuation of sovereign securities across all maturities irrespective of its liquidity and facilitated the pricing of corporate papers and GOI Bond Index.

NSEs Capital Market segment offers a fully automated screen based trading system, known as the National Exchange for Automated Trading (NEAT) system, which operates on a strict price/time priority. It enables members from across the country to trade simultaneously with enormous ease and efficiency.

NSEs Futures &Options segment provides trading of a wide range of derivatives like Index Futures, Index Options, Stock Options and Stock Futures.

NSEs Currency Derivatives segment provides trading on currency futures contracts on the USD-INR which commenced on August 29, 2008.

### *Trading Value of Different Market Segments*

Rs. in crores

| *Segment/Year* | *2010-11* | *2011-12* | *2012-13* | *2013-14* | *2014-15* |
|---|---|---|---|---|---|
| Capital market | 3,577,410 | 2,810,893 | 2,708,279 | 2,808,488 | 4,329,655 |
| Equity Futures& Options | 29,248,221 | 31,349,732 | 31,533,004 | 38,211,408 | 55,606,453 |
| Whole sale Debt Market | 559,447 | 633,179 | 729,214 | 851,434 | 772,369 |
| Currency F&O* | 3,449,788 | 4,674,990 | 5,274,465 | 4,012,513 | 3,023,908 |
| Interest Rate Futures** | 62 | 3,959 | 0.22 | 30,173 | 421,558 |
| Total | **36,834,927** | **39,472,753** | **40,307,962** | **45,914,017** | **64,153,943** |

Note:* Trading in currency Futures commenced on August 28, 2008

** Trading in Interest Rate Futures were Relaunched on January 21, 2010

### *Market Capitalisation of Different Market Segments*

Rs. in Crores

| Segments/Year | Mar-11 | Mar-12 | Mar-13 | Mar-14 | Mar-15 |
|---|---|---|---|---|---|
| CM | 6,702,616 | 6,096,518 | 6,239,035 | 7,277,720 | 9,930,122 |
| WDM | 3,594,877 | 4,272,736 | 4,928,332 | 5,128,733 | 5,739,273 |
| TOTAL | **10,297,493** | **10,369,254** | **11,167,366** | **12,406,453** | **15,669,395** |

### *Records Reached in Different Market Segments (Data from Inception to March 31, 2015)*

#### *Capital Market Segment*

| **Parameter** | **Date** | **Magnitude** |
|---|---|---|
| Number of trades | 16- May-14 | 11,805,386 |
| Traded Quantity(in lakhs) | 26-May -14 | 21,060 |
| Turnover(in crores) | 19-May-09 | 40,152 |
| Market capitalisation(crores) | 5-Nov-10 | 7,560,607 |

#### *Futures&Options Segment*

| | | |
|---|---|---|
| Number of contracts traded | 24-Dec-14 | 24,041,817 |
| Turn over(crores) | 26-Feb-15 | 581,564 |

#### *Currency Derivatives Segment*

| | | |
|---|---|---|
| Number of trades | 20-Jun -13 | 390,049 |
| Number of contracts traded | 20-Jun-13 | 11,534,563 |
| Turn over(crores) | 20-Jun-13 | 69,324 |

#### *Wholesale Debt Market Segment*

| | | |
|---|---|---|
| Number of trades | 25-Aug-03 | 2,074 |
| Turn over(crores) | 25-Aug-03 | 1 3,912 |

Source:www.nseindia.com

## The Securities and Exchange Board of India(SEBI)

Securities Exchange Board of India (SEBI) was set up in 1988 to regulate the functions of securities market. SEBI promotes orderly and healthy development in the stock market but initially SEBI was not able to exercise complete control over the stock market transactions.

It was left as a watch dog to observe the activities but was found ineffective in regulating and controlling them. As a result in May 1992, SEBI was granted legal status. SEBI is a body corporate having a separate legal existence and perpetual succession.

### *The Organisational Structure of SEBI*

1. SEBI is working as a corporate sector.
2. Its activities are divided into five departments. Each department is headed by an executive director.
3. The head office of SEBI is in Mumbai and it has branch office in Kolkata, Chennai and Delhi.
4. SEBI has formed two advisory committees to deal with primary and secondary markets.
5. These committees consist of market players, investors associations and eminent persons.

### *Reasons for Establishment of SEBI*

With the growth in the dealings of stock markets, lot of malpractices also started in stock markets such as price rigging, 'unofficial premium on new issue, and delay in delivery of shares, violation of rules and regulations of stock exchange and listing requirements. Due to these malpractices the customers started losing confidence and faith in the stock exchange. So government of India decided to set up an agency or regulatory body known as Securities Exchange Board of India (SEBI).

### *Purpose and Role of SEBI*

SEBI was set up with the main purpose of keeping a check on malpractices and protect the interest of investors. It was set up to meet the needs of three groups.

#### *1. Issuers*

For issuers it provides a market place in which they can raise finance fairly and easily.

#### *2. Investors*

For investors it provides protection and supply of accurate and correct information.

#### *3. Intermediaries*

For intermediaries it provides a competitive professional market.

### *Objectives of SEBI*

The overall objectives of SEBI are to protect the interest of investors and to promote the development of stock exchange and to regulate the activities of stock market. The objectives of SEBI are:

- To regulate the activities of stock exchange.
- To protect the rights of investors and ensuring safety to their investment.
- To prevent fraudulent and malpractices by having balance between self regulation of business

### *Functions of SEBI*

The SEBI performs functions to meet its objectives. To meet three objectives SEBI has three important functions. These are:

i. Protective functions
ii. Developmental functions
iii. Regulatory functions.

### 1. *Protective Functions*

These functions are performed by SEBI to protect the interest of investor and provide safety of investment.

### *As Protective Functions SEBI Performs following Functions*

#### *(i) It Checks Price Rigging*

Price rigging refers to manipulating the prices of securities with the main objective of inflating or depressing the market price of securities. SEBI prohibits such practice because this can defraud and cheat the investors.

#### *(ii) It Prohibits Insider Trading*

Insider is any person connected with the company such as directors, promoters etc. These insiders have sensitive information which affects the prices of the securities. This information is not available to people at large but the insiders get this privileged information by working inside the company and if they use this information to make profit, then it is known as insider trading, e.g., the directors of a company may know that company will issue Bonus shares to its shareholders at the end of year and they purchase shares from market to make profit with bonus issue. This is known as insider trading. SEBI keeps a strict check when insiders are buying securities of the company and takes strict action on insider trading.

#### *(iii) SEBI Prohibits Fraudulent and Unfair Trade Practices*

SEBI does not allow the companies to make misleading statements which are likely to induce the sale or purchase of securities by any other person.

- SEBI undertakes steps to educate investors so that they are able to evaluate the securities of various companies and select the most profitable securities.
- SEBI promotes fair practices and code of conduct in security market by taking following steps:
- SEBI has issued guidelines to protect the interest of debenture-holders wherein companies cannot change terms in midterm.
- SEBI is empowered to investigate cases of insider trading and has provisions for stiff fine and imprisonment.
- SEBI has stopped the practice of making preferential allotment of shares unrelated to market prices.

### 2. *Developmental Functions*

These functions are performed by the SEBI to promote and develop activities in stock exchange and increase the business in stock exchange. Under developmental categories following functions are performed by SEBI:

i. SEBI promotes training of intermediaries of the securities market.
ii. SEBI tries to promote activities of stock exchange by adopting flexible and adoptable approach in following way:
    a. SEBI has permitted internet trading through registered stock brokers.
    b. SEBI has made underwriting optional to reduce the cost of issue.
    c. Even initial public offer of primary market is permitted through stock exchange.

### 3. *Regulatory Functions*

These functions are performed by SEBI to regulate the business in stock exchange. To regulate the activities of stock exchange following functions are performed:

i. SEBI has framed rules and regulations and a code of conduct to regulate the intermediaries such as merchant bankers, brokers, underwriters, etc.
ii. These intermediaries have been brought under the regulatory purview and private placement has been made more restrictive.
iii. SEBI registers and regulates the working of stock brokers, sub-brokers, share transfer agents, trustees, merchant bankers and all those who are associated with stock exchange in any manner.
iv. SEBI registers and regulates the working of mutual funds etc.
v. SEBI regulates takeover of the companies.
vi. SEBI conducts inquiries and audit of stock exchanges.

### *The Organisational Structure of SEBI*

- SEBI is working as a corporate sector.
- Its activities are divided into five departments. Each department is headed by an executive director.
- The head office of SEBI is in Mumbai and it has branch office in Kolkata, Chennai and Delhi.
- SEBI has formed two advisory committees to deal with primary and secondary markets.
- These committees consist of market players, investors associations and eminent persons.

### *Objectives of the Two Committees are*

1. To advise SEBI to regulate intermediaries.
2. To advise SEBI on issue of securities in primary market.
3. To advise SEBI on disclosure requirements of companies.
4. To advise for changes in legal framework and to make stock exchange more transparent.
5. To advise on matters related to regulation and development of secondary stock exchange.

These committees can only advise SEBI but they cannot force SEBI to take action on their advice.

## Stock Market Indices

A stock index or stock market index is a measurement of the value of a section of the stock market. It is computed from the prices of selected stocks (typically a weighted average). It is a tool used by investors and financial managers to describe the market, and to compare the return on specific investments.

Sensex is an abbreviation of the Bombay Exchange Sensitive Index (Sensex) - the benchmark index of the Bombay Stock Exchange (BSE). It is composed of 30 of the largest and most actively-traded stocks on the BSE. Initially compiled in 1986, the Sensex is the oldest stock index in India

Sensex is an abbreviation of the Bombay Exchange Sensitive Index (Sensex) - the benchmark index of the Bombay Stock Exchange (BSE). It is composed of 30 of the largest and most actively-traded stocks on the BSE. Initially compiled in 1986, the Sensex is the oldest stock index in India.

### *Sensex Calculation*

The index is calculated based on a free-float capitalization method when weighting the effect of a company on the index. This is a variation of the market cap method, but instead of using a company's outstanding shares it uses its float, or shares that are readily available for trading. The free-float method, therefore, does not include restricted stocks, such as those held by company insiders that can't be readily sold.

To find the free-float capitalization of a company, first find its market cap (number of outstanding shares x share price) then multiply its free-float factor. The free-float factor is determined by the percentage of floated shares to outstanding. For example, if a company has a float of 10 million shares and outstanding shares of 12 million, the percent of float to outstanding is 83%. A company with an 83% free float falls in the 80-85% free-float factor, or 0.85, which is then multiplied by its market cap (e.g., $120 million (12 million shares x .$10/share) x 0.85 = $102 million free-float capitalization).

### *Nifty Index*

The Nifty is an indicator of all the major companies of the NSE. The CNX Nifty is a well diversified 50 stock index accounting for 13 sectors of the economy. It is used for a variety of purposes such as benchmarking fund portfolios, index based derivatives and index funds.

CNX Nifty is owned and managed by India Index Services and Products Ltd. (IISL). IISL is India's first specialised company focused upon the index as a core product.

- The CNX Nifty Index represents about 66.17% of the free float market capitalization of the stocks listed on NSE as on March 31, 2015.
- The total traded value for the last six months ending March 2015 of all index constituents is approximately 46.22% of of the traded value of all stocks on the NSE.
- Impact cost of the CNX Nifty for a portfolio size of Rs.50 lakhs is 0.06% for the month March 2015.
- CNX Nifty is professionally maintained and is ideal for derivatives trading

Nifty is calculated using the same methodology adopted by the BSE in calculating the Sensex–but with three differences.

They are:

- The base year is taken as 1995
- The base value is set to 1000
- Nifty is calculated on 50 stocks actively traded in the NSE
- 50 top stocks are selected from 24 sectors

**Sensex Calculation**

The whole nation is obsessed with the rise and fall of the sensex whether or not people are directly or indirectly associated with it. With the increase in economic activity in the nation, the Sensex has become a household term keenly followed by millions each day. But the methodology employed to calculate the Sensex is known to very few people.

**Understanding Sensex**

The Sensex is primarily an index reflecting the Bombay Stock Exchange (BSE). Established in 1875, the stock exchange did not have an official index till Jan 1, 1986 when the Sensex was adopted for gauging the performance of the Indian markets. The other important index in India is the National Stock Exchange (NSE) barometer -- the Nifty. The Sensex comprises of 30 prominent stocks derived from all key sectors which are traded actively in the exchange. Thus, the Sensex truly reflects the movement of the Indian stock markets.

**Calculation Methodology for Sensex**

- Like the other major financial indexes of the world, the Sensex has also shifted to the 'Free Float market capitalization' methodology to determine its figures with effect from September 1, 2003. The level of the index is a direct reflection of the performance of the 30 selected key stocks in the market.
- Free-float market capitalization is defined as that proportion of total shares issued by the company that are readily available for trading in the market. It generally excludes promoters' holding, government holding, strategic holding and other locked-in shares that will not come to the market for trading in the normal course. So, simply put, Free-float market capitalization is the proportion of total shares available for trading to the general public.
- Note: suppose Company A has 1,000 shares in total, of which 200 are held by the promoters, so that only 800 shares are available for trading to the general public. These 800 shares are the so-called 'free-floating' shares. If the price of each share is 120 rupees, then the 'total' market capitalization of the company is 120,000 rupees (1,000 x 120), but its free-float market capitalization is 96,000 rupees (800 x 120)

**Sensex is Calculated through the following Steps**

- The market capitalization of each of the 30 companies comprising the index is first determined by multiplying the price of their stocks with the number of shares issued by that company.
- The market capitalization is then multiplied to the free-float factor to derive the free-float market capitalization. (The free-float factor of a company is the multiple with which the total market capitalization of that company is adjusted to arrive at its free-float market capitalization. It is determined by the BSE based on the information submitted by the companies. The value of the free-float factor lies between 0.05 and 1.00. A free-float factor of say 0.55 means that only 55 pct of the market capitalization of the company will be considered for index calculation.)
- The free-float market capitalization of the Index constituents is then divided by a number known as the Index Divisor. This index divisor is the sole link to the original base period value of the index. (For the Sensex, the base value period, it is 1978-79) This value provides for comparison of the index over a period of time.
- For example, if the days' Market Capitalization based on the performance of the 30 key stocks is 8060000 and the base index of 1978-79 is 60000. The index divisor becomes 100/60000 and the Sensex index value equals 8060000 x 100/60000 = 13433 for that day

## *Uses of Index*

### *Traditional Uses*

- Indicator of Market Movement / Returns
- Indexes reflect highly up-to-date information
- Lead indicator of the economy

### *Higher Applications*

- Index Funds - Passive Fund Management
- Index Derivatives - Index Futures and Index Options

In India, the S&P CNX Nifty is the most scientific Index that was constructed keeping in mind Index funds and Index derivatives.

The S&P CNX Nifty is a market capitalisation-weighted Index with base year as November 03, 1995. The base value has been set at 1000. The S&P CNX Nifty is an event-driven Index i.e., price change in any of the Index securities will lead to a change in the Index. It also takes into account substitutions in the Index set and importantly, corporate actions such as stock splits, rights, etc without affecting the Index value. For the purpose of Indexation, market cap weighted Index offers the advantage of simplifying the day to day management of the fund. As market prices rise or fall, the value of the Index fund rises and falls in tandem with the target Index. Since market price change does not require any rebalancing, there are savings in the number of transactions, thus reducing transaction cost.

# 5. MERCHANT BANKING

### *Introduction*

Merchant banking is the direct, negotiated investment of private money into privately or publicly held companies by financial institutions or professional investors. The investors make private placements of equity and, in return, receive private stock that is not registered with financial regulators for trading on an exchange. In a way, they are becoming financial partners of the companies. Merchant banking has been statutorily brought within the framework of the "Securities and Exchange Board of India".

### *Definition*

Any person who is engaged is the business of the issue management either by making arrangements selling, buying or subscribing to the securities of manager, consult adviser, or one rendering corporate advisory service in the relation to such activities to the management.

## Origin of Merchant Banking

The origin of merchant banking is to be traced to Italy in late medieval times and France during the seventeenth and eighteenth centuries. The Italian merchant bankers introduced into England not only the bill of exchange but also all the institutions and techniques connected with an organized money market. Merchant banking consisted initially of merchants who assisted in financing the transactions of other merchants in addition to their own trade. In France, during seventeenth and eighteenth centuries a merchant banker (le merchand Banquer) was not merely a trader but an entrepreneur par excellence. He invested his accumulated profits in all kinds of promising activities. He added banking business to his merchant activities and became a merchant banker.

### *Merchant Banking in India*

As planning and industrial policy envisaged the setting up of new industries and technology, greater financial sophistication and financial services are required. According to Goldsmith, there is a well proven link between economic growth and financial technology. Economic development requires specialist financial skills: savings banks to marshal individual savings; finance companies for consumer lending and mortgage finance; insurance companies for life and property cover; agricultural banks for rural development; and a range of specialised government or government sponsored institutions. As new units were set up and businesses expanded, they required additional financial services which were then not provided by the banking system. Like the local banking system and the trade before, the local system of family enterprises was unsuited for raising large amounts of capital. A public equity or debt issue was the logical source of funds. Merchant banks serve a dual role within the financial sector. Through deposits or sales of securities they obtain funds for lending to their clients (SEBI forbids lending by them): a function similar to most institutions. Their other role is to act as agents in return for fee. SEBI envisages a mandatory role for merchant banks in exercising due diligence apart from issue management, in buy-backs and public offer in takeover bids. Their underwriting and corporate financial services are all fee based rather than fund based and their significance is not reflected in their total assets of the industry. SEBI has been pressing for merchant banks to be primarily fee based institutions.

## Functions and Services Rendered by Merchant Bankers

Merchant bakers provide all types of financial services. In order to satisfy their clientele merchant bankers specialize in or couple of services as their expertise which allows them to participate in the global financial markets.

### 1. *Corporate Counseling Services*

Earlier business houses had in-house advisors to aid smooth functioning of businesses. With the advent of globalization and increase competition corporate's seek the help of managerial economist who is a merchant banker who guides the client on the areas of achievement of organizational goals, location factors, organization size, operational scale, choice of product, market survey, investment decisions, pricing methods and marketing strategy, capital management and expenditure control etc.

### 2. *Project Counseling Services*

Merchant bankers covers the study of project, offering advisory assistance on the viability and procedural steps for its implementation and following are the activities performed by the merchant bankers:

1. Review the project ideas/project profile.
2. Providing directions on the procedural aspects of project implementation.
3. Review the feasibility of the projects.
4. Assist in the preparation of project reports, market surveys, review of reports, obtain government consents for implementation of projects, obtain approvals/licenses/ permissions/grants in the form of letter of intent, industrial license, DGTD registration.
5. To identify potential investment avenues
6. Guide entrepreneurs for making investment in Indian projects as well as projects overseas.
7. To process capital structuring.
8. To facilitate foreign collaboration, amalgamations, mergers and takeovers.
9. To prepare viability reports after financial study of the projects to advise on the legal framework governing the corporate.
10. Provide assistance to prepare project profiles and feasibility studies based on the preliminary project ideas covering all aspects of the project to ensure the acceptance by financial institutions.
11. Assist and advice clients in the preparation of applications for financial institutions.

### 3. *Pre-investment Services*

Feasibility studies are conducted to explore alternative avenues of investment. They carryout in-depth investigation to assess the feasibility of the project. They also identify projects which will enhance the profitability of the company in the long run. Merchant bankers help foreign companies to identify projects in India which will match their objectives, goals and profitability to facilitate joint ventures.

### 4. *Capital Restructuring Services*

Merchant banks undertake the responsibility of designing the capital structure by analysing various factors influencing capital structure. The factors include nature of industry, type, growth, taxation, control, liquidity, profitability, management policy and company characteristics. Merchant banks also extend their expertise and advice the company as to how to maintain optimum capital structure.

### 5. *Credits Syndication Services*

Credit syndication refers to the process of providing credit for the project by a group of credit institutions. Merchant banks extend credit syndication services ranging from identifying and assessing fund requirements completing the formalities for sanctioning the bank loan and also for availing funds. Merchant banks work includes collaboration with their clients and credit agencies. They also assist in foreign currency loans.

### 6. *Issue Management Services*

Firms issue different kinds of securities like equity shares, preference shares, debentures and bonds to raise funds from primary market. The major activities in issue management are preparation of auction plan and budget for the issue, preparation of applications to SEBI, drafting prospectus and selection of intermediaries. It is mandatory that every issue should have lead managers and merchant banks act as lead managers who will take up entire responsibility of public issue.

### 7. *Portfolio Management Services*

Investors find it difficult to take investment decisions when they do not have adequate knowledge and the skills to buy or sell securities and do not find time to constantly keep track of the developments in capital markets. Merchant banks being professional in investment management offer solution by investing and managing the fund on behalf of the client by keeping in view the investment objectives of the client.

### 8. *Private Equity Services*

Private equity refers to very large investment made in a closely held company (unlisted company) instituted by high net worth individuals and institutional investors. The most common private equity investment strategies include venture capital, LBO (Leveraged Buyout), destruct investment, and debt capital. Merchant banks play an important role in arranging private equity or participating in private equity.

### 9. *Structure Product Services*

Structured products are special kind of financial instruments designed to possess different combination of risk return characteristics. To structure a product, expertise in economic, accountancy, legal aspects and marketing is required. The process of quantification of risk and pricing of the financial product is known as financial engineering. Merchant banks play an important role in designing a structured products and also marketing them. Structured products include equity linked product in which equity is linked with bond.

The following are other services rendered by merchant bankers:

1. Lease financing services
2. Mergers and acquisitions services
3. Venture financing servicing
4. Acceptance credit and bill discounting services
5. Foreign currency financing services
6. Fixed deposit broking services
7. Relief to sick companies
8. Working capital financing services
9. Project appraisal services
10. Non-Resident investments.

### *Organisation of Merchant Banking Units*

The structure of organisation of merchant banks reveals certain similar characteristics:

- a high proportion of professionals to total staff;
- a substantial delegation of decision making;
- a short chain of command;
- rapid decision making;
- flexible organisation structure;
- innovative approaches to problem solving; and
- high level of financial sophistication.

In the words of Skully, a merchant bank could be best defined as a financial institution conducting money market activities and lending, underwriting and financial advice, and investment services whose organisation is characterised by a high proportion of professional staff able to approach problems in an innovative manner and to make and implement decisions rapidly. Merchant banking activities are regulated by (1) Guidelines of SEBI and Ministry of Finance, (2) Companies Act, 1956 and (3) Listing Guidelines of Stock Exchange and (4) Securities Contracts (Regulation) Act, 1956. INVESTMENT BANKING Investment banks in USA are the most important participants in the direct market by bringing financial claims for sale. They specialise in helping businesses and governments sell their new security issues, whether debt or equity in the primary market to finance capital expenditures. Once the securities are sold, investment bankers make secondary markets for the securities as brokers and dealers. In 1990, there was 2500 investment banking firms in USA doing underwriting business. About 100 firms are so large that they dominate the industry. In recent years some investment banking firms have diversified or merged with other financial firms to become full service financial firms.

## Qualities of Merchant Banker

- Ability to analyse
- Abundant knowledge
- Ability to build up relationship
- Innovative approach
- Intergrity.

## Guidelines for Merchant Banking

A merchant banker will require authorization by SEBI to carry out the business. SEBI has classified the merchant bankers into four categories based on the nature and range of the activities and the responsibilities.

**Category I**: It consists of merchant bankers who carry on the business of issue management which consists of preparation of issue management which consists of preparation of prospectus, determining the financial structure, tie-up of the financiers and final allotment/refund of subscription and to act in the capacity of managers, advisors or consultants to an issue, portfolio manager and underwriter.

Minimum networth required is Rs. 1 crore.

**Category II**: It consists of those authorized to act in the capacity of comanger/advisor, consultant underwriter to an issue.

The Minimum networth required is Rs. 50 Lakhs.

**Category III**: It consists of those authorized to act as underwriter, advisor or consultant to an issue.

The Minimum networth required is Rs. 20 Lakhs.

**Category IV**: It consists of Merchant Banker who act as advisor or consultant to an issue.

There is no Minimum networth required.

Every merchant banker should maintain copies of balance sheet, Profit and loss account, Statement of financial position. Half-yearly unaudited result should be submitted to SEBI. SEBI has been vested with the power to suspend or cancel the authorization in case of violation of the guidelines. Every merchant banker shall appoint a 'Compliance Officer' to monitor compliance of the Act. SEBI has the right to send inspecting authority to inspect books of accounts, records etc... of merchant bankers. Inspections will be conducted by SEBI to ensure that provisions of the regulations are properly complied. An initial authorization fee, an annual fee and renewal fee may be collected by SEBI. A lead manager holding a certificate under first category shall accept a minimum underwriting obligation of 5% of size of issue or Rs.25 lakhs whichever is less

## Functions of Merchant Banks

The basic function of a merchant banker is marketing corporate and other securities. Now they are required to take up some allied functions also.

### *A Merchant Bank now Takes up the Following Functions*

### *1. Promotional Activities*

A merchant bank functions as a promoter of industrial enterprises in India He helps the entrepreneur in conceiving an idea, identification of projects, preparing feasibility reports, obtaining Government approvals and incentives, etc. Some of the merchant banks also provide assistance for technical and financial collaborations and joint ventures

### *2. Issue Management*

In the past, the function of a merchant banker had been mainly confined to the management of new public issues of corporate securities by the newly formed companies, existing companies (further issues) and the foreign companies in dilution of equity as required under FERA In this capacity the merchant banks usually act as sponsor of issues.

They obtain consent of the Controller of Capital Issues (now, the Securities and Exchange Board of India) and provide a number of other services to ensure success in the marketing of securities. The services provided by them include, the preparation of the prospectus, underwriting arrangements, appointment of registrars, brokers and bankers to the issue, advertising and arranging publicity and compliance of listing requirements of the stock-exchanges, etc.

They act as experts of the type, timing and terms of issues of corporate securities and make them acceptable for the investors on the one hand and also provide flexibility and freedom to the issuing companies.

### *3. Credit Syndication*

Merchant banks provide specialized services in preparation of project, loan applications for rising short-term as well as long- term credit from various bank and financial institutions, etc. They also manage Euro-issues and help in raising funds abroad.

### *4. Portfolio Management*

Merchant banks offer services not only to the companies issuing the securities but also to the investors. They advise their clients, mostly institutional investors, regarding investment decisions. Merchant bankers even undertake the function of purchase and sale of securities for their clients so as to provide them portfolio management services. Some merchant bankers are operating mutual funds and off shore funds also.

### 5. *Leasing and Finance*

Many merchant bankers provide leasing and finance facilities to their customers. Some of them even maintain venture capital funds to assist the entrepreneurs. They also help companies in raising finance by way of public deposits.

### 6. *Servicing of Issues*

Merchant banks have also started to act as paying agents for the service of debt- securities and to act as registrars and transfer agents. Thus, they maintain even the registers of shareholders and debenture holders and arrange to pay dividend or interest due to them

### 7. *Other Specialised Services*

In addition to the basic activities involving marketing of securities, merchant banks also provide corporate advisory services on issues like mergers and amalgamations, tax matters, recruitment of executives and cost and management audit, etc. Many merchant bankers have also started making of bought out deals of shares and debentures. The activities of the merchant bankers are increasing with the change in the money market.

## SEBI Criteria for Fit and Proper Person Regulation

For determining as to whether an applicant/intermediary seeking registration under any SEBI regulation is a fit and proper person, the SEBI would take in to account any consideration as it deems fit, including but not limited to the following criteria: financial integrity; absence of convictions or civil liabilities; competence; good reputation and character; efficiency and honesty; and absence of any disqualification to act as an intermediary as stipulated in the relevant regulations.

A Person would not be considered as fit and proper person if he incurs any of the following disqualifications:

- The applicant/ intermediary or its whole time director(ie.sponsors/directors/principal officers/trustees/whole time directors of the asset management company of a mutual fund of whole time directors of the trustee company/whole time directors or trustees of a venture capital fund set up a trust and a body corporate respectively) or managing partner has been convicted for any offence involving moral turpitude, economic offence, securities low or fraud
- An order for winding up has been passed against it.
- Has been declared insolvent and has not been discharged.
- An order, other than order of suspension of certificate of registration as an intermediary, restraining/prohibiting/debarring it from dealing in securities in accessing the capital market passed by the SEBI/any other regulatory authority and a period of three years from the date of expiry of the period specification in the order has not elapsed.
- An order cancelling its registration has been passed by the SEBI on ground of its indulging in insider trading, fraudulent and unfair trade practices or market manipulation and a period of three years from the date of the order has not elapsed.
- An order withdrawing/refusing to grant any license/approval to it having a bearing on the capital market has been passed by the SEBI/any other regulatory authority and three years from the date of order has not elapsed.
- Is not financially sound(ie. in terms of the specified capital adequacy or net worth);
- Any other reason, which in the opinion of the SEBI renders it unfit to operate in the capital market.

### *Fee*

A merchant banker has to pay to the SEBI (a) application fee of Rs 25,000 (b) registration, RS 10 lakh and (c) renewal fee of Rs. 5 lakh every three years from the fourth year from the date of initial registration.

### *Conditions of Registration*

The registration/renewal of certificate of a merchant banker would be subject to the following conditions:

- Prior approval of the SEBI would be necessary to continue to act as a merchant banker after change of its status/constitution. Change of status/constitution mean any change in status/constitution of whatsoever nature including
  (a) amalgamation/demerger/consolidation/any other kind of corporate restructuring
  (b) change in its managing/whole time directors and
  (c) any change in control over the body corporate. Change in control means
  (i) If its share is listed, change of control in terms of stipulations of the SEBI Takeover regulations
  (ii) change in its controlling interest in any other case. Controlling interest means direct/indirect interest to the extent of at least 51% of voting rights.
- Enter in to a legally binding contract with the issuer specifying their mutual duties and responsibilities.
- Pay the registration/renewal fee in the prescribed manner.
- Take adequate steps for redressal of investor's grievances within one month of the complaint and keep the SEBI informed about the number, nature and other particulars of such complaints together with the manner of their redressal.
- Abide by the relevant regulations under the SEBI act.

# 6. MUTUAL FUNDS

### *Meaning*

A Mutual fund is a professionally-managed investment fund that pools money from many investors to purchase securities. While there is no legal definition of the term "mutual fund", it is most commonly applied only to those collective investment vehicles that are regulated and sold to the general public. They are sometimes referred to as "investment companies" or "registered investment companies". Hedge funds are not mutual funds, primarily because they cannot be sold to the general public.

The Securities and exchange board of India (mutual funds) regulation, 1996 defines a mutual fund as, "a fund established in the form of a trust to raise money through the sale of units to the public or a section of the public under one or more schemes for investing in securities, including money market instruments or gold or gold related instruments or real estate assets".

According to the above definition, a mutual fund in India can raise resources through sale of units to the public. It can be set up in the form of a trust under the Indian Trust Act. The definition has been further extended by allowing mutual funds to diversify their activities in the following areas:

- Portfolio management services.
- Management of offshore funds
- Providing advice to offshore funds
- Management of pension or provident fund
- Management of venture capital funds
- Management of money market funds
- Management of real estate funds

A mutual fund serves as a link between the investor and the securities market by mobilizing savings from the investors and investing them in the securities market to generate returns. Thus, a mutual fund is akin to portfolio management services (PMS). Although, both are conceptually same, they are different from each other. Portfolio management services are offered to high net worth individuals; taking into account their risk profile, their investments are managed separately.

## Features of Funds

Some of the traditional, distinguishing features of mutual funds include the following:

- Investors purchase mutual fund shares from the fund itself (or through a broker for the fund) instead of from other investors on a secondary market, such as the New York Stock Exchange or Nasdaq Stock Market.
- The price that investors pay for mutual fund shares is the fund's per share net asset value (NAV) plus any shareholder fees that the fund imposes at the time of purchase (such as sales loads).
- Mutual fund shares are "redeemable," meaning investors can sell their shares back to the fund (or to a broker acting for the fund).
- Mutual funds generally create and sell new shares to accommodate new investors. In other words, it sells its shares on a continuous basis, although some funds stop selling when, for example, they become too large.
- The investment portfolios of mutual funds typically are managed by separate entities known as "investment advisers" that are registered with the SEC(Securities and Exchange commission).

## Structure of a Mutual Fund

A mutual fund is set up in the form of a trust, which has sponsor, trustees, asset management company ("AMC") and a custodian. The trust is established by a sponsor or more than one sponsor who is like a promoter of a company. The trustees of the mutual fund hold its property for the benefit of the unit-holders. The AMC, approved by SEBI, manages the funds by making investments in various types of securities. The custodian, who is registered with SEBI, holds the securities of various schemes of the fund in its custody. The trustees are vested with the general power of superintendence and direction over AMC. They monitor the performance and compliance of SEBI Regulations by the mutual fund.

A typical mutual fund structure in India can be graphically represented as follows:

### *Regulatory Regime*

A mutual fund is a fund established in the form of a trust to raise monies through the sale of units to the public or a section of the public under one or more schemes for investing insecurities, including money market instruments. The regulation of mutual funds operating in India falls under the purview of the authority of the Securities and Exchange Board of India ("SEBI"). Any person proposing to set up a mutual fund in India is required, under the Securities and Exchange Board of India (Mutual Funds) Regulations, 1996 ("Mutual Fund Regulations"), to be registered with the SEBI.

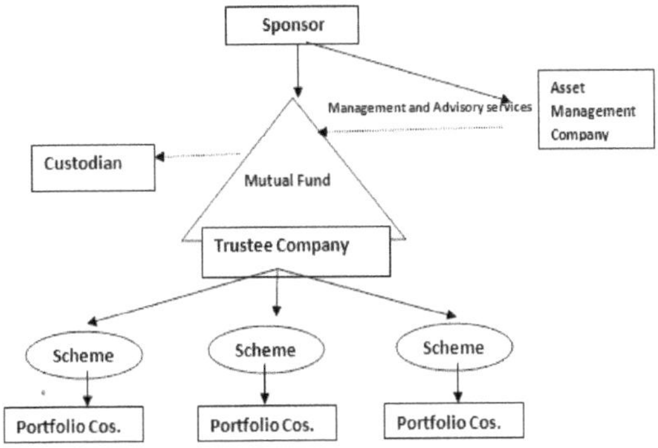


### a. *Mutual Fund*

The Mutual Fund Regulations lay down several criteria that need to be fulfilled in order to be granted registration as a mutual fund. Every mutual fund must be registered with SEBI and must be constituted in the form of a trust in accordance with the provisions of the Indian Trusts Act, 1882. The instrument of trust must be in the form of a deed between the sponsor and the trustees of the mutual fund duly registered under the provisions of the Indian Registration Act, 1908.

### b. *Sponsor*

The sponsor is required, under the provisions of the Mutual Fund Regulations, to have a sound track record3, a reputation of fairness and integrity in all his business transactions. Additionally, the sponsor should contribute at least 40% to the net worth of the AMC. However, if any person holds 40% or more of the net worth of an AMC shall be deemed to be a sponsor and will be required to fulfill the eligibility criteria specified in the Mutual Fund Regulations.

The sponsor or any of its directors or the principal officer employed by the mutual fund should not be guilty of fraud, not be convicted of an offence involving moral turpitude or should have not been found guilty of any economic offence.

### c. *Trustees*

The mutual fund is required to have an independent Board of Trustees, *i.e.* two thirds of the trustees should be independent persons who are not associated with the sponsors in any manner whatsoever. An AMC or any of its officers or employees is not eligible to act as a trustee of any mutual fund. In case a company is appointed as a trustee, then its directors can act as trustees of any other trust provided that the object of such other trust is not in conflict with the object of the mutual fund. Additionally, no person who is appointed as a trustee of a mutual fund can be appointed as a trustee of any other mutual fund unless he is an independent trustee and prior approval of the mutual fund of which he is a trustee has been obtained for such an appointment.

The trustees are responsible for - *inter alia* - ensuring that the AMC has all its systems in place, all key personnel, auditors, registrars *etc.* have been appointed prior to the launch of any scheme. It is also the responsibility of the trustees to ensure that the AMC does not act in a manner that is favorable to its associates such that it has a detrimental impact on the unit holders, or that the management of one scheme by the AMC does not compromise the management of another scheme. The trustees are also required to ensure that an AMC has been diligent in empanelling and monitoring any securities transactions with brokers, so as to avoid any undue concentration of business with any broker. The Mutual Fund Regulations further mandates that the trustees should prevent any conflicts of interest between the AMC and the unit holders in terms of deployment of net worth. The trustees are also responsible for ensuring that there is no change carried out in the fundamental attributes of any scheme or the trust or fees and expenses payable or any other change that would modify the scheme and affect the interest of unit holders, unless each unit holder is provided with written communication thereof. In addition, the unit holders must be given the option to exit at the prevailing Net Asset Value ("NAV") without any exit load. They are obliged to perform a quarterly review of all transactions carried out between the mutual funds, AMC and its associates.

As far as professional indemnity cover for the trustees or the AMC is concerned, industry practice in India reveals that the insurance policy is taken out by an Indian insurance company (as is required by the Insurance Act, 1938) while the risk is subsequently ceded to an overseas re-insurer who underwrites the primary policy issued by the Indian insurance company.

### d. *Asset Management Company*

The sponsor or the trustees are required to appoint an AMC to manage the assets of the mutual fund. Under the Mutual Fund Regulations, the applicant must satisfy certain eligibility criteria in order to qualify to register with SEBI as an AMC:

- The sponsor must have at least 40% stake in the AMC;
- The directors of the AMC should be persons having adequate professional experience in finance and financial services related field and not found guilty of moral turpitude or convicted of any economic offence or violation of any securities laws;
- The AMC should have and must at all times maintain, a minimum net worth of Rs. 100 million;
- The board of directors of such AMC has at least 50% directors, who are not associate of, or associated in any manner with, the sponsor or any of its subsidiaries or the trustees;
- The Chairman of the AMC is not a trustee of any mutual fund.

In addition to the above eligibility criteria and other ongoing compliance requirements laid down in the Mutual Fund Regulations, the AMC is required to observe the following restrictions in its normal course of business:

- Any director of the AMC cannot hold office of a director in another AMC unless such person is an independent director and the approval of the board of the AMC of which such person is a director, has been obtained;
- The AMC shall not act as a trustee of any mutual fund;
- The AMC cannot undertake any other business activities except activities in the nature of portfolio management services, management and advisory services to offshore funds, pension funds, provident funds, venture capital funds, management of insurance funds, financial consultancy and exchange of research on commercial basis if any of such activities are not in conflict with the activities of the mutual fund; However, the AMC may, itself or through its subsidiaries, undertake such activities if it satisfies the Board that the key personnel of the asset management company, the systems, back office, bank and securities accounts are segregated activity wise and there exist systems to prohibit access to inside information of various activities.
- The AMC shall not invest in any of its schemes unless full disclosure of its intention to invest has been made in the offer. However, an AMC shall not be entitled to charge any fees on its investment in that scheme. The AMC is required to take all reasonable steps and exercise due diligence to ensure that the investment of funds pertaining to any scheme are not contrary to the provisions of the Mutual Fund Regulations and the trust deed. An AMC cannot, through any broker associated with the sponsor, purchase or sell securities, which is an average of 5% or more of the aggregate purchases and sale of securities made by the mutual fund in all its schemes. However, the aggregate purchase and sale of securities excludes the sale and distribution of units issued by the mutual fund and the limit of 5% shall apply only for a block of any three months.

### *e. Custodian*

The mutual fund is required, under the Mutual Fund Regulations, to appoint a custodian to carry out the custodial services for the schemes of the fund. Only institutions with substantial organizational strength, service capability in terms of computerization, and other infrastructure facilities are approved to act as custodians. The custodian must be totally delinked from the AMC and must be registered with SEBI. Under the Securities and Exchange Board of India (Custodian of Securities) Guidelines, 1996, any person proposing to carry on the business as a custodian of securities must register with the SEBI and is required to fulfill specified eligibility criteria. Additionally, a custodian in which the sponsor or its associates holds 50% or more of the voting rights of the share capital of the custodian or where 50% or more of the directors of the custodian represent the interest of the sponsor or its associates cannot act as custodian for a mutual fund constituted by the same sponsor or any of its associate or subsidiary company.

### *Schemes*

Under the Mutual Fund Regulations, a mutual fund is allowed to float different schemes. Each scheme has to be approved by the trustees and the offer document is required to be filed with the SEBI. The offer document should contain disclosures which are adequate enough to enable the investors to make informed investment decision, including the disclosure on maximum investments proposed to be made by the scheme in the listed securities of the group companies of the sponsor. If the SEBI does not comment on the contents of the offering documents within 21 days from the date of filing, the AMC would be free to issue the offer documents to public. There are obligations on the AMC and the trustee to ensure that the statements made in the offer documents are true and correct. The AMC is also required to provide an option to the unit-holder to nominate a person in whom the units held by him shall vest in the event of his death. SEBI has also prescribed an Advertising Code that has to be observed while launching a new scheme.

Closed-ended schemes are required to be listed on a recognized stock exchange within six months from the closure of the subscription. However, this requirement is not mandatory if the scheme provides for periodic repurchase facility to all the unit-holders or monthly income or caters to special classes of persons, if the details of such repurchase facility are clearly disclosed in the offer document or if the scheme opens for repurchase within a period of six months from the closure of subscription. The units of closed-ended scheme may be converted into open-ended scheme if the offer document of such scheme discloses the option and the period of such conversion or if the unit-holders are provided with an option to redeem their units in full. A closed-ended scheme is required to be fully redeemed at the end of the maturity period. However, a closed-ended scheme may be allowed to be rolled over if the purpose, period and other terms of the roll over and all other material details of the scheme including the likely composition of assets immediately before the roll over, the net assets and NAV of the scheme, are disclosed to the unit-holders and a copy of the same has been filed with SEBI. Additionally, such a roll over would be permitted only in case of those unit-holders who have expressed their consent in writing and the unit-holders who do not opt for the roll over or have not given written consent shall be allowed to redeem their holdings in full at NAV based price.

The SEBI has restricted a mutual fund from giving guaranteed returns in a scheme unless such returns are fully guaranteed by the sponsor or the AMC or a statement indicating the name of the person who will guarantee the return is made in the offer document or the manner in which the guarantee to be met has been stated in the offer document.

### *Investment Criteria*

The Mutual Fund Regulations lay down certain investment criteria that the mutual funds need to observe. There are certain restrictions on the investments made by a mutual fund. The moneys collected under any scheme of a mutual fund shall be invested only in transferable securities in the money market or in the capital market or in privately placed debentures or securitized debts. However, in the case of securitized debts, such fund may invest in asset backed securities and mortgaged backed securities. Furthermore, the mutual fund having an aggregate of securities which are worth Rs.100 million (approximately USD2.15 million) or more shall be required to settle their transactions through dematerialized securities.

## Types of Mutual Fund

### *Functional Classification of Mutual Funds*

1. **Open-ended schemes**: In case of open-ended schemes, the mutual fund continuously offers to sell and repurchase its units at net asset value (NAV) or NAV-related prices. Unlike closed-ended schemes, open-ended ones do not have to be listed on the stock exchange and can also offer repurchase soon after allotment. Investors can enter and exit the scheme any time during the life of the fund. Open-ended schemes do not have a fixed corpus. The corpus of fund increases or decreases, depending on the purchase or redemption of units by investors. There is no fixed redemption period in open-ended schemes, which can be terminated whenever the need arises.
   The fund offers a redemption price at which the holder can sell units to the fund and exit. Besides, an investor can enter the fund again by buying units from the fund at its offer price. Such funds announce sale and repurchase prices from time-to-time. UTI's US-64 scheme is an example of such a fund.

2. **Closed-ended schemes**: Closed-ended schemes have a fixed corpus and a stipulated maturity period ranging between 2 to 5 years. Investors can invest in the scheme when it is launched. The scheme remains open for a period not exceeding 45 days. Investors in closed-ended schemes can buy units only from the market, once initial subscriptions are over and thereafter the units are listed on the stock exchanges where they are to be bought and sold. The fund has no interaction with investors till redemption except for paying dividend/bonus. In order to provide an alternate exit route to the investors, some closed-ended funds give an option of selling back the units to the mutual fund through periodic repurchase at NAV related prices.
3. **Interval scheme**: Interval scheme combines the features of open-ended and closed-ended schemes. They are open for sale or redemption during predetermined intervals at NAV related prices.

### *Portfolio Classification*

Here, classification is on the basis of nature and types of securities and objective of investment.

1. **Income funds**: The aim of income funds is to provide safety of investments and regular income to investors. Such schemes invest predominantly in income-bearing instruments like bonds, debentures, government securities, and commercial paper. The returns as well as the risk are lower in income funds as compared to growth funds.
2. **Growth funds**: The main objective of growth funds is capital appreciation over the medium-to-long- term. They invest most of the corpus in equity shares with significant growth potential and they offer higher return to investors in the long-term. They assume the risks associated with equity investments. There is no guarantee or assurance of returns. These schemes are usually closed-ended and listed on stock exchanges.
3. **Balanced funds**: The aim of balanced scheme is to provide both capital appreciation and regular income. They divide their investment between equity shares and fixed nice bearing instruments in such a proportion that, the portfolio is balanced. The portfolio of such funds usually comprises of companies with good profit and dividend track records. Their exposure to risk is moderate and they offer a reasonable rate of return.
4. **Money market mutual funds**: They specialize in investing in short-term money market instruments like treasury bills, and certificate of deposits. The objective of such funds is high liquidity with low rate of return.

### *Geographical Classification*

1. **Domestic funds**: Funds which mobilize resources from a particular geographical locality like a country or region are domestic funds. The market is limited and confined to the boundaries of a nation in which the fund operates. They can invest only in the securities which are issued and traded in the domestic financial markets.
2. **Offshore funds**: Offshore funds attract foreign capital for investment in 'the country of the issuing company. They facilitate cross-border fund flow which leads to an increase in foreign currency and foreign exchange reserves. Such mutual funds can invest in securities of foreign companies. They open domestic capital market to international investors. Many mutual funds in India have launched a number of offshore funds, either independently or jointly with foreign investment management companies. The first offshore fund, the India Fund, was launched by Unit Trust of India in July 1986 in collaboration with the US fund manager, Merril Lynch.

### *Others*

1. **Sectoral:** These funds invest in specific core sectors like energy, telecommunications, IT, construction, transportation, and financial services. Some of these newly opened-up sectors offer good investment potential.
2. **Tax saving schemes:** Tax-saving schemes are designed on the basis of tax policy with special tax incentives to investors. Mutual funds have introduced a number of tax saving schemes. These are close--ended schemes and investments are made for ten years, although investors can avail of encashment facilities after 3 years. These schemes contain various options like income, growth or capital application. The latest scheme offered is the Systematic Withdrawal Plan (SWP) which enables investors to reduce their tax incidence on dividends from as high as 30% to as low as 3 to 4%.
3. **Equity-linked savings scheme (ELSS):** In order to encourage investors to invest in equity market, the government has given tax-concessions through special schemes. Investment in these schemes entitles the investor to claim an income tax rebate, but these schemes carry a lock-in period before the end of which funds cannot be withdrawn.
4. **Special schemes:** Mutual funds have launched special schemes to cater to the special needs of investors. UTI has launched special schemes such as Children's Gift Growth Fund, 1986, Housing Unit Scheme, 1992, and Venture Capital Funds.
5. **Gilt funds:** Mutual funds which deal exclusively in gilts are called gilt funds. With a view to creating a wider investor base for government securities, the Reserve Bank of India encouraged setting up of gilt funds. These funds are provided liquidity support by the Reserve Bank.
6. **Load funds:** Mutual funds incur certain expenses such as brokerage, marketing expenses, and communication expenses. These expenses are known as 'load' and are recovered by the fund when it sells the units to investors or repurchases the units from withholders. In other words, load is a sales charge, or commission, assessed by certain mutual funds to cover their selling costs. Loads can be of two types-Front-end-load and back-end load. Front-end-load, or sale load, is a charge collected at the time when an investor enters into the scheme. Back-end, or repurchase, load is a charge collected when the investor gets out of the scheme. Schemes that do not charge a load are called 'No load' schemes. In other words, if the asset management company (AMC) bears the load during the initial launch of the scheme, then these schemes are known as no-load schemes.
7. **Index funds:** An index fund is a mutual fund which invests in securities in the index on which it is based BSE Sensex or S&P CNX Nifty. It invests only in those shares which comprise the market index and in exactly the same proportion as the companies/ weightage in the index so that the value of such index funds varies with the market index. An index fund follows a passive investment strategy as no effort is made by the fund manager to identify stocks for investment/disinvestment. The fund manager has to merely track the index on which it is based. His portfolio will need an adjustment in case there is a revision in the underlying index. In other words, the fund manager has to buy stocks which are added to the index and sell stocks which are deleted from the index. Internationally, index funds are very popular. Around one third of professionally run portfolios in the US are index funds. Empirical evidence points out those active fund managers have not been able to perform well. Only 20-25%of actively managed equity mutual funds out-perform benchmark indices in the long-term. These active fund managers park 80% of their money in an index and do active management on the remaining 20%. Moreover, risk adverse investors like provident funds and pension funds prefer investment in passively managed funds like index funds.

8. **P/I ratio fund:** PIE ratio fund is another mutual fund variant that is offered by Pioneer IT! Mutual Fund. The P/I (Price-Earnings) ratio is the ratio of the price of the stock of a company to its earnings per share (EPS). The P/I ratio of the index is the weighted average price-earnings ratio of all its constituent stocks. The P/I ratio fund invests in equities and debt instruments wherein the proportion of the investment is determined by the ongoing price-earnings multiple of the market. Broadly, around 90% of the investible funds will be invested inequity if the Nifty Index P/I ratio is 12 or below. If this ratio exceeds 28, the investment will be in debt/money markets. Between the two ends of 12 and 28 P/I ratio of the Nifty, the fund will allocate varying proportions of its investible funds to equity and debt. The objective of this scheme is to provide superior risk-adjusted returns through a balanced portfolio of equity and debt instruments.
9. **Exchange traded funds:** Exchange Traded Funds (ETFs) are a hybrid of open-ended mutual funds and listed individual stocks. They are listed on stock exchanges and trade like individual stocks on the stock exchange. However, trading at the stock exchanges does not affect their portfolio. ETFs do not sell their shares directly to investors for cash. The shares are offered to investors over the stock exchange. ETFs are basically passively managed funds that track a particular index such as S&P CNX Nifty. Since they are listed on stock exchanges, it is possible to buy and sell them throughout the day and their price is determined by the demand-supply forces in the market. In practice, they trade in a small range around the value of the assets (NAV) held by them. ETFs offer several distinct advantages. ETFs bring the trading and real time pricing advantages of individual stocks to mutual funds. The ability to trade intraday at prices that are usually close to the actual intra-day NAV of the scheme makes it almost real-time trading.
    - ETFs are simpler to understand and hence they can attract small investors who are deterred to trade in index futures due to requirement of minimum contract size. Small investors can buy minimum one unit of ETF, can place limit orders and trade intra-day. This, in turn, would increase liquidity of the cash market.
    - ETFs can be used to arbitrate effectively between index futures and spot index.
    - ETFs provide the benefits of diversified index funds. The investor can benefit from the flexibility of stocks as well as the diversification.
    - ETFs being passively managed have somewhat higher NAV against an index fund of the same portfolio. The operating expenses of ETFs are lower than even those of similar index funds as they do not have to service investors who deal in shares through stock exchanges.
    - ETFs can be beneficial for financial institutions also. Financial institutions can use ETFs for utilizing idle cash, managing redemptions, modifying sector allocations, and hedging market exposure.

## Benefits of Mutual Funds

An investor can invest directly in individual securities or indirectly through a financial intermediary. Globally, mutual funds have established themselves as the means of investment for the retail investor.

1. **Professional management:** An average investor lacks the knowledge of capital market operations and does not have large resources to reap the benefits of investment. Hence, he requires the help of an expert. It, is not only expensive to 'hire the services' of an expert but it is more difficult to identify a real expert. Mutual funds are managed by professional managers who have the requisite skills and experience to analyses the performance and prospects of companies. They make possible an organized investment strategy, which is hardly possible for an individual investor.

2. **Portfolio diversification**: An investor undertakes risk if he invests all his funds in a single scrip. Mutual funds invest in a number of companies across various industries and sectors. This diversification reduces the riskiness of the investments.
3. **Reduction in transaction costs**: Compared to direct investing in the capital market, investing through the funds is relatively less expensive as the benefit of economies of scale is passed on to the investors.
4. **Liquidity**: Often, investors cannot sell the securities held easily, while in case of mutual funds, they can easily en cash their investment by selling their units to the fund if it is an open-ended scheme or selling them on a stock exchange if it is a closed-ended scheme.
5. **Convenience:** Investing in mutual fund reduces paperwork, saves time and makes investment easy.
6. **Flexibility**: Mutual funds offer a family of schemes, and investors have the option of transferring their holdings from one scheme to the other.
7. **Tax benefits** Mutual fund investors now enjoy income-tax benefits. Dividends received from mutual funds' debt schemes are tax exempt to the overall limit of Rs. 9,000 allowed under section 80L of the Income Tax Act.
8. **Transparency** Mutual funds transparently declare their portfolio every month. Thus an investor knows where his/her money is being deployed and in case they are not happy with the portfolio they can withdraw at a short notice.
9. **Stability to the stock market** Mutual funds have a large amount of funds which provide them economies of scale by which they can absorb any losses in the stock market and continue investing in the stock market. In addition, mutual funds increase liquidity in the money and capital market.
10. **Equity research** Mutual funds can afford information and data required for investments as they have large amount of funds and equity research teams available with them.

### *Disadvantages of Mutual Funds*

The mutual fund not just have advantages to investor but also has disadvantages. The fund manager not always make profits/create loss for not properly managed. The fund has its own strategy for investment to hold, to sell, to purchase unit at particular time period.

1. **Costs Control Not in the Hands of an Investor:** Investor has to pay investment management fees and fund distribution costs as a percentage of the value of his investments (as long as he holds the units), irrespective of the performance of the fund.
2. **No Customized Portfolios:** The portfolio of securities in which a fund invests is a decision taken by the fund manager. Investors have no right to interfere in the decision making process of a fund manager, which some investors find as a constraint in achieving their financial objectives.
3. **Difficulty in Selecting a Suitable Fund Scheme:** Many investors find it difficult to select one option from the plethora of funds/schemes/plans available. For this, they may have to take advice from financial planners in order to invest in the right fund to achieve their objectives.

## RBI Regulation for Mutual Funds

The government of India issued guidelines for mutual funds on February 14, 1992. While issuing the guidelines, the government specifically mentioned that mutual funds had become a major vehicle for mobilization of savings, particularly from the small and house hold sectors, for investment in the stock market in view of their growing importance in the capital market and their expanding investor base.

It was also felt necessary for the government to develop a comprehensive set of prudential guidelines for the all-round development and regulation of mutual funds and ensuring investor protection.

These guidelines are applicable to all mutual funds that invest primarily in the capital market and also partly in money market instruments subject to the following.

1. Money market mutual fund that would invest exclusively in the money market instrument would be regulated by the Reserve Bank of India on the basis of specified guidelines to be laid down by RBI. However, money market schemes of other mutual funds would be regulated by SEBI. These regulations will be in confirmative with the guidelines to be issued by RBI for money market mutual funds investing exclusively in money market instruments.
2. Offshore funds that have non-resident investors and are regulated by provision of the countries where they are registered shall be outside the purview of these guidelines. These funds shall continue to be governed by the rules and procedures laid down for the purpose of approving and monitoring their performance by the Government of India.
3. Mutual funds with special characteristics, for example funds dealing with assets, other than securities, may be specifically exempted by the government from the purview of these guidelines.

The salient features of these guidelines are highlighted as follows.

Mutual funds shall be authorized for business by SEBI. The mutual funds shall be sponsored by registered companies with the sound track record, general reputation and fairness in all their business transactions. They shall be established in the form of trust under Indian Trust Act. The sponsoring institution will be free to work out the details regarding the constitution of the trust. The trust will be then authorized to float one or several different schemes under which units shall be issued to the investors. Mutual funds shall be operated only by separately established Asset Management Companies (AMC's).

## Measurement of Mutual Fund

### *1. Alpha*

Alpha is the measure of a portfolio's return versus a specific benchmark, adjusted for risk. The most common benchmark in use - and the one you can assume is used unless otherwise noted - is the S&P 500. An investment with an alpha greater than zero has provided more return for the given amount of risk assumed. A negative alpha - less than zero - indicates a security which has underperformed the benchmark; it has earned too little for the risk assumed. Investors typically want investments with high alphas.

### *2. Beta*

Beta is the measure of an investment's volatility to another market index, such as the S&P 500. Volatility indicates how likely a security is to experience wide swings in value. If beta is 1.0, the investment moves in sync with the S&P or experiences a measure of volatility similar to the S&P. If beta is positive, the investment moves more than the index; if negative, the investment is less volatile than the index. For example, a beta of 2.0 projects a movement two times that of the market. Assuming a market price change of 15%, the investment could move 30% up or down. Conservative investors typically prefer investments with low betas to reduce volatility in their portfolios.

### 3. *R-Squared Value*

The R-squared value is a measurement of how reliable the beta number is. It varies between zero and 1.0, with zero being no reliability and 1.0 being perfect reliability. The two charts illustrate the variability of return for two funds compared to the volatility of the S&P 500 in the same period. Each y-value represents a fund's returns plotted against the S&P 500 returns (x-values) in the same period. The beta, or the line created by plotting these values, is the same in each case. This suggests that the correlation between each fund and the S&P 500 is identical. However, closer examination indicates that the beta in the second chart is far more reliable than the beta in the first chart as the dispersion of the individual returns (x) is much tighter. Therefore, the R-squared value is higher for the fund in second chart.

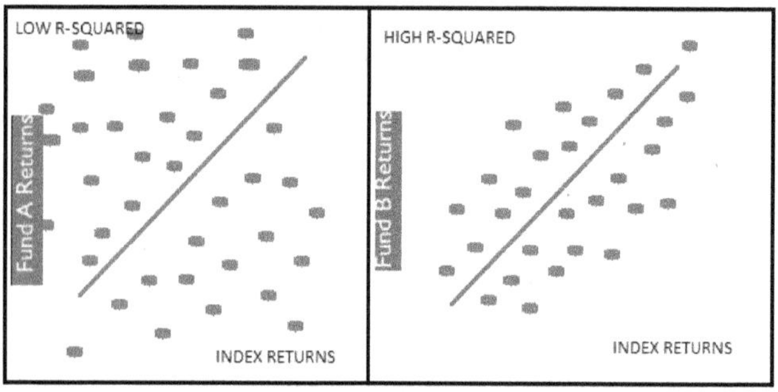


### 4. *Standard Deviation*

While beta typically measures an investment's movement against an index such as the S&P 500, standard deviation measures the volatility of an investment in a different way. Instead of comparing the investment's return to a benchmark, standard deviation compares an investment's individual returns (for example, the closing price each day) over a specific period relative to its average return over the same period. The more individual returns deviate from the investment's average return, the higher the standard deviation. An investment with a standard deviation of 16.5 is more volatile than an investment with a standard deviation of 12.0. According to Morningstar Ratings, the standard deviation for the S&P 500 has been 18.8 for the last five years.

### 5. *Sharpe Ratio*

Developed by Dr. William Sharpe, professor at the Stanford Graduate School of Business and one of the recipients of the Nobel Prize for his contribution to the capital asset pricing model, the Sharpe volatility ratio is a measure of a portfolio's return versus a risk-free return. The risk-free return most often used is the interest rate on a three-month U.S. Treasury bill.

The underlying premise is that an investor should receive a higher return if he assumes more volatility in his portfolio. Theoretically, the higher the ratio, the stronger the portfolio's return has been relative to the risk taken. A ratio of 1.0 indicates that the return was what should be expected for the risk taken, a ratio greater than 1.0 is an indication that the rate was better than expected, and less than 1.0 is an indication that the return did not justify the risk taken. Refinements of return to volatility ratios include the Sortino ratio, the Treynor ratio, and the Modigliani risk adjustment performance measure (RAP).

$$S_p = \frac{R_i - R_f}{\sigma p}$$

$S_p$= Sharpe ratio for the fund

$R_i$=average return on fund

$\sigma p$ = standard deviation of return on fund

$R_f$= return on risk free asset.

**Example**

A manager generates a return of 15% with the risk free-rate of 5%, and a manager's portfolio has a standard deviation of 8%, then find the sharpe ratio for manager portfolio?

**Given**

Expected portfolio return= 15%, Risk free rate= 5% Portfolio standard deviation = 8% Substitute the given values in the formula,

S(x) = (Expected portfolio return - Risk free rate)/Portfolio standard deviation
= (15-5)/8
= (10)/8
= 1.25

### 6. *Capture Ratios*

Capture ratios, or the percent of broad market moves over a specified term reflected in a portfolio, are intended to be a simpler way to reflect a portfolio manager's performance. For example, if the S&P 500 has moved upward 20% while the portfolio being managed has increased 25%, the portfolio has captured more gains than the market move and would have a ratio of 1.25 (25%/20%), an upside capture ratio. If the market falls by 20% and the portfolio drops 25%, the downside capture ratio would also be 1.25, indicating that the portfolio has underperformed the market for the period. Generally, investors would prefer a fund with an upside capture ratio in rising markets greater than 1.0 and a downside capture ratio less than 1.0.

### 7. *Independent Ratings*

Companies such as Lipper and Morningstar have proprietary rating systems to rate mutual funds on a risk-adjusted performance basis. Morningstar uses stars and gives a five-star rating to the top 10% of funds within a fund category. Lipper provides a variety of different ratings depending upon the investor's goal – total return, consistent return, and others. There are a variety of other proprietary ranking services in common use as well, such as Zacks (used by Yahoo! Finance) and The Street. Credit rating services such as Standard & Poor's and Moody's analyze and rank companies on their creditworthiness.

### 8. *Jensen's Ratio*

A risk-adjusted performance measure that represents the average return on aportfolioover and above that predicted by the capital asset pricing model (CAPM), given the portfolio's beta and the average market return. This is the portfolio's alpha. In fact, the concept is sometimes referred to as "Jensen's alpha."

$$E(R_p) = R_f + \beta_p(R_m - R_f)$$

$E(R_p)$ = Expected portfolio return
$R_f$ = risk free return
$\beta_p$= beta of portfolio
$R_m$= market return

**Example**

If there are two mutual funds that both have a 12% return, a rational investor will want the fund that is less risky. Jensen's measure is one of the ways to help determine if a portfolio is earning the proper return for its level of risk. If the value is positive, then the portfolio is earning excess returns.

### *9. Treynor Ratio*

The Treynor ratio (sometimes called the reward-to-volatility ratio or Treynor measure), named after Jack L. Treynor, is a measurement of the returns earned in excess of that which could have been earned on an investment that has no diversifiable risk (e.g., Treasury bills or a completely diversified portfolio), per each unit of market risk assumed. The Treynor ratio relates excess return over the risk-free rate to the additional risk taken; however, systematic risk is used instead of total risk. The higher the Treynor ratio, the better the performance of the portfolio under analysis.

Treynor's ratio is measured through the following equation:

$$T_p = \frac{R_i - R_f}{\beta_p}$$

$R_i$= Average return of fund

$R_f$ = Risk-free rate

$\beta_p$ = Beta of portfolio.

**For Example**

Compare two funds in the large-cap category: Sundaram Growth and HDFC Equity. For Sundaram Growth, the Treynor ratios for the three-, five- and 10-year periods are negative 1.76, negative 4.26, and 16.79, respectively. HDFC Equity's three-, five-, and 10-year Treynor ratios are 6.21, 2.31 and 24.78, respectively.

Based on the Treynor ratios alone, HDFC Equity offers a much more attractive reward-to-volatility profile. Moreover, given that the large-cap category Treynor ratios during the same periods were 0.06, -3.18 and 18.64, we can see that Sundaram Growth lagged the category average significantly over every time period while HDFC Equity handily outpaced the category average.

## Mutual Fund in India

The mutual fund industry in India started in 1963 with the formation of Unit Trust of India, at the initiative of the Government of India and Reserve Bank of India. The history of mutual funds in India can be broadly divided into four distinct phases

### *First Phase - 1964-1987*

Unit Trust of India (UTI) was established in 1963 by an Act of Parliament. It was set up by the Reserve Bank of India and functioned under the Regulatory and administrative control of the Reserve Bank of India. In 1978 UTI was de-linked from the RBI and the Industrial Development Bank of India (IDBI) took over the regulatory and administrative control in place of RBI. The first scheme launched by UTI was Unit Scheme 1964. At the end of 1988 UTI had Rs. 6,700 crores of assets under management.

### *Second Phase - 1987-1993 (Entry of Public Sector Funds)*

1987 marked the entry of non-UTI, public sector mutual funds set up by public sector banks and Life Insurance Corporation of India (LIC) and General Insurance Corporation of India (GIC). SBI Mutual Fund was the first non-UTI Mutual Fund established in June 1987 followed by Canbank Mutual Fund (Dec 87), Punjab National Bank Mutual Fund (Aug 89), Indian Bank Mutual Fund (Nov 89), Bank of India (Jun 90), Bank of Baroda Mutual Fund (Oct 92). LIC established its mutual fund in June 1989 while GIC had set up its mutual fund in December 1990. At the end of 1993, the mutual fund industry had assets under management of Rs. 47,004 crores.

### *Third Phase - 1993-2003 (Entry of Private Sector Funds)*

With the entry of private sector funds in 1993, a new era started in the Indian mutual fund industry, giving the Indian investors a wider choice of fund families. Also, 1993 was the year in which the first Mutual Fund Regulations came into being, under which all mutual funds, except UTI were to be registered and governed. The erstwhile Kothari Pioneer (now merged with Franklin Templeton) was the first private sector mutual fund registered in July 1993.

The 1993 SEBI (Mutual Fund) Regulations were substituted by a more comprehensive and revised Mutual Fund Regulations in 1996. The industry now functions under the SEBI (Mutual Fund) Regulations 1996.

The number of mutual fund houses went on increasing, with many foreign mutual funds setting up funds in India and also the industry has witnessed several mergers and acquisitions. As at the end of January 2003, there were 33 mutual funds with total assets of Rs. 1,21,805 crores. The Unit Trust of India with Rs. 44,541 crores of assets under management was way ahead of other mutual funds.

### *Fourth Phase - Since February 2003*

In February 2003, following the repeal of the Unit Trust of India Act 1963 UTI was bifurcated into two separate entities. One is the Specified Undertaking of the Unit Trust of India with assets under management of Rs. 29,835 crores as at the end of January 2003, representing broadly, the assets of US 64 scheme, assured return and certain other schemes. The Specified Undertaking of Unit Trust of India, functioning under an administrator and under the rules framed by Government of India and does not come under the purview of the Mutual Fund Regulations.

The second is the UTI Mutual Fund, sponsored by SBI, PNB, BOB and LIC. It is registered with SEBI and functions under the Mutual Fund Regulations. With the bifurcation of the erstwhile UTI which had in March 2000 more than Rs. 76,000 crores of assets under management and with the setting up of a UTI Mutual Fund, conforming to the SEBI Mutual Fund Regulations, and with recent mergers taking place among different private sector funds, the mutual fund industry has entered its current phase of consolidation and growth.

### *Trends in Mutual Fund Industry*

### *Number of Schemes under Mutual Funds during the Period 2010-2014*

| Year | Debt | Income | Balanced | ETFs | Overseas | Total |
|---|---|---|---|---|---|---|
| 2010-11 | 679 | 376 | 32 | 26 | 16 | 1131 |
| 2011-12 | 872 | 352 | 30 | 35 | 20 | 1309 |
| 2012-13 | 857 | 347 | 32 | 37 | 21 | 1294 |
| 2013-14 | 1178 | 363 | 30 | 40 | 27 | 1638 |

Source: SEBI

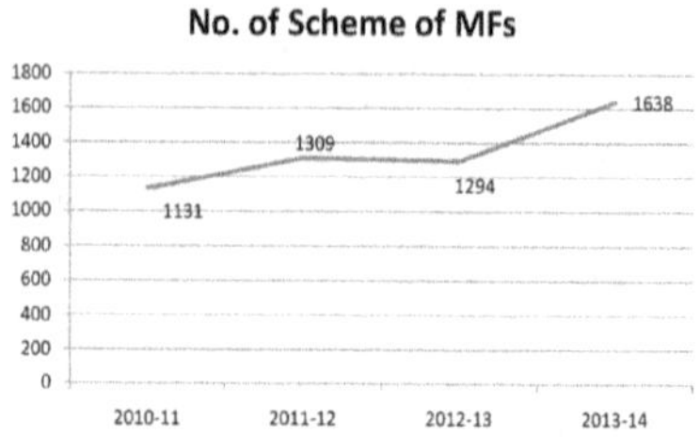


The total number of schemes under MFs have increased during the period 2010-14 and it increased very steeply between 2012-13 to 2013-14. The growth rate of number of schemes in debt is greater than income, balanced, ETFs and overseas.

### *Fund Mobilization under Mutual funds*

**(Rs. in Crore)**

| Year | Debt | Income | Balanced | ETFs | Overseas | Total |
|---|---|---|---|---|---|---|
| 2010-11 | 8777034.17 | 66592.30 | 7490.28 | 7709.25 | 969.39 | 8859515.38 |
| 2011-12 | 6754113.22 | 50618.80 | 5027.29 | 8563.39 | 1355.81 | 6819678.51 |
| 2012-13 | 7213578.19 | 43364.31 | 5204.88 | 5052.35 | 685.53 | 7267885.26 |
| 2013-14 | 9709762.04 | 46092.99 | 3434.89 | 6869.63 | 1941 | 9768100.54 |

Source: SEBI

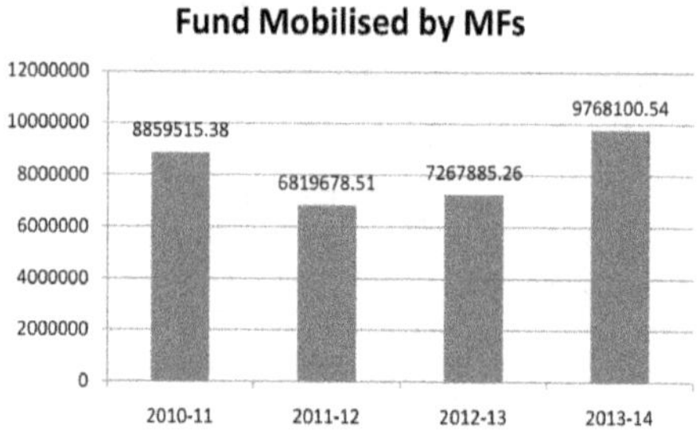


The total Fund mobilized by the mutual fund have declined in the year 2011-12 from Rs. 8859515.38 crore to 6819679.51 crore but again the industry gained momentum and it increased to 9768100.54 in 2013-14. The major chunk of mutual fund industry is invested in debt securities where as the share of investment in balanced and ETFs is more or less same. Thus we can conclude from above that the mutual fund industry is one of the major investor in the debt securities of the capital market.

### *Net Assets under Mutual Funds during 2010-11 to 2103-14*

**(Rs. in Crore)**

| Year | Debt | Income | Balanced | ETFs | Overseas | Total |
|---|---|---|---|---|---|---|
| 2010-11 | 369049.22 | 95322.39 | 18445.09 | 6916.67 | 2516.17 | 592249.53 |
| 2011-12 | 374856.70 | 182075.86 | 16261.10 | 11492.58 | 2530.31 | 587216.56 |
| 2012-13 | 497451.17 | 172507.78 | 16307.21 | 13124.33 | 2052.87 | 701443.37 |
| 2013-14 | 600944.82 | 191107.08 | 6792.61 | 13204.83 | 3190.80 | 825240.14 |

Source: SEBI

The Net Assets under mutual funds have remained almost stagnant during 2010-11 to 2011-12 and it increased very steeply between 2012-13 to 2013-14.

### *Way Forward*

The Mutual fund industry needs to have an outside-in perspective as compared to inside-out perspective. Understanding investors" needs should be followed by a product channel alignment. Increasing financial literacy will be the key to unlock the doors to B-15 and also to remove the perception that equates mutual fund to only equity. Investor awareness campaigns should be conducted to increase the AUM (Assets under management) in smaller cities which would help industry to progress in a holistic manner. Knowledge about mutual fund industry should be included in educational curriculum.

Fund houses may need to find and partner with the right distributor to make the products available to investors in smaller cities. Therefore, Banks and IFAs (Index Fund Advisors) could play a pivotal role in reaching the investor base. Also, distributors should be incentivized enough to ensure that they project mutual funds as a long-term investment for fulfilling financial goals. For future growth, tax could act as an enabler as tax benefits can be a pull factor for investors. For example, fund of funds does not get the required tax benefit from the government. May be, government could look at such funds and few offshore funds from India for tax benefits. Technology can act as a key enabler and help the fund houses reach investors at a low cost and more efficient manner. AMCs need to make the relevant investments in technology to help reach investors to help ensure transactions on the channels of their choice.

## Reasons for Slow Growth of Mutual Fund in India

- ***Poor Investor Interest***

Assets managed by mutual funds are falling. For the month ended March 2012, assets under management with all mutual funds plunged 13 per cent to Rs 5,87,000 crore, according to Association of Mutual funds in India (AMFI) data. This is the lowest since June 2009. This means investors have pulled out money. While March usually sees a high outflow of funds as corporate India pulls out money to meet tax and other working capital requirement, the absence of a diverse retail base hurts. The industry needs more common people to own mutual fund units and not just large corporates to park their money.

- ***Other Attractive Investment Avenues***

For the common man, the Indian government offers saving schemes with sovereign guarantee. With high interest rates and tax rebates, post office schemes like public provident fund or National Saving certificate offer better returns to investors. Individuals have Rs 5,19,162crore invested in the post office or government guarantee schemes, according to Karvy, securities firm. Employee Provident fund and public provident funds manage another Rs 2,81,000crore. This is more than the size of the total mutual fund industry in India. High bank deposit rates also reduce the risk appetite. Indian individuals own fixed deposits and government guaranteed bonds worth Rs 22,16,307 crore, according to Karvy. Another Rs 6,20,000crore is held in savings bank accounts with public and private sector banks.

- ***Equity Assets Stagnant***

Mutual funds manage Rs 1,82,000 crore in equity assets, according to the AMFI data. This is barely 3 per cent of the total market capitalization of the Bombay Stock Exchange. Foreign institutional investors control five times of that. A successful asset management business is evaluated on the basis of the equity assets it manages. However, with sovereign guarantee schemes dominating most of the household investible surplus, it is a challenge to ask individuals to take risks.

- ***Individuals Prefer Direct Equity Investment***

Direct equity holding is estimated at Rs 22,73,043 crore, more than 11 times equity assets managed by mutual funds and a third of the BSE market cap. This means investors prefer to buy or sell shares on their own and not rely on mutual funds. Mutual funds have failed to educate this segment to allocate resources to them.

- ***Tough Business to be in***

Fidelity, one of the biggest mutual fund manager in the world, sold its India business to L&T Finance Holdings recently. They are not the first foreign company to exit. Most of the foreign exits from India were due to global restructuring or M&A. Fidelity's exit from a loss-making India business highlights problems of doing business in India. It is not clear yet why Fidelity decided to exit. However, an exit by one of the largest mutual fund company in the world should not be taken lightly.

- ***Restrictive Mandate***

The mutual fund industry in US relies heavily on US state and private pension funds to manage a large amount of money. So Fidelity and Templeton are engaged by state pension funds to manage a portion of the pension money. In India, pension reforms are part of a major political wrangle. Politicians do not allow government pension funds to invest in equity markets. Even if some agree, they are not able to push through any reforms that could push up assets under management for mutual funds.

## Selection of Mutual Fund

- ***Performance Ranking***

More than the recent or long term performance of any scheme its ranking among peers should be looked at. To find out the ranking you need to check out the quartile ranking which will show how the fund has performed quarter on quarter among its peer group. In quartile ranking each quartile comprises of 25 percent of peer group schemes. So one may select the scheme which has remained in top quartile most of the time. If at all you find your scheme going below 3rd quartile in a couple of consecutive quarters it hints that time has come to exit the scheme.

- ***Ratio Analysis***

Risk and return ratios like standard deviation, Sharpe ratio etc. I have discussed in my earlier article on Measuring Mutual funds risk. Along with those ratios, one also should check out the ALPHA of the fund. Alpha tells us what extra or less the fund manager has generated out of a given portfolio in comparison to benchmark. In other words alpha is the performance ranking of the fund manager. You may check how often the fund manager has generated positive alpha in last few quarters and also keep a watch on its consistency going forward.

- ***Total Expense Ratio***

Expense ratio is very important parameter to be looked at while selecting any mutual fund scheme. All fund management and distribution related expenses are borne by the scheme. This means high expense ratio will affect the fund's returns. Though mutual fund's total expense ratio has been capped by SEBI, still lower the better unless we get some extraordinary return by paying higher expenses for fund management according to the total expenses ratio.

- ***Fund Manager Tenure and Experience***

Fund manager plays a very important role in the fund's performance. Though it is a process oriented approach but still fund manager is the ultimate decision maker and his experience and view point counts a lot. The investors should know who the fund manager of the scheme is and what his past track record is. Also look at the performance of other funds which he is managing. If the fund manager of the scheme has recently been changed, then watch the performance by looking at alpha and quarter to quarter performance.

- ***Scheme Asset Size***

This parameter is different for debt and equity schemes. In equity the comfortable asset size in hundreds of crores, in debt it should be in thousands of crores as the investment value per investor is higher in debt funds. 90 percent of total assets under management (AUM) of the mutual fund industry are invested in debt funds, so your selected scheme assets should also have a considerable AUM. Less AUM in any scheme is very risky as you don't know who the investors are and what quantum of investments they have in this particular scheme. Exit of any big investor out of any mutual fund may impact its overall performance very badly and the remaining investors in a scheme will have to bear the impact. In schemes with larger AUMs this risk gets minimised. The observation of all the above mentioned parameters is overlapping each other in some way or the other. A good fund manager will automatically result in better performance and thus improve the quartile ranking and would also generate good alpha. High scheme assets will help in reducing the total expense ratio of the scheme. But, as the popular saying goes- 'There is no scientific way to choose tomorrow's best funds today', so one should review the current selection every quarter or half yearly.

### *Net Asset Value Method*

**Net asset value (NAV)** is the value of an entity's assets minus the value of its liabilities, often in relation to open-end or mutual funds, since shares of such funds registered with the U.S. Securities and Exchange Commission are redeemed at their net asset value. This may also be the same as the book value or the equity value of a business. Net asset value may represent the value of the total equity, or it may be divided by the number of shares outstanding held by investors, thereby representing the net asset value *per share.*

Net asset value and other accounting and recordkeeping activities are the result of the process of fund accounting (also known as securities accounting, investment accounting, and portfolio accounting). Fund accounting systems are sophisticated computerized systems used to account for investor capital flows in and out of a fund, purchases and sales of investments and related investment income, gains, losses and operating expenses of the fund. The fund's investments and other assets are valued regularly; daily, weekly, or monthly, depending on the fund and associated regulatory or sponsor requirements. There is no universal method or basis of valuing assets and liabilities for the purposes of calculating the net asset value used throughout the world, and the criteria used for the valuation will depend upon the circumstances, the purposes of the valuation and any regulatory and/or accounting principles that may apply. For example, for U.S.-registered open-ended funds, investments are commonly valued each day the New York Stock Exchange is open, using closing prices (meant to represent fair value),[2] typically 4:00 p.m. Eastern Time.

### *Example of Investment Formula*

Based on the market price, the mutual fund DEF has $3,576,000 total assets and the liabilities are $1,250,000. To calculate the net asset value for mutual fund DEF is the following:

**Net asset value = total assets - liabilities = $3,576,000 - $1,250,000 = $2,326,000**

The mutual fund DEF's net asset value is $2,326,000. Assuming that the total outstanding unit of mutual fund is 1,500,000. The calculation for net asset value per share for mutual fund DEF is the following:

**Net asset value per share = net asset value/total outstanding shares = $2,326,000/1,500,000 = $1.55**

Every mutual fund DEF unit share has a net asset value per share of $1.55. Companies of mutual fund will treat this net asset value per share as a base price in selling the mutual fund to the public.

The total assets of ABC Corporation are $2,000,000 and its intangible asset is $1,000,000 and its liabilities are $500,000. The calculation for net asset value of ABC Corporation is the following:

**Net asset value = total assets - intangible assets - liabilities = 2,000,000 - $1,000,000 - $500,000 = $500,000**

The net asset value for ABC Corporation is $500,000.

# 7. Credit Rating

## *Meaning*

It is the evaluation of credit worthiness of debtor, financial instruments, corporations etc. An evaluation into the credit worthiness of an individual is called as credit reporting. It is done by credit bureaus, consumer credit agencies.

Credit rating is the opinion of the rating agency on the relative ability and willingness of tile issuer of a debt instrument to meet the debt service obligations as and when they arise. Rating is usually expressed in alphabetical or alphanumeric symbols. Symbols are simple and easily understood tool which help the investor to differentiate between debt instruments on the basis of their underlying credit quality. Rating companies also publish explanations for their symbols used as well as the rationale for the ratings assigned by them, to facilitate deeper understanding.

India was perhaps the first amongst developing countries to set up a credit rating agency in 1988. The function of credit rating was institutionalized when RBI made it mandatory for the issue of Commercial Paper(CP) and subsequently by SEBI. When it made credit rating compulsory for certain categories of debentures and debt instruments. In June 1994, RBI made it mandatory for Non-Banking Financial Companies (NBFCs) to be rated. Credit rating is optional for Public Sector Undertakings (PSUs) bonds and privately placed non-convel1ible debentures upto Rs. 50 million. Fixed deposits of manufacturing companies also come under the purview of optional credit rating

## Features

1. **Rating is based on information:** Any rating based entirely on published information has serious limitations and the success of a rating agency will depend, to a great extent, on its ability to access privileged information. Cooperation from the issuers as well as their willingness to share even confidential information are important pre-requisites. The rating agency must keep information of confidential nature possessed during the rating process, a secret.
2. **Many factors affect rating:** Rating does not come out of a predetermined mathematical formula. Final rating is given taking into account the quality of management, corporate strategy, economic outlook and international environment. To ensure consistency and reliability a number of qualified professionals are involved in the rating process. The Rating Committee, which assigns the final rating, consists of specialised financial and credit analysts. Rating agencies also ensure that the rating process is free from any possible clash of interest.
3. **Rating by more than one agency:** In the well developed capital markets, debt issues are, more often than not, rated by more than one agency. And it is only natural that ratings given by two or more agencies differ from each other e.g., a debt issue, may be rated 'AA+' by one agency and 'AA' or 'AA-' by another. It will indeed be unusual if one agency assigns a rating of AA while another gives a 'BBB'.
4. **Monitoring the already rated issues:** A rating is an opinion given on the basis of information available at particular point of time. Many factors may affect the debt servicing capabilities of the issuer. It is, therefore, essential that rating agencies monitor all outstanding debt issues rated by them as part of their investor service. The rating agencies should put issues under close credit watch and upgrade or downgrade the ratings as per the circumstances after intensive interaction with the issuers.
5. **Publication of ratings:** In India, ratings are undertaken only at the request of the issuers and only those ratings which are accepted by the issuers are published. Thus, once a rating is accepted it is published and subsequent changes emerging out of the

monitoring by the agency will be published even if such changes are not found acceptable by the issuers.

6. **Right of appeal against assigned rating:** Where an issuer is not satisfied with the rating assigned, he may request for a review, furnishing additional information, if any, considered relevant. The rating agency will undertake a review and thereafter give its final decision. Unless the rating agency had over looked critical information at the first stage chances of the rating being changed on appeal are rare.
7. **Rating of rating agencies:** Informed public opinion will be the touchstone on which the rating companies have to be assessed and the success of a rating agency is measured by the quality of the services offered, consistency and integrity.
8. **Rating is for instrument and not for the issuer company:** The important thing to note is that rating is done always for a particular issue and not for a company or the Issuer. It is quite possible that two instruments issued by the same company carry different ratings, particularly if maturities are substantially different or one of the instruments is backed by additional credit reinforcements like guarantees. In many cases, short-term obligations, like commercial paper(CP) carry the highest rating even as the risk profile changes for longer maturities.

2. **Rating not applicable to equity shares:** By definition, credit rating is an opinion on the issuers capacity to service debt. In the case of equity there is no pre-determined servicing obligation, as equity is in the nature of venture capital. So, credit rating does not apply to equity shares.
3. **Credit vs. financial analysis:** Credit rating is much broader concept than financial analysis. One important factor which needs consideration is that the rating is normally done at the request of and with the active co-operation of the issuer. The rating agency has access to unpublished information and the discussions with the senior management of issuers give meaningful insights into corporate plans and strategies. Necessary adjustments are made to the published accounts for the purpose of analysis. Rating is carried out by specialised professionals who are highly qualified and experienced. The final rating is assigned keeping in view the number of factors.
4. **Time taken in rating process:** The rating process is a fairly detailed exercise. It involves, among other things analysis of published financial information, visits to the issuers offices and works, 'intensive discussion with the senior executives of issuers, discussions with auditors, bankers, creditors etc. It also involves an in-depth study of the industry itself and a degree of environment scanning. All this takes time, a rating agency may take 6 to 8 weeks or more to arrive at a decision. For rating short-term instruments like commercial paper (CP), the time taken may vary from 3 to 4 weeks, as the focus will be more on short-term liquidity rather than on long-term fundamentals. Rating agencies do not compromise on the quality of their analysis or work under pressure from issuers for quick results. Issuers are always advised to. Approach the rating agencies sufficiently in advance so that issue schedules can be adhered to.

## Symbols

| CREDIT RATING SYMBOLS AND WHAT THEY MEAN | |
|---|---|
| **High Investment Grades:** | |
| AAA | Highest Safety |
| AA | High Safety |
| **Investment Grades:** | |
| A | Adequate Safety |
| BBB | Moderate Safety |
| **Speculative Grades:** | |
| BB | Inadequate Safety |
| B | High Risk |
| C | Substantial Risk |
| D | In Default |

## Validity

When a company, government agency or municipality issues any debt security, a credit rating is usually sought. The rating is published so investors can judge the creditworthiness of the issuer and determine more effectively the risks associated with investing in debt from that issuer. There are several credit rating agencies that provide a thorough analysis of an issuer's finances and assign a rating according to their findings. The rating is reviewed and restated quarterly in most instances, with full analysis annually for higher volume issuers.

There are three main credit rating agencies followed by investors around the globe. Moody's, Standard & Poor's and Fitch all provide objective opinions on an issuer, so investors can make wise decisions. The process of rating a bond begins with an initial meeting between an analyst at the credit rating agency and management of the issuer to go over basic financial statements of the company. Financial strength ratios are calculated to help the analyst determine the likelihood of the indenture being repaid. The initial review and rating process can take around four weeks, according to Moody's. After the analyst judges the financial strength of the company, a board of ratings analysts meets to collaborate on finding an appropriate rating for the issuer's current state. The final rating is revealed to the issuer and the public via press release.

After the initial rating, the assigned analyst keeps in contact with the issuing company's finance team and reviews its rating periodically. Ratings are most often reviewed, upgraded or downgraded each quarter, after a company releases quarterly earnings information.

## Functions

A credit rating agency serves following functions:

- **Provides unbiased opinion:** An independent credit rating agency is likely to provide an unbiased opinion as to relative capability of the company to service debt obligations because of the following reasons:
  i. It has no vested interest in an issue unlike brokers, financial intermediaries.
  ii. Its own reputation is at stake.
- **Provides quality and dependable information**: A credit rating agency is in a position to provide quality information on credit risk which is more authenticate and reliable because:
  i. It has highly trained and professional staff who has better ability to assess risk.
  ii. It has access to a lot of information which may not be publicly available.
- **Provides information at low cost**: Most of the investors rely on the ratings assigned by the ratings agencies while taking investment decisions. These ratings are published in the form of reports and are available easily on the payment of negligible price. It is not possible for the investors to assess the creditworthiness of the companies on their own.
- **Provide easy to understand information**: Rating agencies first of all gather information, then analyse the same. At last these interpret and summarize complex information in a simple and readily understood formal manner. Thus in other words, information supplied by rating agencies can be easily understood by the investors. They need not go into details of the financial statements.
- **Provide basis for investment**: An investment rated by a credit rating enjoys higher confidence from investors. Investors can make an estimate of the risk and return associated with a particular rated issue while investing money in them.
- **Healthy discipline on corporate borrowers:** Higher credit rating to any credit investment enhances corporate image and builds up goodwill and hence it induces a healthy/ discipline on corporate.

- **Formation of public policy:** Once the debt securities are rated professionally, it would be easier to formulate public policy guidelines as to the eligibility of securities to be included in different kinds of institutional port-folio.

### *Functions of Credit rating agencies in India*

The credit rating agencies in India offer varied services like mutual consulting services, which comprises of operation up gradation, risk management.

They have special sections to carry on research and development work of the industries. They provide training to the employees and executives of the companies for better management. They examine the risk involved in a new project, chalk out plans to fight with the problem successfully and thus ameliorate the percentage of risk to a great extent. For this they carry on thorough research into the respective industry. They have started offering services to the mutual fund sector through the application of fund utilization services. The major industries currently graded by the credit rating agencies include agriculture, health care industry, infrastructure, and maritime industry.

## Benefits

Different benefits accrue from use of rated instruments to different class of investors or the company. These are explained as under:

### *A. Benefits to Investors*

1. **Safety of investments.** Credit rating gives an idea in advance to the investors about the degree of financial strength of the issuer company. Based on rating he decides about the investment. Highly rated issues gives an assurance to the investors of safety of Investments and minimizes his risk.
2. **Recognition of risk and returns.** Credit rating symbols indicate both the returns expected and the risk attached to a particular issue. It becomes easier for the investor to understand the worth of the issuer company just by looking at the symbol because the issue is backed by the financial strength of the company.
3. **Freedom of investment decisions.** Investors need not seek advise from the stock brokers, merchant bankers or the portfolio managers before making investments. Investors today are free and independent to take investment decisions themselves. They base their decisions on rating symbols attached to a particular security. Each rating symbol assigned to a particular investment suggests the creditworthiness of the investment and indicates the degree of risk involved in it.
4. **Wider choice of investments.** As it is mandatory to rate debt obligations for every issuer company, at any particular time, wide range of credit rated instruments are available for making investment. Depending upon his own ability to bear risk, the investor can make choice of the securities in which investment is to be made.
5. **Dependable credibility of issuer.** Absence of any link between the rater and rated firm ensures dependable credibility of issuer and attracts investors. As rating agency has no vested interest in issue to be rated, and has no business connections or links with the Board of Directors. In other words, it operates independent of the issuer company, the rating given by it is always accepted by the investors.
6. **Easy understanding of investment proposals.** Investors require no analytical knowledge on their part about the issuer company. Depending upon rating symbols assigned by the rating agencies they can proceed with decisions to make investment in any particular rated security of a company.

7. **Relief from botheration to know company.** Credit agencies relieve investors from botheration of knowing the details of the company, its history, nature of business, financial position, liquidity and profitability position, composition of management staff and Board of Directors etc. Credit rating by professional and specialised analysts reposes confidence in investors to rely upon the credit symbols for taking investment decisions.
8. **Advantages of continuous monitoring.** Credit rating agencies not only assign rating symbols but also continuously monitor them. The Rating agency downgrades or upgrades the rating symbols following the decline or improvement in the financial position respectively.

### *B. Benefits of Rating to the Company*

A company who has got its credit instrument or security rated is benefited in the following ways:

1. **Easy to raise resources.** A company with highly rated instrument finds it easy to raise resources from the public.
   Even though investors in different sections of the society understand the degree of risk and uncertainty attached to a particular security but they still get attracted towards the highly rated instruments.
2. **Reduced cost of borrowing.** Investors always like to make investments in such instrument, which ensure safety and easy liquidity rather than high rate of return. A company can reduce the cost of borrowings by quoting lesser interest on those fixed deposits or debentures or bonds, which are highly rated.
3. **Reduced cost of public issues.** A company with highly rated instruments has to make least efforts in raising funds through public. It can reduce its expenditure on press and publicity. Rating facilitates best pricing and timing of issues.
4. **Rating builds up image.** Companies with highly rated instrument enjoy better goodwill and corporate image in the eyes of customers, shareholders, investors and creditors. Customers feel confident of the quality of goods manufactured, shareholders are sure of high returns, investors feel secured of their investments and creditors are assured of timely payments of interest and principal.
5. **Rating facilitates growth.** Rating motivates the promoters to undertake expansion of their operations or diversify their production activities thus leading to the growth of the company in future. Moreover highly rated companies find it easy to raise funds from public through new issues or through credit from banks and FIs to finance their expansion activities.
6. **Recognition to unknown companies.** Credit rating provides recognition to relatively unknown companies going for public issues through wide investor base. While entering into market, investors rely more on the rating grades than on 'name recognition'.

### *C. Benefits to Intermediaries*

Stock brokers have to make less efforts in persuading their clients to select an investment proposal of making investment in highly rated instruments. Thus rating enables brokers and other financial intermediaries to save time, energy costs and manpower in convincing their clients.

## Credit Rating Process

The rating process begins with the receipt of formal request from a company desirous of having its issue obligations rated by credit rating agency. A credit rating agency constantly monitors all ratings with reference to new political, economic and financial developments and industry trends. The process/procedure followed by all the major credit rating agencies in the country is almost similar and usually comprises of the following steps.

1. **Receipt of the request**: The rating process begins, with the receipt of formal request for rating from a company desirous of having its issue obligations under proposed instrument rated by credit rating agencies. An agreement is entered into between the rating agency and the issuer company. The agreement spells out the terms of the rating assignment and covers the following aspects:
   i. It requires the CRA (Credit Rating Agency) to keep the information confidential.
   ii. It gives right to the issuer company to accept or not to accept the rating.
   iii. It requires the issuer company to provide all material information to the CRA for rating and subsequent surveillance.
2. **Assignment to analytical team**: On receipt of the above request, the CRA assigns the job to an analytical team. The team usually comprises of two members/analysts who have expertise in the relevant business area and are responsible for carrying out the rating assignments.
3. **Obtaining information:** The analytical team obtains the requisite information from the client company. Issuers are usually provided a list of information requirements and broad framework for discussions. These requirements are derived from the experience of the issuers business and broadly confirms to all the aspects which have a bearing on the rating. The analytical team analyses the information relating to its financial statements, cash flow projections and other relevant information.
4. **Plant visits and meeting with management**: To obtain classification and better understanding of the client's operations, the team visits and interacts with the company's executives. Plants visits facilitate understanding of the production process, assess the state of equipment and main facilities, evaluate the quality of technical personnel and form an opinion on the key variables that influence level, quality and cost of production A direct dialogue is maintained with the issuer company as this enables the CRAs to incorporate non-public information in a rating decision and also enables the rating' to be forward looking. The topics discussed during the management meeting are wide ranging including competitive position, strategies, financial policies, historical performance, risk profile and strategies in addition to reviewing financial data.
5. **Presentation of findings**: After completing the analysis, the findings are discussed at length in the Internal Committee, comprising senior analysts of the credit rating agency. All the issue having a bearing on rating are identified. An opinion on the rating is also formed. The findings of the team are finally presented to Rating Committee.
6. **Rating committee meeting**: This is the final authority for assigning ratings. The rating committee meeting is the only aspect of the process in which the issuer does not participate directly. The rating is arrived at after composite assessment of all the factors concerning the issuer, with the key issues getting greater attention.
7. **Communication of decision**: The assigned rating grade is communicated finally to the issuer along with reasons or rationale supporting the rating. The ratings which are not accepted are either rejected or reviewed in the light of additional facts provided by the issuer. The rejected ratings are not disclosed and complete confidentiality is maintained.
8. **Dissemination to the public**: Once the issuer accepts the rating, the credit rating agencies disseminate it through printed reports to the public.

9. **Monitoring for possible change**: Once the company has decided to use the rating, CRAs are obliged to monitor the accepted ratings over the life of the instrument. The CRA constantly monitors all ratings with reference to new political, economic and financial developments and industry trends. All this information is reviewed regularly to find companies for major rating changes. Any changes in the rating are made public through published reports by CRAs.

## Credit Rating Agencies

The credit rating agencies in India mainly include ICRA and CRISIL. ICRA was formerly referred to the Investment Information and Credit Rating Agency of India Limited. Their main function is to grade the different sector and companies in terms of performance and offer solutions for up gradation.

### *CRISIL*

CRISIL (Credit Rating and Information Services of India Limited) was set up in the year 1987 in order to rate the firms and then entered into the field of assessment service for the banks. Highly skilled members manage the agency. Ms.RoopaKudva who acts as the Managing Director and Chief Executive Officer of the company heads it. The company has set up large number of committees to look after dispersal of various services offered by the company for example, investor grievance committee, investment committee, rating committee, allotment committee, compensation committee and so on. The head office of the company is located at Mumbai and it has established offices outside India also.

### *ICRA*

ICRA (Investment Information and Credit Rating Agency) was established in the year 1991 by the collaboration of financial institutions, investment companies, and banks. The company has formed the ICRA group together with its subsidiaries. The company is headed by Mr.Piyush G. Mankad and offers products like short-term debt schemes, Issue-specific long-term rating and offers fund based as well as non-fund based facilities to its clients.

### *Moody's*

It is one of the oldest credit rating agency. It is also the first rating agency to be recognised by NSRO in 1975. The company became public in 2000.

### *Standard & Poor's*

The agency is owned by McGraw-Hill Inc. It has been published any stock indices of the world, most famous being S&P 500 index which is the most watched index in the world.

### *Fitch*

Fitch is smallest among the top three agencies. It is a part of Fitch Group, a subsidiary of Fimalac S.A FIM.PA. Was the third agency to become an NRSRO in 1975. From 1975 to 1992, four other agencies were recognized as NRSROs and all subsequently merged with Fitch.

### *DBRS*

DBRS (Dominion Bond Rating Service) is privately owned Canadian ratings agency. Has been the top ratings agency in Canada for 30 years. It became the fourth NRSRO in 2003. DBRS believes that it can compete with the big three but is not favored by authorities.

### *Egan-Jones*

Egan-Jones is a Philadelphia-based agency founded in 1995. It was granted NRSRO status in December 2007 after a nine-year process. Although they are paid by investor-subscribers, Egan-Jones will give out their ratings to anyone who asks.

### *A.M Best*

A.M Best was founded in 1899 in New York City and became an NRSRO in 2005. It specializes exclusively on the insurance marketplace and so not a competitor with the others per se. But has recently begun issuing debt and financial-strange ratings for small and mid-sized commercial banks.

### *Japan Credit Rating Agency Limited*

Japan Credit rating Agency was established in 1985 and based in Tokyo and it became an NRSRO in 2007. It is a small agency when compared to competitors. it has a staff of just 90.

### *Rating and Investment Information Inc*

The second Japanese credit ratings agency to become an NRSRO in 2007. It was set up in 1975, now based in Nihonbashi. New York office was set up in 2005.

### *LACE Financial*

It was founded in 1984, and became a NRSRO in 2008. The second NRSRO after Egan-Jones to operate on investor-paid business model.

### *Realpoint LLC*

Realpoint LLC became a NRSRO in 2008. It is one of the smallest NRSROs and is paid by issuers. Obtained an exemption in 2008 from the SEC regulation that an NRSRO is prohibited from rating an issuer that contributes 10 percent or more of its revenue.

## Limitations

1. Biased and misrepresentations
2. Static study
3. Concealment of material information
4. Rating is no guarantee for soundness of company
5. Human bias
6. Reflection of temporary adverse conditions
7. Rating under unfavourable conditions
8. Difference in rating of two agencies

## Problems in Credit Rating

1. Rating agencies cannot perform an audit but has to rely on the information provided by the companies
2. Rating agencies have to offer financial and consultancy services to the companies they rate.
3. The rating given by the agency is not the final
4. Gradings are revised frequently which becomes a hassle and time consuming.

# 8. Venture Capital

The term venture capital consists of two words namely, Venture and Capital. The term "Venture" means to undertake a risky or daring journey or course of action. The term "Capital" means wealth in the form of money or other assets for the purpose of starting a company or investing. To represent risk and adventure of such fund, the term venture capital is introduced.

Venture capital is often considered as financing of companies with high end or new technology. The investment is done often in innovative and new technologies started by new, professionally qualified individuals, who have inadequate funds to start their own companies or companies which have limited operating history but have high potential to grow in future. The conventional financers will be reluctant to invest in new technologies rather they would want to invest in those companies which use proven technologies and have established markets. Thus, Venture capital is money provided by an outside investor to finance a new, growing, or troubled business who have good prospects in future.

Venture Capital is also called "unsecured high risk financing". The high risk in venture capital is often compensated by high returns usually in the form of capital gains in medium term. As a shareholder, the venture capitalist's return is dependent on the growth and profitability of the business. This return is generally earned when the venture capitalist "exits" by selling its shareholding in the business .Venture capital can also include managerial and technical expertise. The Venture capitalists not only provide funds but also necessary skills and expertise needed to start the firm, design and market the products and to organise and manage the firm. Most venture capital comes from a group of wealthy investors, investment banks and other financial institutions that pool such investments or partnerships.

Venture Capital is not a passive finance. It may be in any stages of business or production cycle ie; start up, expansion, or to improve a process or product which have both risk and reward. The venture capital makes higher capital gains through appreciation in value of such investments when a technology succeeds. Thus, a return that is sought by a venture capitalist is basically capital gains, rather than steady interest or dividend yield.

### *Definition of Venture Capital*

"Start-up companies with a potential to grow need a certain amount of investment. Wealthy investors like to invest their capital in such businesses with a long-term growth perspective. This capital is known as venture capital and the investors are called venture capitalists." ~ Economic Times

"Funds flowing into a company, generally during pre-IPO process, in the form of an investment rather than a loan. Controlled by an individual or small group known as venture capitalists, these investments require a high rate of return and are secured by a substantial ownership position in the business. "~ Small Business Encyclopaedia

"Venture Capital is the support given by investors with entrepreneurial talent with finance and business skills to exploit market opportunities and thus obtain capital gains"

A venture capital may be injected in the company not only in the early stage of the company but also in the developmental stage of the company too. A venture capital involves long term commitment of funds usually in the form of equity, with an intention to have capital gain in the investment rather than income, with active involvement in the management of the company which they are investing.

## Characteristics of Venture Capital Fund

- **Illiquidity:** Easy liquidity by getting out of the investment in the short-term is not an option for venture capital funding. An IPO or buyout of a venture is how venture capitalists disinvest. An investor will most likely have to wait until the company is able to attract a buy-out or issue an IPO. A liquidity risk premium is a characteristic of the initial investment.
- **Long-term commitment:** Venture capital funds need to be locked in for a period of at least three to five years before disinvestment. This is mostly due to the time lag between starting a company and bringing it to a buy-out or IPO.
- **High Risk:** Venture Capital financing is highly risky and the chances of failure is high. A venture capital assumes four types of risk:
  - **Management Risk:** Inability of management teams to work together
  - **Market Risk:** Product may fail in Market
  - **Product Risk:** Product may not be commercially viable
  - **Operation Risk:** Operations may not be cost effective leading to increased cost and decreased gross margins
- **Difficulty in determining current market values:** It is difficult to evaluate the current market value of the portfolio of a VC. Since these assets do not trade in an active marketplace it's difficult to determine an objective value for the business and the investment.
- **Limited historical risk and return data and limited information:** Venture capital funds more often invest in new and cutting edge industries of a sector, where there is little historical data or continuous trading data. It is also difficult to estimate cash flows or the probability of success.
- **Entrepreneurial/management mismatches:** Entrepreneurs may face difficulties when there is dilution of ownership and control. Bad management choices may scuttle a good venture. Entrepreneurs sometimes find it difficult to step up as the venture gains size. Management styles that did well in the early stages may not work as the organisation grow.
- **Equity Participation & Capital Gains:** Investments are generally in equity and quasi equity participation through direct purchase of shares, options, convertible debentures where the debt holder has the option to convert the loan instruments into stock of the borrower or a debt with warrants to equity investment. The funds in the form of equity help to raise term loans that are cheaper source of funds. In the early stage of business, because dividends can be delayed, equity investment implies that investors bear the risk of venture and would earn a return commensurate with success in the form of capital
- **Fund manager incentive mismatches:** Investors interested in well performing rather than large sized funds need to find managers who match their investment objectives. Managers may be rewarded for the size of their fund, not its performance.
- **Knowledge of competition:** Almost business' that are funded are from nascent industries it is difficult to assess the competition, than in established industries. Competitive valuations are difficult to find in the marketplace
- **Vintage Cycles:** Economic conditions vary from year to year. The volume of business start-ups is dependent on the economic climate - some years offer more and better opportunities than others. It all depends on the market and who and when firms are entering and exiting the marketplace.

- **Extensive Operation Analysis and Advice:** Venture capital funds that plan to invest in technology companies may not have the required expertise to assess them. Financial investment knowledge alone is not sufficient. Good fund managers therefore require both operating and financial analysis and advising skills. A fund manager who does not understand the business will impede rather than improve it.

## Evolution of Venture Capital in India

In 1972, a committee on Development of Small and Medium Enterprises highlighted the need to foster venture capital as a source of funding new entrepreneurs and technology. This resulted in a few incremental steps being taken over the next decade-and-a-half to facilitate venture capital funds into needy technology oriented small and medium Enterprises (SMEs), namely:

- Risk Capital Foundation, sponsored by IFCI, was set-up in 1975 to promote and support new technologies and businesses.
- Seed Capital Scheme and the National Equity Scheme was set up by IDBI in1976.
- Programme for Advancement of Commercial Technology (PACT) Scheme was introduced by ICICI in 1985.

These schemes provided some succour to a limited number of SMEs but the activity of venture capital industry did not gather momentum as the funding was based on investment evaluation processes that remained largely collateral based, rather than being holistic, and the policy framework remained unaltered, without the instruments to inject dynamism in the VC industry. Also, there was no policy in place to encourage and involve the private sector in the venture capital activity.

The first major analysis on risk capital for India was reported in 1983 [Chitale 1983]. It indicated that new companies often confront serious barriers to entry into capital market for raising equity finance which undermines their future prospects of expansion and diversification. It also indicated that on the whole there is a need to revive the equity cult among the masses by ensuring competitive return on equity investment. This brought out the institutional inadequacies with respect to the evolution of venture capital. The role of venture capital was met initially by the following institutions:

- Industrial Development Bank of India.
- Industrial Credit and Investment Corporation of India
- State Finance Corporations and
- Small Industries Development Bank of India

Venture capital was almost absent till 1975 when Industrial Finance Corporation of India (IFCI) set up Risk Capital Foundation (RCF). This was considered as the first step in the direction of venture capital. In the year 1976, initiative had been taken by the Government of India to create Technical Development Fund (TDF) in the Ministry of Industry with the assistance of World Bank. The main intention was to ensure sufficient rupee resources to finance the modernisation programs. In the year 1986, Government of India announced the setting up of venture capital fund (VCF) to encourage the enterprise based on indigenous technology and upgradation of existing technology. Grindlays Bank of Australia set up Indian Technology Fund Ltd. (ITFL) with the objective of providing venture capital assistance to young and growing companies seeking funds at early stages.

State Bank of India and Canara Bank have entered in the business of venture capital. SBI Capital Markets (SBI Caps), a subsidiary of SBI's merchant banking has set up a venture capital fund for "brought out deals". Under this scheme SBI Caps invests in the equity- shares of new companies. The Industrial Credit and Investment Corporation of India (ICICI) also entered in the field of venture capital by establishing a venture capital fund for assisting small and medium entrepreneurs with initial equity capital. This was provided for developing and commercialising the indigenous technology. India has taken a unique step in introducing venture capital in the area of bio-technology. The Bangalore based Bangalore GeneiPvt. Ltd. will be India's first ever venture capital biotechnology company engaged in the manufacture of enzymes used in genetic engineering manipulations in research and technology.

A significant feature of venture capital financing in India, which is little recognised, is the support the commercial banks provide to small scale industries. The small scale industries in India run both the risks inherent in a venture capital project-the failure of management and the high risks in the venture. The venture capital providers in India (other than the commercial banks' efforts as stated above) can be divided into following categories.

1. Specialised financial institutions and their financing schemes.
2. Funds promoted by state level institutions.
3. Funds promoted by public sector banks.
4. Private agencies.
5. Overseas venture capital funds.

### 1. *Special/Seed Financial Institutions and their Financing Schemes*

In India, the Industrial Financial Corporations of India (IFCI), Industrial Development Bank of India (IDBI) and the Industrial Credit and Investment Corporation of India (ICICI) are the major three institutions, which are engaged in the financing of high tech new ventures. The difference and similarities between three schemes of IFCI, IDBI and ICICI are discernible from the objectives sought to be pursued under the broad characteristics of the schemes precisely explained below.

### A. *Risk Capital Scheme of IFCI*

The IFCI began its equity financing through its Risk CapitalFoundation (RCF) by providing risk capital assistance on soft terms to first generation entrepreneurs. The corporation envisages to provide assistance to technologists and the professionals who do not have adequate resources of their own for contributing to equity capital of the industrial projects undertaken by them with a view to enlarging entrepreneurial base for wider dispersal of ownership and control of industry in the national interest. The corporation is continuing its efforts through the newly formed Risk Capital and Technology Finance Corporation Ltd. (RCTFC) set up in 1988 as a wholly owned subsidiary of the IFCI. RCTFC was established with an objective of providing financial support to such activities in the area of innovative technology, energy conservation and environmental pollution. Some of the projects financed under the new scheme of IFCI include development of artificial intelligence software, three Dimensional Computer animation, educational robots, hybrid seeds etc. In addition to operating its own schemes, the RCTC also manages a Venture Capital Unit Scheme VECAUS-III (started in mid-1991) with a resource base of Rs. 30 crores with participation from the UTI, IFCI and World Bank in equal proportions.

### B. *Technology Development & Information Company of India Ltd. (TDICI) of ICICI*

Encouraged by the response to technology financing, ICICI floated a separate company-Technology Development and Information Company of India (TDICI) in collaboration with UTI in 1988. Apart from Venture Capital financing TDICI activity profile includes technology consultancy services and technology escort services such as marketing, business management, export marketing and guidance for individual venture capital projects etc. TDICI makes investments in highly risky projects promising high return in future. It gives preference to companies, which are unable to raise public share capital and would not be financed by anyone else. In addition to equity participation (upto a maximum of 49%) undertaken by typical venture capital companies, TDICI offers the unique option of conditional loans. The entrepreneur neither pays interest on it nor does he have to repay the principal amount. If the venture succeeds, TDICI recovers back its investment in the form of royalty on sales which ranges between 2 % to 8 %. On the contrary, if venture fails to take off even after 5 years, TDICI will consider writing off the loan. TDICI usually has a nominee on the Boards of companies with whom it enters into long-term contracts. TDICI assists such venture projects in arranging working capital finance, recruiting senior executives. It also takes advise of the outside experts in taking various decisions. Some of the projects financed by ICICI includes:

i. **Mastek** a Bombay based software firm in which TDICI invested Rs. 42 lakh in equity in 1989 went public in 1992. It showed an annual growth of 70% to 80% in the turnover.
ii. **Temptation Foods** which exports frozen vegetables and fruits, went public in November, 1992. The TOICI invested Rs. 50 lakhs in its equity.

### *C. SEED Capital Scheme or Venture Capital Fund of IDBI*

IDBI's scheme is known as "Seed Capital Scheme" intended to help create a new generation of entrepreneurs who have the requisite traits of entrepreneurship but who lack financial resources to promote industrial ventures. The assistance is provided for meeting the risk capital requirements of entrepreneurs. IDBI is doing well under the venture capital fund scheme by assisting the projects which are engaged in the promotion and development of indigenous technology that is new and untested in India. The financial assistance is provided under this scheme in the areas of chemical, software electronics, biotechnology, food products and medical equipment.

The project cost varies between Rs. 5 lakh to Rs. 250 lakh. IDBI provides assistance both for financing the cost of fixed assets as well as for meeting the operating expenses in the form of unsecured loans carrying a concessional interest rate of 6% p.a. during the early stages of development.

## *2. Funds Promoted by State Level Institutions*

Funds promoted by state level institutions include:

### *a. APIDC- Venture Capital Ltd. (A VCL)*

This is wholly owned by the Andhra Pradesh Industrial Development Corporation Ltd. It aims at specialising venture fund Management Company. It has been entrusted with the management of a fund, namely APIDC - Venture Capital Fund. It is established with a capital of 13.5 crores contributed by APIDC, IDBI, Andhra Bank and IOB and few small organisations. The A VCL undertakes investments with the objective of bringing technological innovations in order to improve quality, reduce energy consumption, increase competition and enhanced exports.

### *b. Gujarat Venture Finance Ltd. (GVFL)*

The GVFL has been promoted by Gujarat Industries Investment Corporation Ltd., (GIIC) in association with Gujarat Lease Finance Corporation Ltd., Gujarat Alkalies and Chemicals Ltd. and Gujarat State Fertiliser Corporation Ltd. GIIC holds 40% of the equity capital of the GVFL and the rest is contributed by other three organisations. The GVFL is a fund management company, and presently acts as a trustee manager of a venture fund, namely (GVCF) Gujarat Venture Capital Fund, started in 1990. GVFL provides finance for innovations in technology leading to an improvement - in product quality and energy conservation, for launching new products based on imported technology.

### 3. *Funds Promoted by Public Sector Banks Such as Canara Bank Venture Capital Fund (CVCF)*

This fund has been promoted by Canara Bank and its subsidiary Canbank Financial Services Ltd. (CANFINA). It was set up in 1989 as a trust. It provides finance in the form *of* equity, conditional loans, conventional loans or both. Its capital base is Rs. 24 crores. The Fund aims at providing financial support for commercial exploitation *of* new technologies, technology upgradation to improve quality etc.

### 4. *Private Agencies*

Venture capital funds set up in the private sector include

1. Credit Capital Venture Fund (CCVF)
2. 20th Century Venture Capital Fund
3. India Investment Fund
4. Indus Venture Capital Fund (IVCF)
5. SBI Capital Venture Capital Fund

1. **Credit Capital Venture Fund (CCVF)**: The Credit Capital Venture Fund (India) was established in 1986. It has a capital base of 10.8 crores. The principal shareholders are Credit Capital Finance Corporation, Bank of India, Asian Development Bank, Common Wealth Development Corporation. It finances ventures promising high returns with maximum assistance limited to Rs. 50 lakhs. It also provides value added services in an advisory role and actively participates in marketing, recruitment and management affairs. -Thus it helps the entrepreneurs to realise maximum returns. It has recently launched 10 state funds of Rs. 10 crore each. It is now known as Lazard Credit Capital Fund (India) Ltd. (LCCVF).
2. **20th Century Venture Capital Fund**: It was promoted by 20th Century Finance Ltd. and has a resource base of Rs. 20 crores. The fund aims at reviving the sick industries and help first generation entrepreneurs.
3. **India Investment Fund**: It is India's first private venture capital fund mainly subscribed by Non-Resident Indians (NRIs). The Fund is "an offshore company owned predominantly by NRI investors incorporated in early 1987. The fund provides equity or equity linked finance to new projects or often young as well as established Indian companies which can demonstrate a potential for sustained growth. The maximum assistance made available to one venture is limited to Rs. One crore. The principal investment objectives of the fund is long term capital appreciation. Merchant Banking Division of Grindlays Bank has been retained as the advisers for the Fund which evaluates and recommends specific investment proposals. The fund follows hands off approach in making the investment.
4. **Indus Venture Capital Fund (IVCF):** This fund was promoted by Shri T. Thomas, the former Director of Unilever. The Indus Venture Management Ltd. (IVML) has been entrusted with the management of (IVCF). IVCF has a capital resource of Rs. 21 crores contributed by IVML, the IDB!, IFCI, Deutsche Bank, International Finance Corporation (Washington) and a few other national/international organisations.
5. **SBI Capital Venture Capital Fund:** This fund has been set up by the SBI Capital Markets Ltd. to finance ventures through its "bought out deals". The objective behind the fund is to promote new capital issues by purchasing them when capital market is sluggish and disposing them off at times when market picks-up. The fund has a capital base of Rs. 10 crore.

### 5. *Overseas Venture Capital Funds*

Overseas Venture Capital Funds look for investment in areas ensuring high and guaranteed returns such as tourism, hospitals, air transport, information technology, communication, pharmaceutical, consumer durables, food processing industry, machinery components and textiles etc. Following are some of the examples where foreign venture capitalists have undertaken investments:

- The global insurance giant, AIG, has tied up with IL & FS to float a 150 million venture fund.
- The IL & FS is also planning to launch a $ 100 million fund with the ADB.
- George, Sors has already floated the Indocean Fund.
- NIKKO Securities has tied up with Walden and San Francis Company to float a venture capital fund with a minimum capital of $ 50 million.

## The Stages in Venture Capital (VC) Investing

Angel investors are most often individuals (friends, relations or entrepreneurs) who want to help other entrepreneurs get their businesses off the ground - and earn a high return on their investment. The term "angel" comes from the practice in the early 1900s of wealthy businessmen investing in Broadway productions. Usually they are the bridge from the self-funded stage of the business to the point that the business needs true venture capital. They typically offer expertise, experience and contacts in addition to money.

1. ***Seed*** - The first stage of venture capital financing. Seed-stage financings are often comparatively modest amounts of capital provided to inventors or entrepreneurs to finance the early development of a new product or service. These early financings may be directed toward product development, market research, building a management team and developing a business plan. A genuine seed-stage company has usually not yet established commercial operations - a cash infusion to fund continued research and product development is essential. These early companies are typically quite difficult business opportunities to finance, often requiring capital for pre-startup R&D, product development and testing, or designing specialized equipment. An initial seed investment round made by a professional VC firm typically ranges from $250,000 to $1 million.

   Seed-stage VC funds will typically participate in later investment rounds with other equity players to finance business expansion costs such as sales and distribution, parts and inventory, hiring, training and marketing.
2. ***Early Stage*** - For companies that are able to begin operations but are not yet at the stage of commercial manufacturing and sales, early stage financing supports a step-up in capabilities. At this point, new business can consume vast amounts of cash, while VC firms with a large number of early-stage companies in their portfolios can see costs quickly escalate.
   - **Start-up** - Supports product development and initial marketing. Start-up financing provides funds to companies for product development and initial marketing. This type of financing is usually provided to companies just organized or to those that have been in business just a short time but have not yet sold their product in the marketplace. Generally, such firms have already assembled key management, prepared a business plan and made market studies. At this stage, the business is seeing its first revenues but has yet to show a profit. This is often where the enterprise brings in its first "outside" investors.

- **First Stage** - Capital is provided to initiate commercial manufacturing and sales. Most first-stage companies have been in business less than three years and have a product or service in testing or pilot production. In some cases, the product may be commercially available.

3. ***Formative Stage*** - Financing includes seed stage and early stage.
4. ***Later Stage*** - Capital provided after commercial manufacturing and sales but before any initial public offering. The product or service is in production and is commercially available. The company demonstrates significant revenue growth, but may or may not be showing a profit. It has usually been in business for more than three years.
    - **Third Stage** - Capital provided for major expansion such as physical plant expansion, product improvement and marketing.
    - **Expansion Stage** - Financing refers to the second and third stages.
    - **Mezzanine (bridge)** - Finances the step of going public and represents the bridge between expanding the company and the IPO
5. ***Balanced-stage*** financing refers to all the stages, seed through mezzanine.

## Advantages of Venture Capital

Following are some of the advantages of venture capital:

- Business expertise. Aside from the financial backing, obtaining venture capital financing can provide a start-up or young business with a valuable source of guidance and consultation. This can help with a variety of business decisions, including financial management and human resource management. Making better decisions in these key areas can be vitally important as your business grows.
- Additional resources. In a number of critical areas, including legal, tax and personnel matters, a VC firm can provide active support, all the more important at a key stage in the growth of a young company. Faster growth and greater success are two potential key benefits.
- Connections. Venture capitalists are typically well connected in the business community. Tapping into these connections could have tremendous benefits.
- No repayment schedule: Since VC funding is not a loan scheme, there is no repay schedule; which means you don't have to repay debt as a cost of doing business.

### *Disadvantages of Venture Capital*

Following are some of the disadvantages of venture capital:

- Loss of control. The drawbacks associated with equity financing in general can be compounded with venture capital financing. With a large injection of cash and professional—and possibly aggressive—investors, it is likely that VC partners will want to be involved in management. The size of their stake could determine how much say they have in shaping company's direction.
- Minority ownership status. Depending on the size of the VC firm's stake in the company, which could be more than 50%, there may be lose management control. Essentially, it could be giving up ownership of your own business.
- Confidentiality: Though they generally treat information confidentially, VC firms usually refuse to sign a non-disclosure agreement due to the legal ramifications of doing so. This can put the ideas at risk, especially when it's new.

## Forms of Venture Capital Financing in India

Venture capital is typically available in three forms in India, they are:

- **Equity:** All VCFs in India provide equity but generally their contribution does not exceed 49 percent of the total equity capital. Thus, the effective control and majority ownership of the firm remains with the entrepreneur. They buy shares of an enterprise with an intention to ultimately sell them off to make capital gains.
- **Conditional Loan:** It is repayable in the form of a royalty after the venture is able to generate sales. No interest is paid on such loans. In India, VCFs charge royalty ranging between 2 to 15 percent; actual rate depends on other factors of the venture such as gestation period, cost-flow patterns, riskiness and other factors of the enterprise.
- **Income Note:** It is a hybrid security which combines the features of both conventional loan and conditional loan. The entrepreneur has to pay both interest and royalty on sales, but at substantially low rates.
- **Other Financing Methods:** A few venture capitalists, particularly in the private sector, have started introducing innovative financial securities like participating debentures, introduced by TCFC is an example.
- **A Case on Technology Development & Information Company Of India Ltd.**
- TDICI was incorporated in January 1988 with the support of the ICICI and the UTI. The country's first venture fund managed by the TDICI called VECAUS ( Venture Capital Units Scheme) was started with an initial corpus of Rs.20 crore and was completely committed to 37 small and medium enterprises. The first project of the TDICI was loan and equity to a computer software company called Kale Consultants.
- Present Status: At present the TDICI is administering two UTI -mobilised funds under VECAUS-I and II, totaling Rs.120 crore. the Rs.20 crore invested under the first fund, VECAUS-I, has already yielded returns totalingRs. 16 crore to its investors.

**Some of the projects financed by the TDICI are discussed below.**

- MASTEK, a Mumbai based software firm, in which the TDICI invested Rs.42 lakh in equity in 1989, went public just three years later, in November 1992. It showed an annual growth of 70-80 percent in the turnover.
- TEMPTATION FOODS, located in PUNE, which exports frozen vegetables and fruits, went public in November 1992. The TDICI invested Rs.50 lakh in its equity.
- RISHABH INSTRUMENTS of Nasik got Rs.40 lakh from the TDICI. It manufactures a range of meters used in power stations in collaboration with the ABB Metra Watt of Germany. After making cash losses totaling Rs.25 lakh in two bad years, it turned around in 1989 and showed an increase of over 70 percent in the turnover.
- SYNERGY ART FOUNDATION, which runs art galleries in Mumbai and Chennai and plans to set up in Pune and Delhi too, had received Rs.25 lakh from the TDICI as convertible loans which were converted into equity on March 31, 1994. Most of this money has been used for the company's innovative art library scheme at least paintings to corporate clients.

(Source: http://www.indianmba.com/faculty_column/fc159/fc159.html)

## Venture Capital in India and Abroad

- Venture capital investments in India have crossed $1 billion mark for the first time in 2015. In just the first nine months of 2015, Venture Capital investments in India - at 323 deals worth $1,438 million - have crossed the previous historical high of 2014 (which had witnessed 304 investments worth $1,170 million across the entire year), according to data from Venture Intelligence a research service focused on private company financials, transactions and their valuations.

- The main action was concentrated in the Early Stage investment segment (Seed, First and Second Round investments in companies not more than 5 years old) which, for the first time ever, has attracted over $1 billion in investments in 2015 ($1,018 million across 266 investments in the first nine months) - compared to the previous high of $553 million (across 167 transactions) in 2011 (full year).
  The overwhelming attraction of Information Technology and IT-Enabled Services (IT & ITES companies - especially Internet & Mobile firms - to Venture Capitalists continued in Q3'15 with the industry accounting for 79 investment worth $376 million (71% of the VC investments in volume terms and 70% in value terms).
  (Source:http://economictimes.indiatimes.com/articleshow/49383670.cms?utm_source=contentofinterest&utm_medium=text&utm_campaign=cppst)
- San Francisco led the list of the cities that received the largest share of venture capital funding with $13 billion of VC investments, followed by Beijing ($6.4 billion), New York ($5.7 billion), Palo Alto ($3.2 billion) and Bengaluru ($2.6 billion).
- Among top five countries, India received 3rd largest share of venture capital funding ($4.6 billion) after the United States of America ($58.9 billion) and China ($8.9 billion). Great Britain ($3.2 billion) ranked fourth, followed by Germany ($1.7 billion), rounds out the Top Five.

### *Venture Capital Investments around the World: Top Cities*

1. San Francisco, $13 billion
2. Beijing, $6.4 billion
3. New York, $5.7 billion
4. Palo Alto, $3.2 billion
5. Bengaluru, $2.6 billion

### *Venture Capital Investments around the World: Top Countries*

1. **The United States of America,** $58.9 billion, 8,730 Rounds
2. **China,** $8.9 billion, 236 Rounds
3. **India,** $4.6 billion, 383 Rounds
4. **Great Britain**, $3.2 billion, 767 Rounds
5. **Germany,** $1.7 billion, 277 Rounds
   (Source:http://www.huffingtonpost.in/amarendra-bhushan-dhiraj/top-5-cities-countries-th_b_6560620.html)

### *Top Deals in 2014 in India*

| Company | Funds | Value($M) |
|---|---|---|
| FlipKart | Naspers, Tiger Global Mgmt, Accel Partners, Morgan Stanley Investment Mgmt, DST Advisors, GIC, Sofina, Iconiq Capital | 1000 |
| FlipKart | Qatar Investment Authority, DST Advisors, Greenoaks Ventures, GIC, Iconiq Capital, Tiger Global, Steadview Capital, T. Rowe Price, Baillie Gifford & Co. | 700 |
| Snapdeal.com | BlackRock, Tybourne Capital Mgmt., Temasek, SoftBank, PI Opportunities Fund I, Myriad Asset Mgmt. | 636 |
| Unitech Corporate Parks | Brookfield | 581 |
| Kotak Mahindra Bank | Canada Pension Plan Investment Board (CPPIB) | 376 |
| Shriram Capital | Piramal Enterprises | 334 |
| L&T IDPL | CDPQ, CPPIB, State General Reserve Fund (SGRF) | 323 |
| Jaiprakash Power Ventures | IDFC Private Equity, PSP Investments | 316 |
| Sutherland Global Services | TPG Capital | 300 |
| Minacs | CX Partners, others | 260 |

## *Key Exits in 2014*

| Investor exited | Investee | Sector | Comments |
|---|---|---|---|
| IDFC Alternatives | Galaxy Mercentiles Limited and Blueridge SEZ | Real Estate | IDFC Alternatives has made a complete exit from these investment and selling assets to realty funds managed by Blackstone |
| Essar Global Fund | Aegis Limited USA Inc | IT & ITES | Essar Global Fund Limited is selling Aegis USA Inc, outsourcing company for a consideration of US$ 610 Mn to paris based outsourcing firm Teleperformance |
| Chrys Capital | HCL Technologies | IT & ITES | The fund, which invested US $180 for HCL Stake , offloaded 2% for close to $500 million in open deal Markets |
| Bain Capital Partners | Hero MotoCorp Limited | Automotive | Bain Capital Partners has sold 7.08% of its remaining holding in Hero MotoCorpLtd via secondary market share sale taking its total exit value to over $700 million (including Dividends) |
| Temasek | Mederich Ltd | Pharma, Healthcare and Biocare | Temasek held close to 33% in Medreich which it had picked nine years ago for around US $25mn. Japanese Meiji Seika Pharma acquired Medreichfor US $ 290 Mn |
| The Carlyle Group | Thirumala Milk Products Pvt Limited | Retail and Consumer | Lactalis acquired Tirumala giving Carlyle an exit from its original investment in May 2010 |
| Providence | Idea Cellular | Telecom | The PE Firm exited through Open Market Sale |
| SAIF Partners | Just Dial Pvt Ltd | IT & ITES | SAIF Partners, one of the early investors in local search provider just Dial, has sold one third of the stake held |
| The Carlyle Group | Cyberoam Technologies | IT & ITES | Carlyle is exiting its seven year old investment in Ahmedabad based Cyberoam Technologies. The PE Fund is selling 80% stake in the company to UK's Sophos Group. |

Source: http://gtw3.grantthornton.in/assets/The_Fourth_wheel_2015.pdf

## *Investment Value- $ Bn*

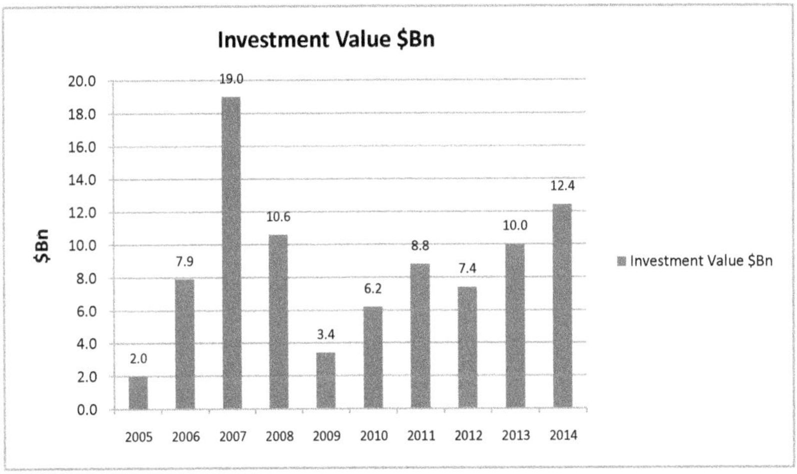

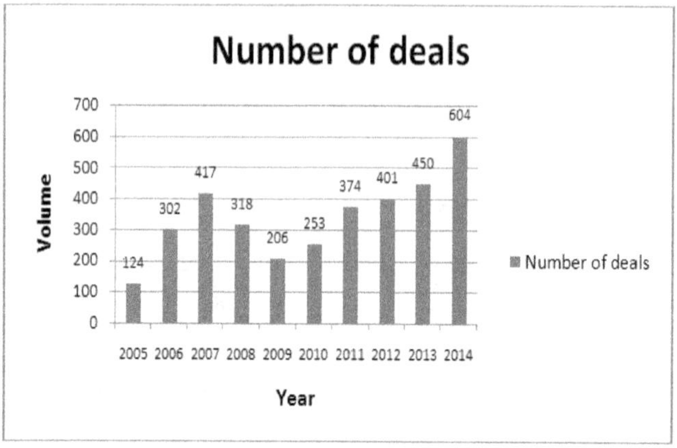


(Source: http://gtw3.grantthornton.in/assets/The_Fourth_wheel_2015.pdf)

| | **TOP 10 DEALS 2005-2014** | | | | |
|---|---|---|---|---|---|
| Year | Investor | Investee | Sector | $Mn | Stake |
| 2007 | Temasek Holdings | BhartiAirtel Ltd | Telecom | 1907 | 5% |
| 2013 | Qatar Foundation Endowment | BhartiAirtel Ltd | Telecom | 1260 | 5% |
| 2006 | Kohlberg Kravis Roberts & Co | Flextronics Software Systems | IT&ITeS | 1035 | 85% |
| 2007 | Temasek Holdings, The Investment Corporation of Dubai, Goldman Sachs, Macquaire, AIF Capital, Citigroup and India Equity Partners | BhartiInfratel ( Subsidiary Of BhartiAirtel Ltd) | Telecom | 1000 | 10% |
| 2014 | Morgan Stanley Investment Management, GIC, Accel Partners, DST Global, Iconiq Capital and Sofina | Flipkart Online Services Pvt Ltd | IT&ITeS | 1000 | N.A |
| 2012 | Bain Capital | Genpact Ltd from GA and Oak Hill Capital | IT&ITeS | 1000 | 30% |
| 2011 | Bain Capital, Government of Singapore | Hero Investment Pvt Ltd | Automotive | 848 | 30% |
| 2007 | ICICI Venture Funds Management Company | JaypeeInfratech ( Subsidiary of Jaypee Group) | Real Estate and Infrastructure Manangement | 800 | N.A |
| 2007 | George Soros hedge fund, Eton Park Capital, Deutsche Asset Management, Capital International, Citigroup, T Rowe Price, Credit Agricole, UBS and Kotak Mahindra | GMR Infrastructure | Real Estate and Infrastructure Manangement | 767 | N.A |
| 2014 | Baillee Gifford, Greenoaks Capital, Steadview Capital, T Rowe Price Associates and Qatar Invesment Authority and existing investors | Flipkart Online Services Pvt Ltd | IT&ITeS | 700 | N.A |

(Source: http://gtw3.grantthornton.in/assets/The_Fourth_wheel_2015.pdf)

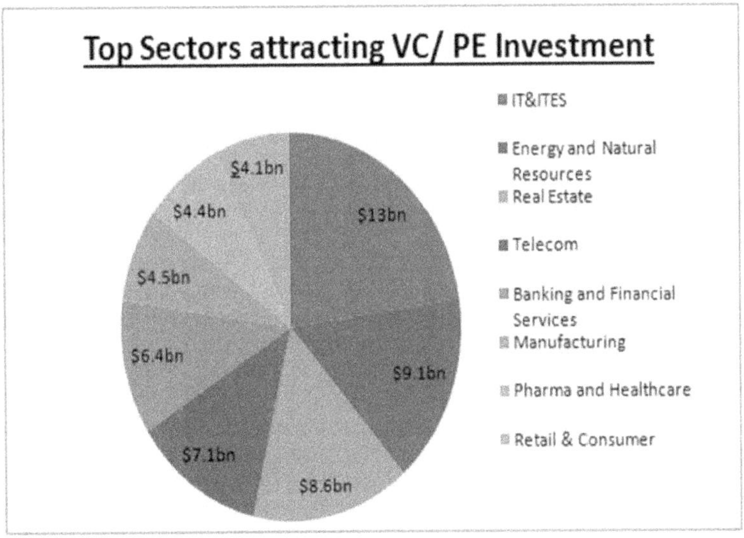


(Source: http://gtw3.grantthornton.in/assets/The_Fourth_wheel_2015.pdf)

***Sector Wise Investment***

| By ValueUS$mn | 2007 | 2008 | 2009 | 2010 | 2011 | 2012 | 2013 | 2014 | Total |
|---|---|---|---|---|---|---|---|---|---|
| IT & ITES | 371 | 488 | 215 | 398 | 1443 | 2057 | 2046 | 5274 | 13222 |
| Energy & Natural Resources | 476 | 947 | 431 | 1676 | 1053 | 360 | 476 | 473 | 9102 |
| Real Estate | 82 | 3313 | 801 | 627 | 962 | 718 | 954 | 1559 | 9015 |
| Telecom | 114 | 1397 | 144 | 515 | 61 | 1 | 1260 | 110 | 7107 |
| Banking & Financial Services | 84 | 819 | 364 | 594 | 810 | 707 | 1106 | 1356 | 6440 |
| Manufacturing | 231 | 939 | 155 | 491 | 829 | 217 | 514 | 338 | 4562 |
| Pharma, Healthcare & Biotech | 225 | 337 | 148 | 320 | 281 | 907 | 1376 | 632 | 4415 |

# 9. Securitization

Securitization is the financial practice of pooling various types of contractual debt such as residential mortgages, commercial mortgages, auto loans or credit card debt obligations (or other non-debt assets which generate receivables) and selling their related cash flows to third party investors as securities, which may be described as bonds, pass-through securities, or collateralized debt obligations (CDOs). Investors are repaid from the principal and interest cash flows collected from the underlying debt and redistributed through the capital structure of the new financing. Securities backed by mortgage receivables are called mortgage-backed securities (MBS), while those backed by other types of receivables are asset-backed securities (ABS).

Critics have suggested that the complexity inherent in securitization can limit investors' ability to monitor risk, and that competitive securitization markets with multiple securitizers may be particularly prone to sharp declines in underwriting standards. Private, competitive mortgage securitization is believed to have played an important role in the U.S. subprime mortgage crisis.

In addition, off-balance sheet treatment for securitizations coupled with guarantees from the issuer can hide the extent of leverage of the securitizing firm, thereby facilitating risky capital structures and leading to an under-pricing of credit risk. Off-balance sheet securitizations are believed to have played a large role in the high leverage level of U.S. financial institutions before the financial crisis, and the need for bailouts.

The granularity of pools of securitized assets can mitigate the credit risk of individual borrowers. Unlike general corporate debt, the credit quality of securitized debt is non-stationary due to changes in volatility that are time- and structure-dependent. If the transaction is properly structured and the pool performs as expected, the credit risk of all tranches of structured debt improves; if improperly structured, the affected tranches may experience dramatic credit deterioration and loss.

Securitization has evolved from its beginnings in the late 18th century to an estimated outstanding of $10.24 trillion in the United States and $2.25 trillion in Europe as of the 2nd quarter of 2008. In 2007, ABS issuance amounted to $3.455 trillion in the US and $652 billion in Europe.WBS (Whole Business Securitization) arrangements first appeared in the United Kingdom in the 1990s, and became common in various Commonwealth legal systems where senior creditors of an insolvent business effectively gain the right to control the company.

## Structure

### *Pooling and Transfer*

The originator initially owns the assets engaged in the deal. This is typically a company looking to either raise capital, restructure debt or otherwise adjust its finances (but also includes businesses established specifically to generate marketable debt (consumer or otherwise) for the purpose of subsequent securitization). Under traditional corporate finance concepts, such a company would have three options to raise new capital: a loan, bond issue, or issuance of stock. However, stock offerings dilute the ownership and control of the company, while loan or bond financing is often prohibitively expensive due to the credit rating of the company and the associated rise in interest rates.

The consistently revenue-generating part of the company may have a much higher credit rating than the company as a whole. For instance, a leasing company may have provided $10m nominal value of leases, and it will receive a cash flow over the next five years from these. It cannot demand early repayment on the leases and so cannot get its money back early if required. If it could sell the rights to the cash flows from the leases to someone else, it could transform that income stream into a lump sum today (in effect, receiving today the present value of a future cash flow). Where the originator is a bank or other organization that must meet capital adequacy requirements, the structure is usually more complex because a separate company is set up to buy the assets.

A suitably large portfolio of assets is "pooled" and transferred to a "special purpose vehicle" or "SPV" (the issuer), a tax-exempt company or trust formed for the specific purpose of funding the assets. Once the assets are transferred to the issuer, there is normally no recourse to the originator. The issuer is "bankruptcy remote", meaning that if the originator goes into bankruptcy, the assets of the issuer will not be distributed to the creditors of the originator. In order to achieve this, the governing documents of the issuer restrict its activities to only those necessary to complete the issuance of securities. Many issuers are typically "orphaned". In the case of certain assets, such as credit card debt, where the portfolio is made up of a constantly changing pool of receivables, a trust in favor of the SPV may be declared in place of traditional transfer by assignment (see the outline of the master trust structure below).

Accounting standards govern when such a transfer is a true sale, a financing, a partial sale, or a part-sale and part-financing.[17] In a true sale, the originator is allowed to remove the transferred assets from its balance sheet: in a financing, the assets are considered to remain the property of the originator.[18] Under US accounting standards, the originator achieves a sale by being at arm's length from the issuer, in which case the issuer is classified as a "qualifying special purpose entity" or "qSPE".

Because of these structural issues, the originator typically needs the help of an investment bank (the arranger) in setting up the structure of the transaction.

### *Issuance*

To be able to buy the assets from the originator, the issuer SPV issues tradable securities to fund the purchase. Investors purchase the securities, either through a private offering (targeting institutional investors) or on the open market. The performance of the securities is then directly linked to the performance of the assets. Credit rating agencies rate the securities which are issued to provide an external perspective on the liabilities being created and help the investor make a more informed decision.

In transactions with static assets, a depositor will assemble the underlying collateral, help structure the securities and work with the financial markets to sell the securities to investors. The depositor has taken on added significance under Regulation AB. The depositor typically owns 100% of the beneficial interest in the issuing entity and is usually the parent or a wholly owned subsidiary of the parent which initiates the transaction. In transactions with managed (traded) assets, asset managers assemble the underlying collateral, help structure the securities and work with the financial markets in order to sell the securities to investors.

Some deals may include a third-party guarantor which provides guarantees or partial guarantees for the assets, the principal and the interest payments, for a fee.

The securities can be issued with either a fixed interest rate or a floating rate under currency pegging system. Fixed rate ABS set the “coupon” (rate) at the time of issuance, in a fashion similar to corporate bonds and T-Bills. Floating rate securities may be backed by both amortizing and non-amortizing assets in the floating market. In contrast to fixed rate securities, the rates on “floaters” will periodically adjust up or down according to a designated index such as a U.S. Treasury rate, or, more typically, the London Interbank Offered Rate (LIBOR). The floating rate usually reflects the movement in the index plus an additional fixed margin to cover the added risk.

### *Credit Enhancement and Tranching*

Unlike conventional corporate bonds which are unsecured, securities created in a securitization are "credit enhanced", meaning their credit quality is increased above that of the originator's unsecured debt or underlying asset pool. This increases the likelihood that the investors will receive the cash flows to which they are entitled, and thus enables the securities to have a higher credit rating than the originator. Some securitizations use external credit enhancement provided by third parties, such as surety bonds and parental guarantees (although this may introduce a conflict of interest).

The issued securities are often split into tranches, or categorized into varying degrees of subordination. Each tranche has a different level of credit protection or risk exposure: there is generally a senior ("A") class of securities and one or more junior subordinated ("B", "C", etc.) classes that function as protective layers for the "A" class. The senior classes have first claim on the cash that the SPV receives, and the more junior classes only start receiving repayment after the more senior classes have been repaid. Because of the cascading effect between classes, this arrangement is often referred to as a cash flow waterfall.[20] If the underlying asset pool becomes insufficient to make payments on the securities (e.g. when loans default within a portfolio of loan claims), the loss is absorbed first by the subordinated tranches, and the upper-level tranches remain unaffected until the losses exceed the entire amount of the subordinated tranches. The senior securities might be AAA or AA rated, signifying a lower risk, while the lower-credit quality subordinated classes receive a lower credit rating, signifying a higher risk.[19]

The most junior class (often called the equity class) is the most exposed to payment risk. In some cases, this is a special type of instrument which is retained by the originator as a potential profit flow. In some cases the equity class receives no coupon (either fixed or floating), but only the residual cash flow (if any) after all the other classes have been paid.

There may also be a special class which absorbs early repayments in the underlying assets. This is often the case where the underlying assets are mortgages which, in essence, are repaid whenever the properties are sold. Since any early repayments are passed on to this class, it means the other investors have a more predictable cash flow.

If the underlying assets are mortgages or loans, there are usually two separate "waterfalls" because the principal and interest receipts can be easily allocated and matched. But if the assets are income-based transactions such as rental deals one cannot categorise the revenue so easily between income and principal repayment. In this case all the revenue is used to pay the cash flows due on the bonds as those cash flows become due.

Credit enhancements affect credit risk by providing more or less protection for promised cash flows for a security. Additional protection can help a security achieve a higher rating, lower protection can help create new securities with differently desired risks, and these differential protections can make the securities more attractive.

In addition to subordination, credit may be enhanced through:

- **A reserve or spread account**, in which funds remaining after expenses such as principal and interest payments, charge-offs and other fees have been paid-off are accumulated, and can be used when SPE expenses are greater than its income.
- Third-party insurance, or guarantees of principal and interest payments on the securities.
- **Over-collateralisation**, usually by using finance income to pay off principal on some securities before principal on the corresponding share of collateral is collected.

- **Cash funding or a cash collateral account,** generally consisting of short-term, highly rated investments purchased either from the seller's own funds, or from funds borrowed from third parties that can be used to make up shortfalls in promised cash flows.
- A third-party letter of credit or corporate guarantee.
- A back-up servicer for the loans.
- Discounted receivables for the pool.

### *Servicing*

A servicer collects payments and monitors the assets that are the crux of the structured financial deal. The servicer can often be the originator, because the servicer needs very similar expertise to the originator and would want to ensure that loan repayments are paid to the Special Purpose Vehicle.

The servicer can significantly affect the cash flows to the investors because it controls the collection policy, which influences the proceeds collected, the charge-offs and the recoveries on the loans. Any income remaining after payments and expenses is usually accumulated to some extent in a reserve or spread account, and any further excess is returned to the seller. Bond rating agencies publish ratings of asset-backed securities based on the performance of the collateral pool, the credit enhancements and the probability of default.[18]

When the issuer is structured as a trust, the trustee is a vital part of the deal as the gate-keeper of the assets that are being held in the issuer. Even though the trustee is part of the SPV, which is typically wholly owned by the Originator, the trustee has a fiduciary duty to protect the assets and those who own the assets, typically the investors.

### *Repayment Structures*

Unlike corporate bonds, most securitizations are amortized, meaning that the principal amount borrowed is paid back gradually over the specified term of the loan, rather than in one lump sum at the maturity of the loan. Fully amortizing securitizations are generally collateralised by fully amortizing assets, such as home equity loans, auto loans, and student loans. Prepayment uncertainty is an important concern with fully amortizing ABS. The possible rate of prepayment varies widely with the type of underlying asset pool, so many prepayment models have been developed to try to define common prepayment activity. The PSA prepayment model is a well-known example.

A controlled amortization structure can give investors a more predictable repayment schedule, even though the underlying assets may be nonamortising. After a predetermined "revolving period", during which only interest payments are made, these securitizations attempt to return principal to investors in a series of defined periodic payments, usually within a year. An early amortization event is the risk of the debt being retired early.[19]

On the other hand, bullet or slug structures return the principal to investors in a single payment. The most common bullet structure is called the soft bullet, meaning that the final bullet payment is not guaranteed to be paid on the scheduled maturity date; however, the majority of these securitizations are paid on time. The second type of bullet structure is the hard bullet, which guarantees that the principal will be paid on the scheduled maturity date. Hard bullet structures are less common for two reasons: investors are comfortable with soft bullet structures, and they are reluctant to accept the lower yields of hard bullet securities in exchange for a guarantee.

Securitizations are often structured as a sequential pay bond, paid off in a sequential manner based on maturity. This means that the first tranche, which may have a one-year average life, will receive all principal payments until it is retired; then the second tranche begins to receive principal, and so forth. Pro rata bond structures pay each tranche a proportionate share of principal throughout the life of the security.

### *Structural Risks and Misincentives*

Some originators (e.g. of mortgages) have prioritised loan volume over credit quality, disregarding the long-term risk of the assets they have created in their enthusiasm to profit from the fees associated with origination and securitization. Other originators, aware of the reputational harm and added expense if risky loans are subject to repurchase requests or improperly originated loans lead to litigation, have paid more attention to credit quality

## Securing Assets

Is the process whereby interests in loans and receivables are packaged and sold in the form of asset backed securities. They are the bonds or notes backed by some financial assets. It consists of receivables such as mortgage loans, credit card receivables, auto loans, manufactured housing contracts and home equity loans. The duration is upto 5 years.

## Role of Institutions

Increasing numbers of financial institutions employ securitization to transfer the credit risk of the assets they originate from their balance sheets to those of other financial institutions, such as banks, insurance companies, and hedge funds. They do it for a variety reasons. It is often cheaper to raise money through securitization, and securitized assets were then less costly for banks to hold because financial regulators had different standards for them than for the assets that underpinned them. In principle, this "originate and distribute" approach brought broad economic benefits too—spreading out credit exposures, thereby diffusing risk concentrations and reducing systemic vulnerabilities.

## Benefits

- Lower cost
- Alternative investor base
- Matching of assets and liabilities
- Issuer rating irrelevant
- Multiplies asset creation ability
- Non conventional source; may allow higher funding
- Off balance sheet financing – removal of accounts
- Frees up regulatory capital
- Improves capital structure
- Higher trading on equity with no increased risk
- Extends credit pool
- Not regulated as loan
- Reduces credit concentration
- Risk management by risk transfer
- Arbitraging opportunities
- Avoids interest rate risk
- Improves accounting profits

## Conditions

The SPV pre-designs the type of bonds to be issued depending on the deal structure. The broad type of securitisation structures include:

- **Cash vs. Synthetic Structures:** Most transactions world over follow the cash structure in which the originator sells assets and receives cash instead. In a synthetic transaction, the seller keeps his title and investment on the assets unaffected. In other words, he does not sell assets for cash but merely transfers risks/rewards relating to the asset by entering into a derivative transaction. When securities are issued by the SPV, they carry such embedded derivative. Synthetic securitisation is gaining popularity in Europe and Asia.
- **True Sale vs. Secured Loan Structures:** The true sale structure involves sale of a specific pool of assets where the originator transfers both the legal and the beneficial interest in the assets. In a secured loan structure, the originator takes a loan similar to any secured lending. Investor rights in this case are protected by creating a fixed and a floating charge over the undertaking of the originator in favour of a security trustee. The assets are generic assets of the originator and the trustee is empowered to take possession of the assets at times of certain trigger events to prevent the assets from being burdened any further. The use of secured loan structure depends on the legal provisions of the country concerned. The secured loan structure is more popular in the UK.
- **Pass Through vs. Collateral Structure:** In a pass through structure, the SPV issues participation certificates that enable investors to take a direct exposure on the performance of the securitised assets. Investors are serviced as and when cash is actually generated by the underlying assets. Risks like delay/disruptions in cash flows is mitigated via credit enhancement. (As investors do not have recourse to the Originator, they seek comfort through credit enhancement methods by which risks intrinsic to the transaction are re-allocated.) Pass through structure is the most basic and simplest way of securitisation in mortgage markets. In a collateral structure (also known as pay through structure), the SPV retains the assets to be securitised with it and gives investors only a charge against the securitised assets. The SPV issues debt that is collateralised by the assets that are transferred by the originator. This is also referred to as the Pay through structure and popularly known as collateralised mortgage obligations (CMO).
- **Discreet Trust vs. Master Trust:** Discreet trust implies one SPV for a single identified pool of assets where investors participate in the cash flow of the pool. In the creation of a master trust, the Originator sets up a large fund in which large pools of receivables are transferred, much larger than the size of the funding raised by investors. Several security issuances can be created from this fund either concurrently or consecutively. The master trust serves as a tool to create disparities between the repayment structures and the tenure of the securities and assets in the pool. Master trusts are increasingly becoming the preferred mode of securitisation as a result of their flexibility.
- **Conduit vs. Standalone Transactions:** In conduit transactions, the purchaser or conduit sources the assets from multiple originators and securitises the assets by issuing asset-backed commercial paper. Since commercial papers of short term duration, it becomes necessary for the conduit to avail of short term or bridge financing from banks. In standalone transactions, the conduit purchases the assets from a single originator. In this case the conduit issues securities of a maturity matching the maturity of the underlying asset pool.

## Securitisation in India and Abroad

The credit of starting securitisation goes to America, where the first structured asset securitised financing came into being in 1970. Although firstly it was backed by mortgage loans the securities issued by it were called "Mortgage pass through securities". However in 1985non mortgage collaterals started getting securitised in USA. Securitisation is gaining popularity in UK also in recent years. Like America the concept firstly backed by mortgage. Securitisation is popular in countries like Italy, Australia, Canada, Japan, France etc.

### *Early Regulation of Securitization in India*

There is no comprehensive single regulatory framework for the securitization market per se. In effect, only the financial sector has a clear framework for participating in securitization.

The recommendations of the High Level Committee on Corporate Debt and Securitisation (Chairman: Dr.R.H.Patil) in 2005 proved to be the turning point towards the development of the corporate debt and securitization market.

The Reserve Bank accepted several of its recommendations and in February 2006, issued guidelines for securitisation of standard assets by Banks, FIs and NBFCs. These guidelines provided the regulatory framework for several critical aspects of securitisation.

In 2007, the Securities Contracts (Regulation) Act 1956 was amended in 2007 to include "securitised instruments" in the definition of "securities". The amendment has paved the way for listing and trading of securitised debt on stock exchanges.

Consequently, the Securities and Exchange Board of India (SEBI) released draft regulations for "Public Offer and Listing of Securitised Debt Instruments" in June 2007 which is yet to be formalized. However, these guidelines envisage a very different transaction structure compared to current market practices.

The graph below indicates that the issuances in the Eurozone have been on a low key post the crisis. There has been some activity which is closer to the level of issuances in 2000s.

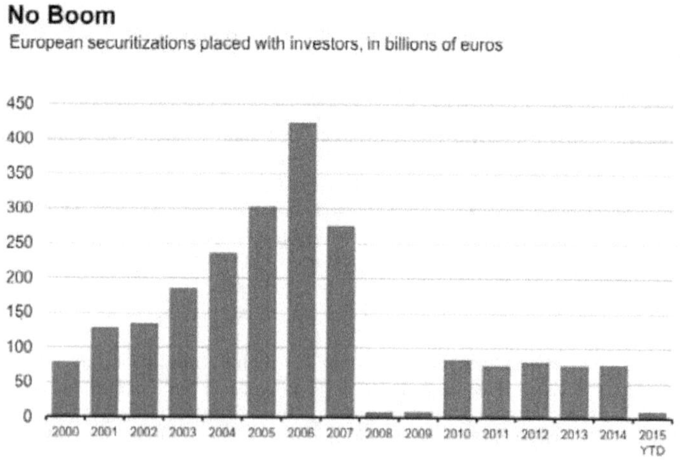


Source: Barclays, WSJ.com

The graph below indicates China overtaking South Korea in securitisation transactions in terms of deal values

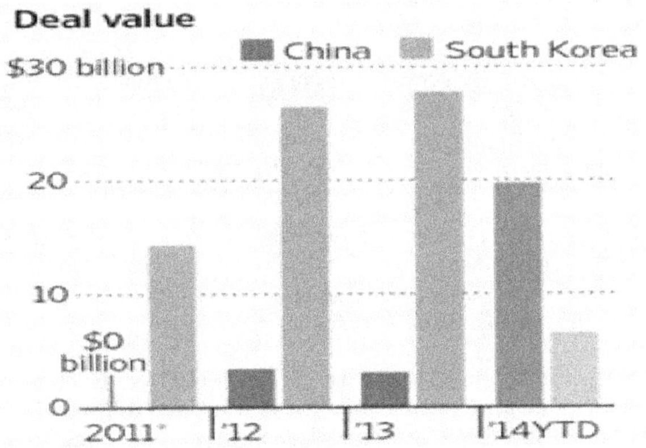


### *Role of the Reserve Bank of India in regulation of Securitisation*

The Reserve Bank of India (RBI) is the regulator of the major players in the Indian financial system (banks, financial institutions and NBFCs) and has to ensure that financial intermediaries engage in Securitisation prudently.

The Reserve Bank issued the first set of comprehensive guidelines applicable to banks, financial institutions and non-banking financial companies (NBFCs) on Securitisation in India way back in February 2006. The guidelines covered following aspects relating to Securitisation transactions:

- Broad definitions on important securitisation related concepts such as securitisation, SPV, bankruptcy remote, credit enhancement, first loss facility, liquidity facilities, service provider and underwriting facilities.
- Prescribed detailed 'true sale' criteria and criteria to be met by originators and SPVs. Some important criteria included that originators should not indulge in market making on securities issued by SPV, originators shall not invest in more than 10% of securities issued by SPV, securities cannot have any put option, etc.
- Detailed policy for originators and third parties on provision of credit enhancements, liquidity support/ facilities, underwriting facilities, servicing arrangements, etc.
- Capital adequacy norms for Credit Enhancement-First loss credit enhancement is deducted from capital and second loss facility is risk weighted according to the rating. Credit enhancement cannot be withdrawn/ reduced by the provider throughout the life of the transaction except to cover the losses suffered by SPV.
- Prudential Norms for investment in the securities issued by SPVs.
- Accounting treatment for securitisation transactions - An important feature was that profit/premium arising on account of sale should be amortized over the life of the securities issued or to be issued by the SPV.

Due diligence framework for securitisation transactions and disclosures to be made by the SPVs/ Trustee and originators.

# 10. DERIVATIVES

Derivative is a financial instrument whose value is derived from the value of another asset which is known as the underlying. When the price of underlying asset changes the value of derivative also changes. The underlying assets could be prices of traded securities of gold, copper, aluminium and may even cover prices of flowers and fruits. The derivative itself is a contract between two or more parties based upon the asset or assets. Its value is determined by fluctuations in the underlying asset. The most common underlying assets include stocks, bonds, commodities, currencies, interest rates and market indexes. There are 3 types of traders in derivatives market: hedger, speculator, and arbitrageur. The derivate are traded

- OTC (over the counter) or off-exchange trading is to trade derivatives between two parties without going through an exchange or other intermediary.
- Exchange traded derivatives: Exchange traded derivatives contract (ETD) are those derivatives instruments that are traded via specialized Derivatives exchange or other exchanges

The origin of derivatives can be traced back to the need of farmers to protect themselves against fluctuations in the price of their crop. The first step towards introduction of financial derivatives trading in India was the promulgation at the securities laws (Amendment) ordinance 1995. It provided for withdrawal at prohibition on options in securities. The last decade, beginning the year 2000, saw lifting of ban of futures trading in many commodities. Derivatives such as options and futures are traded actively on many exchanges.

## Types and Classification of Derivatives

1. Derivatives can be classified as linear and non-linear derivatives or financial and non-financial derivatives.

(a)Linear derivatives: Those derivatives whose Over-the-counter (OTC) traded derivative: These values depend linearly on the underlying's value are called linear derivatives. They are following:

- Forwards
- Futures
- Swaps

(b) Non-linear derivatives: Those derivatives whose value is a non-linear function of the underlying are called non-linear derivatives. They are following:

- Options
- Convertibles
- Equity linked bonds
- Reinsurance

2. On the basis of financial and non-financial: On the basis of this classification the derivatives can be classified into two category namely financial derivatives and non-financial derivatives.

(a) Financial derivatives: Those derivatives which are of financial nature are called financial derivatives. They are following:

- Forwards
- Futures
- Options
- Swaps

The above financial derivatives may be credit derivatives, forex, currency fixed-income, interest, insider trading and exchange traded.

(b) Non-financial derivatives: Those derivatives which are not of financial nature are called non-financial derivatives. They are following:

- Commodities
- Metals
- Weather
- Others

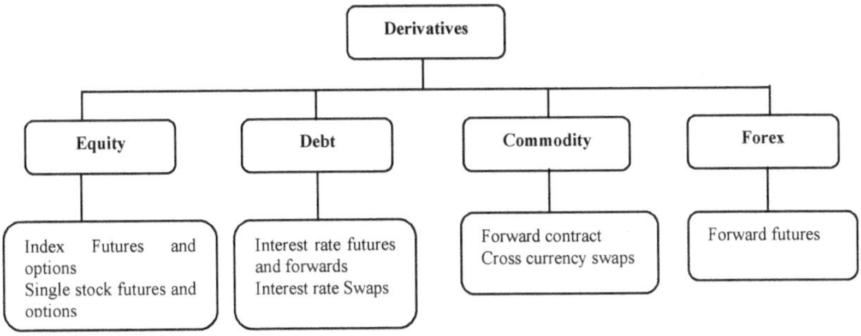


### *Benefits of Financial Derivatives*

Some of the uses and applications of financial derivatives can be enumerated as following:

#### 1. *Management of Risk*

One of the most important services provided by the derivatives is to control, avoid, shift and manage efficiently different types of risk through various strategies like hedging, arbitraging, spreading etc. Derivative assist the holders to shift or modify suitable the risk characteristics of the portfolios. These are specifically useful in highly volatile financial conditions like erratic trading, highly flexible interest rates, volatile exchange rates and monetary chaos.

#### 2. *Price Discovery*

The important application of financial derivatives is the price discovery which means revealing information about future cash market prices through the future market. Derivative markets provide a mechanism by which diverse and scattered opinions of future are collected into one readily discernible number which provides a consensus of knowledgeable thinking.

#### 3. *Liquidity and Reduce Transaction Cost*

As we see that in derivatives trading no immediate full amount of the transaction is required since most of them are based on margin trading. As a result, large number of traders, speculators, arbitrageurs operates in such markets. So, derivatives trading enhance liquidity and reduce transaction cost in the markets of underlying assets. Measurement of Market: Derivatives serve as the barometers of the future trends in price which result in the discovery of new prices both on the spot and future markets. They help in disseminating different information regarding the future markets trading of various commodities and securities to the society which enable to discover or form suitable or correct or true equilibrium price in the markets. As a result, the assets will be in an appropriate and superior allocation of resources in the society.

### 4. *Efficiency in Trading*

Financial derivatives allow for free trading of risk components and that leads to improving market efficiency. Traders can use a position in one or more financial derivatives as a substitute for a position in underlying instruments. In many instances, traders find financial derivatives to be a more attractive instrument than the underlying security. This is mainly because of the greater amount of liquidity in the market offered by derivatives as well as the lower transaction costs associated with trading a financial derivative as compared to the costs of trading the underlying instruments in cash market.

### 5. *Speculation and Arbitrage*

Derivatives can be used to acquire risk, rather than to hedge against risk. Thus, some individuals and institutions will enter into a derivative contract to speculate on the value of the underlying asset, betting that the party seeking insurance will be wrong about the future value of the underlying asset. Speculators look to buy an asset in the future at a low price according to a derivative contract when the future market price is high, or to sell an asset in the future at a high price according to derivative contract when the future market price is low. Individual and institutions may also look for arbitrage opportunities, as when the current buying price of an asset falls below the price specified in a futures contract to sell the asset.

### 6. *Hedging*

Hedge or mitigate risk in the underlying, by entering into a derivative contract whose value moves in the opposite direction to their underlying position and cancels part or all of it out. Hedging also occurs when an individual or institution buys an asset and sells it using a future contract. They have access to the asset for a specified amount of time, and can then sell it in the future at a specified price according to the futures contract of course; this allows them the benefit of holding the asset.

### 7. *Price Stabilization Function*

Derivative market helps to keep a stabilizing influence on spot prices by reducing the short term fluctuations. In other words, derivatives reduce both peak and depths and lends to price stabilization effect in the cash market for underlying asset.

### 8. *Gearing of Value*

Special care and attention about financial derivatives provide leverage (or gearing), such that a small movement in the underlying value can cause a large difference in the value of the derivative.

### 9. *Develop the Complete Markets*

It is observed that derivative trading develop the market towards "complete markets" complete market concept refers to that situation where no particular investors be better of than others, or patterns of returns of all additional securities are spanned by the already existing securities in it, or there is no further scope of additional security.

### 10. *Encourage Competition*

The derivatives trading encourage the competitive trading in the market, different risk taking preference at market operators like speculators, hedgers, traders, arbitrageurs etc. resulting in increase in trading volume in the country. They also attract young investors, professionals and other experts who will act as catalysts to the growth of financial market.

### *11. Other Uses*

The other uses of derivatives are observed from the derivatives trading in the market that the derivatives have smoothen out price fluctuations, squeeze the price spread, integrate price structure at different points of time and remove gluts and shortage in the markets. The derivatives also assist the investors, traders and managers of large pools of funds to device such strategies so that they may make proper asset allocation increase their yields and achieve other investment goals.

### *Major Players in the Financial Derivatives Trading*

There are three major players in the financial derivatives trading:

1. Hedgers: Hedgers are traders who use derivatives to reduce the risk that they face from potential movements in a market variable and they want to avoid exposure to adverse movements in the price of an asset. Majority of the participants in derivatives market belongs to this category.
2. Speculators: Speculators are traders who buy/sell the assets only to sell/buy them back profitably at a later point in time. They want to assume risk. They use derivatives to bet on the future direction of the price of an asset and take a position in order to make a quick profit. They can increase both the potential gains and potential losses by usage of derivatives in a speculative venture.
3. Arbitrageurs: Arbitrageurs are traders who simultaneously buy and sell the same (or different, but related) assets in an effort to profit from unrealistic price differentials. They attempt to make profits by locking in a riskless trading by simultaneously entering into transaction in two or more markets. They try to earn riskless profit from discrepancies between futures and spot prices and among different futures prices.

## Growth of Derivatives in India and Abroad

The first record of organized trading in futures comes from 17th century Japan. Feudal Japanese landlords would ship surplus rice to storage warehouses in the cities and then issue tickets promising future delivery of the rice. The tickets represented the right to take delivery of a certain quantity of rice at a future date at a specified price. These rice tickets were traded on the Dojima rice market near Osaka and in 1730.Trading in rice tickets allowed landlords and merchants to lock the prices at which rice was bought and sold, reducing the risk they faced. The tickets also provided flexibility. Someone holding a rice ticket but not a holder of a rice ticket but not wanting to take delivery could sell it in the market. The rules governing the trading on the Dojima market were similar to those of modern-day futures markets.

Moving forward 200 years, Chicago was central to the 19th century development of futures contracts in the US. As in Japan, the seasonal nature of agricultural production was the main impetus behind the development of these financial instruments. Farmers would traditionally bring their harvest to market once a year in search of buyers creating a seasonal glut and driving prices to extremely low levels.

The history of derivatives is surprisingly longer than what most people think. Some texts even find the existence of the characteristics of derivative contracts in incidents of Mahabharata. Traces of derivative contracts can even be found in incidents that date back to the ages before Jesus Christ. However, the advent of modern day derivative contracts is attributed to the need for farmers to protect themselves from any decline in the price of their crops due to delayed monsoon, or over production. The first 'futures' contracts can be traced to the Yodoya rice market in Osaka, Japan around1650. These were evidently standardized contracts, which made them much like today's futures.

The Chicago Board of Trade (CBOT), the largest derivative exchange in the world, was established in 1848 where forward contracts on various commodities were standardizedaround1865. From then on, futures contracts have remained more or less in the same form as we know them today.

Derivatives have had a long presence in India. The commodity derivative market has been functioning in India since the nineteenth century with organized trading in cotton through the establishment of Cotton Trade Association in 1875. Since then contracts on various other commodities have been introduced as well. Exchange traded financial derivatives were introduced in India in June 2000 at the two major stock exchanges, NSE and BSE. There are various contracts currently traded on these exchanges.

The National Stock Exchange of India Limited (NSE) commenced trading in derivatives with the launch of index futures on June 12, 2000. The futures contracts are based on the popular benchmark S&P CNX Nifty Index. The Exchange introduced trading in Index Options (also based on Nifty) on June 4, 2001. NSE also became the first exchange to launch trading in options on individual securities from July 2, 2001. Futures on individual securities were introduced on November 9, 2001.

## Forward Contract

A forward contract is a customized contract between the buyer and the seller where settlement takes place on a specific date in future at a price agreed today. In case of a forward contract the price which is paid/received by the parties is decided at the time of entering into contract. It is simplest form of derivative contract mostly entered by individual in day to day life.

The holder of a long (short) forward contract has an agreement to buy (sell) an asset at a certain time in the future for a certain price, which is agreed upon today. The buyer (or seller) in a forward contract

Acquires a legal obligation to buy (or sell) an asset (known as the underlying asset)

- At some specific future date (the expiration date)
- At a price (the forward price) which is fixed today

The basic features of a contract are given in brief here as under:

1. Forward contracts are bilateral contracts, and hence, they are exposed to the counter party risk. There is risk of non-performance of obligation either of the parties, so these are riskier than to futures contracts.
2. Each contract is custom designed, and hence, is unique in terms of contract size, expiration date, the asset type, quality etc.
3. In forward contract, one of the parties takes a long position by agreeing to buy the asset at a certain specified future date. The other party assumes a short position by agreeing to sell the same asset at the same date for the same specified price. A party with no obligation offsetting the forward contract is said to have an open position. A party with a close position is, sometimes, called a hedger.
4. The specified price in a forward contract is referred to as the delivery price. The forward price for a particular forward contract at a particular time is the delivery price that would apply if the contract were entered into at that time. It is important to differentiate between the forward price and the delivery price. Both are equal at the time the contact is entered into. However, as time passes, the forward price is likely to change whereas the delivery price remains the same.
5. In the forward contract, derivative asset can often be contracted from the combination of underlying assets; such assets are often known as synthetic assets in the forward market.

6. In the forward market, the contract has to be settled by delivery of the asset on expiration date. In case the party wishes to reverse the contract, it has to compulsory go to the same counter party, which may dominate and command the price it wants as being in a monopoly situation.
7. In a forward contract, covered party or cost of carry relations are relation between the prices of forward and underlying asset's.
8. Forward contract are very popular in foreign exchange market as well as interest rate bearing instruments. Most of the large and international banks quote the forward rate through their forward desk lying within their foreign exchange trading room. Forward foreign exchange quotes by these banks are displayed with the spot rates.

**Example 1:** If a person in India is expecting 1000$ from his relative in USA, then the question is how much INR he will get for one US Dollar. Here the person is comparing the domestic currency with the foreign currency. He will be happy if USD to INR conversion is more.

So they go to a bank, explain their situation and after fulfilling the below two conditions:

- minimum deposit required (amount depends upon the financial institution).
- 200, 000 USD should reach their bank from US Client on a specified date in a month.

This contract is called as Forward Contract. Upon signing the forward contract, the bank agrees to pay conversion rate of 53 rupees per month, on 5th of every month for the next 12 months.

## *Forward Contract Types*

- **Time option forward contract:** This is a forward contract that allows access to the funds between two pre-determined dates eg. 01/04/00 - 31/08/00. This is of particular benefit when, for example a car delivery is not precisely known, and therefore funds may be needed earlier. It is important to remember that the last date is not flexible and physical delivery of the currency can take place before but no later than that date.
- **Drawdown forward contract:** This is similar to a time option forward contract, however, if a portion of the funds are required during the life of the contract then they may be drawn down against the said contract at the original buy rate, thereby reducing the final balance. This would particularly suit either a boat or house purchase where large sums maybe needed to settle stage payments. Its structure also lends itself to corporate clients with large capital payments as the minimum is circa. Â£75,000. Draw down payments will incur a small fee.
- **Fixed term forward contract:** A Fixed-Term Forward Contract gives you the ability to fix a currency rate with a view to take physical delivery of the said currency in the future. The rate is guaranteed irrespective of market fluctuations for the duration of the Contract.

A deposit is required on each Forward Contract and must be received within two (2) working days of the contract date. The balance of the contract must be settled no later than the maturity date. We recommend that our clients settle the outstanding balance on their contracts five (5) working days prior to the contract matures. Should the delivery of the currency not be required upon maturity, the said currency can usually be held on account at no additional charge or penalty.

### *The advantages of Forward Contracts are as Follows*

1) They can be matched against the time period of exposure as well as for the cash size of the exposure.
2) Forwards are tailor made and can be written for any amount and term.
3) It offers a complete hedge.
4) Forwards are over-the-counter products.
5) The use of forwards provide price protection.
6) They are easy to understand.

## Options Contracts

Options are derivative contract that give the right, but not the obligation to either buy or sell a specific underlying security for a specified price on or before a specific date. In theory, option can be written on almost any type of underlying security. Equity (stock) is the most common, but there are also several types of non-equity options, based on securities such as bonds, foreign currency, indices or commodities such as gold or oil.

The person who buys an option is normally called the buyer or holder. Conversely, the seller is known as the seller or writer. Again we can say "An option is a particular type of a contract between two parties where one person gives the other person the right to buy or sell a specific asset at a specified price within a specified time period." Today, options are traded on a variety of instruments like commodities, financial assets as diverse as foreign exchange, bank times deposits, treasury securities, stock, stock indexes, petroleum products, food grains, metals etc.

The main characteristics of options are following:

1. Options holders do not receive any dividend or interest.
2. Option yield only capital gains.
3. Options holder can enjoy a tax advantages.
4. Options are traded on OTC and in all recognized stock exchanges.
5. Options holders can control their rights on the underlying assets.
6. Options create the possibility of gaining a windfall profit.
7. Options holder can enjoy a much wider risk- return combinations.
8. Options can reduce the total portfolio transaction costs.
9. Options enable with the investors to gain a better returns with a limited amount of investment.

A call which is the right to buy shares under a negotiable contract and which do not carry any obligation. The buyers have the right to receive the delivery of assets are known as call option.

In this option the owner has the right to sell the underlying asset under the negotiable contract. Put option holder has the right to receive the payment by surrendering the asset.

The writer of an option is a stock broker, member or a security dealer. The buyer of an option pays a price depending on the risk of underlying security and he as an investor or a dealer or trader.

### *Features*

1. The option is exercisable only by the owner namely the buyer of the option.
2. The owner has limited liability.
3. Owners of options have no voting rights and dividend right.
4. Options have high degree of risk to the option writers.
5. Options involving buying counter positions by the option sellers.

6. Flexibility in investor's needs
7. No certificates are issued by the company.
8. Options are popular because they allow the buyer profits from favorable movement in exchange rate.

### *Options can be Classified into Different Categories Like*

- Call options
- Put options
- Exchange traded options
- OTC traded options
- American options
- European options
- Commodity options
- Currency options
- Stock options
- Stock Index options

### *Terminology*

- X` Underlying: Specific security or asset.
- Option premium: Price paid.
- Strike price: Pre-decided price.
- Expiration date: Date on which option expires.
- Exercise date: Option is exercised.
- Open interest: Total numbers of option contracts that have not yet been expired.
- Option holder: One who buys option.
- Option writer: One who sells option.
- Option class: All listed options of a type on a particular instrument.
- Option series: A series that consists of all the options of a given class with the same expiry date and strike price.
- Put-call ratio: The ratio of puts to the calls traded in the market.

### *Example*

Rajesh purchases one lot of Infosys Technologies May 3000 call and pays a premium of Rs.250. At this time the share price was Rs.2900.

This means, under this contract, Rajesh has the rights to buy one lot of 100 Infosys shares at Rs 3000 per share any time between now and the month of May. He paid a premium of Rs 250 per share. He thus pays a total amount of Rs 25,000 to enjoy this right to sell.

Now, suppose the share price of Infosys rises over Rs 3,000 to Rs 3200, Rajesh can consider exercising the option and buying at Rs 3,000 per share. He would be saving Rs 200 per share; this can be considered a tentative profit. However, he still makes a notional net loss of Rs 50 per share once you take the premium amount into consideration. For this reason, Rajesh may choose to actually exercise the option once the share price crosses Rs 3,250 levels. Otherwise, he can choose to let the option expire without being exercised.

Rajesh believes that the shares of Company X are currently overpriced and bets on them falling in the next few months. Since he wants to secure his position, he takes a put option on the shares of Company X.

### *Quotes for Stock X*

| Month | Price | Premium |
|---|---|---|
| February (Current month) | Rs 1040 Spot | NA |
| May | Rs 1050 Put | Rs 10 |
| May | Rs 1070 Put | Rs 30 |

Rajesh buys 1000 shares of Company X Put at a strike price of 1070 and pays Rs 30 per share as premium. His total premium paid is Rs 30,000.

**If the spot price for Company X falls below** the Put option Rajesh bought, say to Rs 1020; Rajesh can safeguard his money by choosing to sell the put option. He will make Rs 50 per share (Rs 1070 minus Rs 1020) on the trade, making a net profit of Rs 20,000 (Rs 50 x 1000 shares - Rs 30,000 paid as premium).

**Alternately, if the spot price for Company X rises higher** than the Put option, say Rs 1080; he would be at a loss if he decided to exercise the put option at Rs 1070. So, he will choose, in this case, to not exercise the put option. In the process, he only loses Rs 30,000 - the premium amount; this is much lower than if he had exercised his option.

### *Benefits of Options*

Following are the benefits of trading options

### *Cost Efficiency*

They have a great leveraging power. Any investor can obtain an option position that will mimic a stock position almost identically, but at a huge cost saving.

### *Less Risk*

Options can be less risky for investors because they require less financial commitment than equities, and they can also be less risky due to their relative imperviousness to the potentially catastrophic effects of gap openings.

### *Higher Potential Returns*

Options offer a higher return because the investor pays less amount for an option position and when they make a same amount of profit the return is higher when is there is a pay off.

### *More Strategic Alternatives*

Options are flexible investment tools. Options can be used many ways to recreate positions. It can be used to achieve investment goals. It allows the trader to trade not stock movements but also passage of time and movements in volatility.

## Futures Contract

Futures contract is an agreement between two parties to buy or sell a specified quantity of an asset at a specified price and at a specified time and place. Future contracts are normally traded on an exchange which sets the certain standardized norms for trading in futures contracts.

The features of a futures contract may be specified as follows:

1. Futures are traded only in organized exchanges.
2. Futures contract required to have standard contract terms.
3. Futures exchange has associated with clearing house.
4. Futures trading required margin payment and daily settlement.
5. Futures positions can be closed easily.
6. Futures markets are regulated by regulatory authorities like SEBI.

7. The futures contracts are executed on expiry date.
8. The futures prices are expressed in currency units, with a minimum price movement called a tick size. The quality of positive economic theory explains about its ability with precision clarity and simplicity.

The main characteristics of futures explained by a good economic theory are as follows:

1. There are a limited number of actively traded products with futures contracts.
2. The trading unit is large and indivisible.
3. It has no more than maturity of 3 months.
4. The success ratio of new contract is about 25% in the world financial markets.
5. Futures are seldom used by farmers.
6. There are both commercial and non-commercial users of futures contract in interest rates and foreign exchange.
7. The main use of the future by the commercial users is to hedge corresponding cash and forward positions.
8. The positions of the non-commercial users take almost entirely speculative positions. In foreign exchange futures, the positions of the commercials users are unbalanced.

There are different types of contracts in financial futures which are traded in the various futures market of the world. The followings are the important types of financial futures contract:

1. **Stock future or equity futures:** This kind of future contract has a stock as its underlying and stock price defines the value of a future contract. generally settled in cash or stock
2. **Stock index futures:** This type of equity future has a index as its underlying. Like Dow Jones future. It settles in cash settlement only on a specified date.
3. **Currency futures:** Futures contract to exchange one currency for another at a specified date in the future at a price (exchange rate) that is fixed on the purchase date. On NSE the price of a future contract is in terms of INR per unit of other currency e.g. US Dollars.
4. **Interest rate futures:** A futures contract with an interest-bearing instrument as the underlying asset. It is a particular type of interest rate derivative. Examples include Treasury-bill futures, Treasury-bond futures and Eurodollar futures.

### *Economic Importance of the Futures Market*

Futures market is both highly active and central to the global marketplace, it's a good source for vital market information and sentiment indicators.

### *Price Discovery*

Due to its highly competitive nature, the futures market has become an important economic tool to determine prices based on today's and tomorrow's estimated amount of supply and demand. Futures market prices depend on a continuous flow of information from around the world and thus require a high amount of transparency. Factors such as weather, war, debt default, refugee displacement, land reclamation and deforestation can all have a major effect on supply and demand and, as a result, the present and future price of a commodity. This kind of information and the way people absorb it constantly changes the price of a commodity. This process is known as price discovery.

### *Risk Reduction*

Futures markets are also a place for people to reduce risk when making purchases. Risks are reduced because the price is pre-set, therefore letting participants know how much they will need to buy or sell. This helps reduce the ultimate cost to the retail buyer because with less risk there is less of a chance that manufacturers will jack up prices to make up for profit losses in the cash market.

### *Margin*

A margin is an amount of a money that must be deposited with the clearing house by both buyers and sellers in a margin account in order to open a futures contract. It ensures performance of the terms of the contract. Its aim is to minimize the risk of default by either counterparty.

There are different types of margin:

- Initial Margin - Deposit that a trader must make before trading any futures. Usually, 10% of the contract size.
- Maintenance Margin - When margin reaches a minimum maintenance level, the trader is required to bring the margin back to its initial level. The maintenance margin is generally about 75% of the initial margin.
- Variation Margin - Additional margin required to bring an account up to the required level.
- Margin call – If amount in the margin A/C falls below the maintenance level, a margin call is made to fill the gap.

### *Marking to Market*

This is the practice of periodically adjusting the margin account by adding or subtracting funds based on changes in market value to reflect the investor's gain or loss. This leads to changes in margin amounts daily. 'This ensures that there are o defaults by the parties

**Expiry**: Is the time and the day that a particular delivery month of a futures contract stops trading, as well as the final settlement price for that contract.

- Contract size – The amount of the asset that has to be delivered under one contract. All futures are sold in multiples of lots which is decided by the exchange board.
  Eg. If the lot size of Tata steel is 500 shares, then one futures contract is necessarily 500 shares.
- Contract cycle – The period for which a contract trades.
- The futures on the NSE have one (near) month, two (next) months, three (far) months expiry cycles.
- Expiry date – usually last Thursday of every month or previous day if Thursday is public holiday.
- Strike price – The agreed price of the deal is called the strike price.
- Cost of carry – Difference between strike price and current price.

There are different type of future contracts:

- Stock Futures Trading (dealing with shares)
- Commodity Futures Trading (dealing with gold futures, crude oil futures)
- Index Futures Trading (dealing with stock market indices)

### *Closing a Futures Position*

Most futures contracts are not held till expiry, but closed before that. If held till expiry, they are generally settled by delivery. (2-3%). By closing a futures contract before expiry, the net difference is settled between traders, without physical delivery of the underlying

### *Advantages*

- Futures are Highly Leveraged Investments
- Low Commission and execution cost
- Speculators make fast money
- Great for diversification or hedging

### *Limitation*

- Counter Party Risk
- Low Liquidity

**Example 1:** If you want to purchase a single July futures contract of ABC Ltd., you would have to do so at the price at which the July futures contracts are currently available in the derivatives market. Let's say that ABC Ltd July futures are trading at Rs 1,000 per share. This means, you are agreeing to buy/sell at a fixed price of Rs 1,000 per share on the last Thursday in July. However, it is not necessary that the price of the stock in the cash market on Thursday has to be Rs 1,000. It could be Rs 992 or Rs 1,005 or anything else, depending on the prevailing market conditions. This difference in prices can be taken advantage of to make profits.

**Example 2:** If the index stands at 3550 points in the cash market today and you decide to purchase one Nifty 50 July future, you would have to purchase it at the price prevailing in the futures market.

This price of one July futures contract could be anywhere above, below or at Rs 3.55 lakh (i.e., 3550*100), depending on the prevailing market conditions. Investors and traders try to profit from the opportunity arising from this difference in prices

## Swaps

A swap is an agreement between two or more people or parties to exchange sets of cash flows over a period in future. It is a funding technique which permits borrower to access one market and then exchange the liability for another type of liability.

Swaps are agreements between two parties to exchange assets at predetermined intervals. Swaps are generally customized transactions. The swaps are innovative financing which reduces borrowing costs, and to increase Page control over interest rate risk and FOREX exposure. The swap includes both spot and forward transactions in a single agreement.

Swaps are at the centre of the global financial revolution.

### *Benefits*

Swaps are useful in avoiding the problems of unfavourable fluctuation in FOREX market. The parties that agree to the swap are known as counter parties. They are favourable because they work on the concept of comparative advantage. The basic principle is that some companies have a comparative advantage when borrowing in fixed rate markets while others have a comparative advantage in floating rate markets. This may lead to some companies borrowing in fixed markets when the need is of floating rate loan and vice versa.

### *Types*

There are 2 main types of swaps:

- Plain vanilla fixed for floating swaps or simply interest rate swaps.
- Fixed for fixed currency swaps or simply currency swaps

### *Interest Rate Swap*

A company agrees to pay a pre-determined fixed interest rate on a notional principal for a fixed number of years. In return, it receives interest at a floating rate on the same notional principal for the same period of time. The principal is not exchanged. Hence, it is called a notional amount.

### *Floating Interest Rate Swaps*

LIBOR – London Interbank Offered Rate. It is the average interest rate estimated by leading banks in London. It is the primary benchmark for short term interest rates around the world. Similarly, we have MIBOR i.e. Mumbai Interbank Offered Rate. It is calculated by the NSE as a weighted average of lending rates of a group of banks.

Usually two non-financial companies don't directly arrange a swap. They deal with a financial intermediary such as a bank who then structures the plain vanilla swap in such a way so as to earn a margin or spread. In international markets they earn about 3 basis points on a pair of offsetting transactions.

### *Currency Swap*

It is a swap that includes exchange of principal and interest rates in one currency for the same in another currency. It is considered to be a foreign exchange transaction. It is not required by law to be shown in the balance sheets. The principal may be exchanged either at the beginning or at the end of the tenure. However, if it is exchanged at the end of the life of the swap, the principal value may be very different. It is generally used to hedge against exchange rate fluctuations.

Example:

ABC Company and XYZ Company enter into one-year interest rate swap with a nominal value of $1 million. ABC offers XYZ a fixed annual rate of 5% in exchange for a rate of LIBOR plus 1%, since both parties believe that LIBOR will be roughly 4%. At the end of the year, ABC will pay XYZ $50,000 (5% of $1 million). If the LIBOR rate is trading at 4.75%, XYZ then will have to pay ABC Company $57,500 (5.75% of $1 million, because of the agreement to pay LIBOR plus 1%).

Therefore, the value of the swap to ABC and XYZ is the difference between what they receive and spend. Since LIBOR ended up higher than both companies thought, ABC won out with a gain of $7,500, while XYZ realizes a loss of $7,500. Generally, only the net payment will be made. When XYZ pays $7,500 to ABC, both companies avoid the cost and complexities of each company paying the full $50,000 and $57,500.

# 11. COMMODITIES MARKET

A commodity market is a market that trades in primary economic sector rather than manufactured products. Soft commodities are agricultural products such as wheat, coffee, cocoa and sugar. Hard commodities are mined, such as gold and oil.

## Types

Commodities can be categorised as soft and hard.

### *Soft Commodities*

They are usually grown and includes crops such as Corn, wheat, soybean, Soybean oil, and sugar. They are subject to severe volatility since there is a huge risk of spoilage. Predicting the supply of such commodities is very difficult because weather plays a very important role in their production and the same is very unstable and never constant.

### *Hard Commodities*

They are typically mined from the ground or taken from other natural resources and include gold, oil, aluminium etc., In many cases, initial products are refined into further commodities, as oil is refined into gasoline. Investors focus mainly on these commodities because they are easy to handle than the soft products and they can be further integrated into industrial goods.

The commodities can be further classified as Non- Agriculture commodities and agriculture commodities.

### *Agriculture Commodities*

Over 58.4% of India's population depend on agriculture for their primary income and it also accounts for approximately one-fifth of total gross domestic product (GDP). Agriculture contributes about 10 per cent of the total export earnings. Agriculture has been the primary source of raw material to a large number of industries. India has been the largest producer of agricultural commodities because it has huge mass of land under cultivation compared to other countries and yet Indian agriculture has one of the lowest yields in most commodities because nearly 55.7% of area sown is dependent on rainfall. Clearly while there are challenges there are huge potentials as well.

- ***Edible Oil Complex***

Commodities like soya beans, refined soya oil, soya meal, Mustard seed and Crude palm oil are actively traded under edible oil complex and they contribute to more than 50% of the exchange volume. Their prices move in tandem with the international markets because they have a global appeal compared to other agricultural commodities traded at the domestic market. Prices in domestic exchanges enjoy high correlation with their global counterparts. Chicago Board of Trade (CBOT) which has integrated e trading is considered to be benchmark for Soya complex pricing and similarly Bursa Malaysia Exchange is considered to be benchmark for Crude Palm oil pricing. Products traded comprise of soya complex, mustard seed, crude palm oil, castor seed, cotton seed oil cake.

- ***Pulses***

Commodities like Chana, Tur, Urad, Moong are some of the major pulses grown in the country while India stands the largest producer of pulses globally. 40% of the total pulse production in India is Chana and is also the only commodity traded in the segment. India remains the only platform for this kind of trade globally. The commodity is highly liquid due to its high correlation with the physical market prices which has attracted large volume of trade in this counter. It remains very attractive for hedging and arbitrage perspective due to its profound use in food industry

- ***Grains***

India has evolved to become the largest exporter of grains compared to being an importer in the past. India has a 20% share in the world production as well as tenth largest in the wheat production. It remains the second largest producer of rice next to China. It accounts to 200 million tonnes of different variety of grains produced annually and is self-sufficient. Grains will grow to be a major foreign exchange in the future. India accounts for an annual production of 230-240 million tonnes while the commodities traded include rice, jawar, bajra, maize, wheat, gram and pulses.

- ***Spice***

India has a rich history of being the monopoly in the production of spice and it is rightly called as 'The home of spices'. India contributes 40% of the world spice demand. It is also the leading consumer and exporter of spices. India produces around 2.75 million tons of different spices valued at approximately 4.2 billion US $, and holds the premier position in the world spices market. The commodities traded are Chilli, Coriander, Jeera, Pepper, Turmeric and cardamom etc., The performance of these contracts illustrates the success of efficient price discovery in the Indian domestic market through derivatives trading. Albeit the fact is that no other futures contracts of spices are actively traded on any of leading international exchanges.

- ***Others***

Cotton and sugar are very important commodities in India and the derivative market for these are in the nascent stage. India is the largest producer of cotton and largest consumer of sugar in the world. They remain an important source of income to thousands of farmers, traders and exporters in the country and thus has become the most politically sensitive product.

### *Non- Agriculture Commodities*

Non-agricultural commodities are anything that are not grown but mined and processed and in the derivative segment has evolved in Industrial Metals, Energy and Precious Metals. India remains the major consumer of gold and has huge deposits of natural resources in the form of minerals like copper, iron ore, bauxite, and gold. India being a developing country the demand for these products will continue to rise.

- ***Precious Metal***

ETFs are a convenient and liquid means of purchasing and selling gold, silver or platinum. The demand for these precious metals are driven not only by their practical use but also by their role as investments and a store of value. Gold remains as an alternative asset class in India. Silver moves closely with gold but is the cheapest precious metal. Platinum is the costliest of the above two but it is commonly used in industries. Gold and silver are few of the highly liquid commodities on Indian and global commodity exchanges. Physical market for these metals is equally developed.

- ***Base Metal Complex***

It is alternatively know as Non-Ferrous complex and includes metals like - Copper, Aluminium, Lead, Nickel and Zinc. They are extensively used in industries. This complex has attracted the attention of the investment community giving different dimension to their importance. London Metal Exchange (LME) is considered to be benchmark for base metals pricing. It includes copper, aluminium, steel, nickel, led, zinc.

- ***Energy***

It can be categorised into and non-renewable. We get most of our energy from non-renewable energy sources, which include the fossil fuels - crude oil, natural gas, and coal.

Crude oil remains the major source of energy for the nations around the world and its further processed into fuels for transportation. Price fluctuations for crude oil is highly volatile making it most risky asset class. It is the most liquid commodity

Natural gas is gaining significant importance as a form of fuel and will soon replace coal as a source of power generation and fuel.

## Commodity Futures Market

A commodity futures contract is a commitment to make or accept delivery of a specified quantity and quality of a commodity during a specific month in the future date at a price agreed upon when the commitment is made.

Commodities traded in the commodity exchanges are required to be delivered at the contracted price, ignoring all the changes in the market prices. Both the participants (Buyers & Sellers) are allowed to liquidate their respective positions by way of cash settlement of price between the contracted and liquidated price, no later than the last trading session of the specified expiry date.

An effective and efficient market for trading in commodities futures requires:

- Volatility in the prices of the underlying commodities.
- Large numbers of buyers and sellers with diverse risk profiles (hedgers, speculators and arbitrageurs).
- The underlying physical commodities to be fungible, i.e. they should be exchangeable.

### *Features of Commodity Futures*

1. **Organized:** Commodity Futures contracts always trade on an organized exchange, e.g. NCDEX, MCX, etc in India and NYMEX, LME, COMEX etc. internationally.
2. **Standardized:** Commodity Futures contracts are highly standardized with the quality, quantity, and delivery date, being predetermined.
3. **Eliminates Counterparty Risk:** Commodity Futures exchanges use clearing houses to guarantee that the terms of the futures contract are fulfilled. The Clearing House guarantees that the contract will be fulfilled, eliminating the risk of any default by the other party.
4. **Facilitates Margin Trading:** Commodity Futures traders do not have to put up the entire value of a contract. Rather, they are required to post a margin that is roughly 4 to 8% of the total value of the contract (this margin varies across exchanges and commodities). This facilitates taking of leveraged positions.
5. **Closing a Position:** Futures markets are closely regulated by government agencies, e.g. Forward Markets Commission (FMC) in India, Commodity Futures Trading Commission in (CFTC) USA, etc. This ensures fair practices in these markets.
6. **Regulated Markets Environment:** Commodity Futures contracts are highly standardized with the quality, quantity, and delivery date, being predetermined.
7. **Physical Delivery:** Actual delivery of the commodity can be made or taken on expiry of the contract. Physical delivery requires the member to provide the exchange with prior delivery information and completion of all the delivery related formalities as specified by the exchange.

The OTC markets are essentially spot markets and are localised for specific commodities. Almost all the trading that takes place in these markets is delivery based.

The buyers as well as the sellers have their set of brokers who negotiate the prices for them. This can be illustrated with the help of the following example:

A farmer, who produces castor, wishing to sell his produce would go to the local 'mandi.' There he would contact his broker who would in turn contact the brokers representing the buyers. The buyers in this case would be wholesalers or refiners.

In event of a deal taking place, the goods and the money would be exchanged directly between the buyer and the seller. Thus, it can be seen that this market is restricted to only those people who are directly involved with the commodity.

In addition to the spot transactions, forward deals also take place in these markets. However, they too happen on a delivery basis and hence are restricted to the participants in the spot markets.

The exchange-traded markets are essentially only derivative markets and are similar to equity derivatives in their working. That is, everything is standardised and a person can purchase a contract by paying only a percentage of the contract value. A person can also go short on these exchanges.

Also, even though there is a provision for delivery most of the contracts are squared-off before expiry and are settled in cash. As a result, one can see an active participation by people who are not associated with the commodity.

The commodity exchanges do facilitate delivery, although it has been observed world-over that only 2 per cent of all the trades result in actual delivery.

## Commodity Exchange Platform

A commodities exchange is an exchange where various commodities and derivatives products are traded. Most commodity markets across the world trade in agricultural products and other raw materials (like wheat, barley, sugar, maize, cotton, cocoa, coffee, milk products, pork bellies, oil, metals, etc.) and contracts based on them. These contracts can include spot prices, forwards, futures and options on futures. Other sophisticated products may include interest rates, environmental instruments, swaps, or ocean freight contracts.

Commodities exchanges usually trade futures contracts on commodities, such as trading contracts to receive something, say corn, in a certain month. A farmer raising corn can sell a future contract on his corn, which will not be harvested for several months, and guarantee the price he will be paid when he delivers; a breakfast cereal producer buys the contract now and guarantees the price will not go up when it is delivered. This protects the farmer from price drops and the buyer from price rises.

Speculators and investors also buy and sell the futures contracts in attempt to make a profit and provide liquidity to the system. However, due to the financial leverage provided to traders by the exchange, commodity futures traders face a substantial risk.

### *Five Largest Commodity Exchanges*

Commodity exchanges began as paper contract transactions. Modern day commodities exchange markets have developed into a complex market. The world's largest commodities exchanges deal in trillions of dollars of exchange commodities. The highest performing and largest worldwide commodities are listed below.

- **New York Mercantile Exchange**: The world's largest physical commodities exchange dealing in futures.
- **London Metal Exchange**: Offers an exchange platform for metals such as gold, silver, aluminum and copper.
- **Chicago Mercantile Exchange**: The first US commodities exchange market. The Chicago Mercantile Exchange is still one of the world's largest commodities platforms.
- **Chicago Board of Trade**: Founded in 1973 as the first US options exchange, Chicago Board of Trade has a complex trading system and is still a world leader in options trading.
- **Shanghai Metals Exchange:** This is the largest metal exchange in China and one of the largest in the world.

(Source: http://valuestockguide.com/guide-stock-commodities-exchanges/)

In India there are 12 recognized Commodity Exchanges of which 6 are National Commodity Exchanges and 6 are Commodity Specific Regional Exchanges. The following table shows various commodity exchanges in India:

Table 1

| Sr. No. | *Name of the Exchanges* |
|---|---|
| A. | **National Multi Commodity Exchanges** |
| 1 | Multi Commodity Exchange of India Ltd., Mumbai (MCX) |
| 2 | National Commodity & Derivatives Exchange Ltd., Mumbai (NCDEX) |
| 3 | ACE Derivatives and Commodity Exchange, Mumbai. (ACE) |
| 4 | National Multi Commodity Exchange of India Ltd., Ahmedabad (NMCE) |
| 5 | Indian Commodity Exchange Ltd., Mumbai (ICEX) |
| 6 | Universal Commodity Exchange Ltd, Navi Mumbai (UCX) |
| B. | **Commodity Specific Regional Exchanges** |
| 7 | The Chamber of Commerce, Hapur |
| 8 | Rajkot Commodity Exchange Ltd., Rajkot |
| 9 | India Pepper & Spice Trade Association, Kochi |
| 10 | Bombay Commodity Exchange Ltd, Mumbai |
| 11 | Spices & Oilseeds Exchange Ltd, Sangli |
| 12 | Cotton Association of India, Mumbai |

Source: Annual Reports, 2011-14, FMC

The regulatory body is Forward Markets Commission (FMC) which was set up in 1953. As of September 2015, FMC is merged with Securities Exchange Board of India (SEBI), the regulator of capital market. As a unified regulator for commodities and capital market, SEBI will be able to control and monitor commodity future trading and to check wild speculations. With a strong regulatory backup, commodity market can facilitate huge volumes of trade, in a manner that every participant is confident of trading.

Given below are the major commodities that are traded in various commodity exchanges in India

Table 2

| | |
|---|---|
| Bullion | Gold and Silver |
| Oil & Oilseeds | Castor Seeds, Soy Seeds, Castor Oil, Refined Soy Oil, Soy meal, Crude Palm Oil, Groundnut Oil, Mustard Seed, Mustard Seed Oil, Cottonseed Oilcake, Cottonseed |
| Spices | Pepper, Red Chilli, Jeera, Turmeric, Cardamom |
| Metals | Steel Long, Steel Flat, Copper, Nickel, Tin, Steel, Aluminium Zinc ingots |
| Fibre | Kapas, Long Staple Cotton, Medium Staple Cotton |
| Pulses | Chana, Urad, Yellow Peas, Tur, Yellow Peas |
| Grains | Rice, Basmati Rice, Wheat, Maize, Sarbati Rice, Jeera |
| Energy | Crude Oil, Natural Gas, Brent Crude |
| Others | Rubber, Guar Seed, Guar gum, Cashew, Cashew Kernel, Sugar, Gur, Coffee, Silk, Sugar. |

Source: www.motilaloswal.com

The following table shows value of various commodities traded in India. The market share of Various commodities in terms of value shows that Bullion was maximum traded in all the three periods, whereas agricultural commodities were least traded during these period.

Table 3

| | | | | | | | |
|---|---|---|---|---|---|---|---|
| | | | | | | Value - In Crores | |
| | | 2013-14 | | 2012-13 | | 2011-12 | |
| **Sl.No** | **Name Of Commodity** | **Value** | **Share%** | **Value** | **Share%** | **Value** | **Share%** |
| A | Bullion | 4308938 | 42% | 7862679 | 46% | 10181957 | 56% |
| B | Metals other than Bullion | 1761360 | 17% | 3260051 | 19% | 2896721 | 16% |
| C | Agricultural Commodities | 1602402 | 16% | 2155700 | 13% | 2196150 | 12% |
| D | Energy | 2472095 | 24% | 3768409 | 22% | 2851269 | 16% |
| E | Other | | 0% | 1.28 | 0% | 1.35 | 0% |
| F | Plastic | | 0% | | 0% | 6.45 | 0% |
| | Grand Total | 10144795 | 100% | 17046840 | 100% | 18126104 | 100% |

Source: Annual Reports 2011-14, FMC

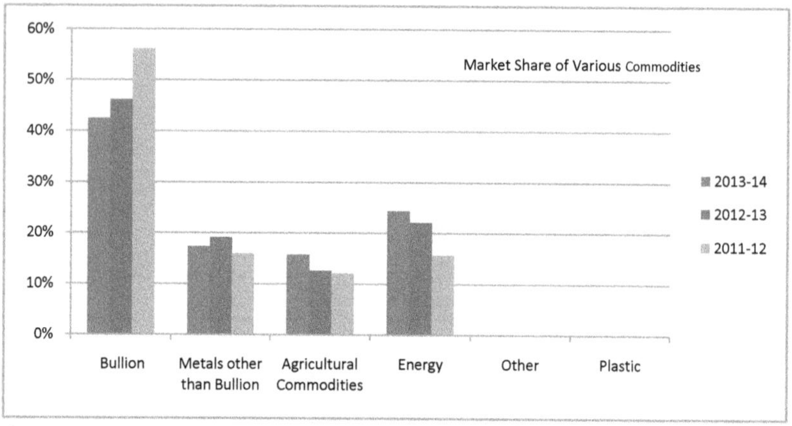


An exchange that allows trading of different commodities is known as commodity exchanges. Today apart from numerous regional exchanges, India has six national commodity exchanges, viz; Multi Commodity Exchange (MCX), National Commodity and Derivative Exchange (NCDEX), National Multi Commodity Exchange (NMCE), Indian Commodity Exchange (ICEX), Ace Derivatives Exchange (ACE) and Universal Commodity Exchange (UCX).

The following table shows the market share of various commodity exchanges in India

Table 4

| Name Of Commodity Exchange | 2013-14 | 2012-13 | 2011-12 |
|---|---|---|---|
| MCX | 84.89% | 87% | 86.05% |
| NCDEX | 11.30% | 10% | 9.90% |
| NMCE | 1.51% | 1% | 1.48% |
| ICEX | 0.84% | 1% | 1.42% |
| ACE | 0.46% | 1% | 0.76% |
| Others | 0.72% | 1% | 0.30% |

Source: Annual Reports 2011-14, FMC

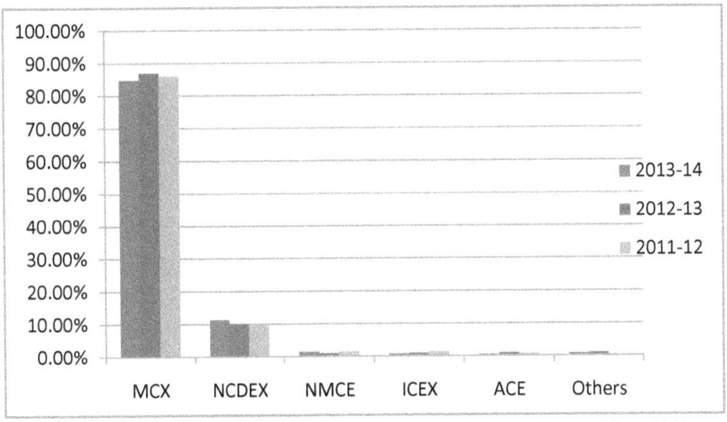


The table shows that MCX enjoys the maximum market share of more than 80% in all the three years followed by NCDEX and NMCE. ACE and ICEX have the least market share among all the commodity exchanges.

There are three main national level commodity exchanges to trade in all permitted commodities.

They are:

***1. Multi Commodity Exchange of India Ltd, Mumbai (MCX)***

www.mcxindia.com

MCX is an independent and de-mutualised multi commodity exchange. MCX features amongst the world's top three bullion exchanges and top four energy exchanges. Its key shareholders are Financial Technologies (I) Ltd., State Bank of India and it's associates, National Bank for Agriculture and Rural Development (NABARD), National Stock Exchange of India Ltd. (NSE), Fid Fund (Mauritius) Ltd. - an affiliate of Fidelity International, Corporation Bank, Union Bank of India, Canara Bank, Bank of India, Bank of Baroda, HDFC Bank and SBI Life Insurance Co. Ltd.

***2. National Commodity and Derivative Exchange, Mumbai (NCDEX)***

www.ncdex.com

A consortium of institutions promotes NCDEX. These include the ICICI Bank Limited (ICICI Bank), Life Insurance Corporation of India (LIC), National Bank for Agriculture and Rural Development (NABARD) and National Stock Exchange of India Limited (NSE).

***3. National Multi Commodity Exchange of India Ltd, Ahmedabad(NMCE)***

www.nmce.com

It is the first de-mutualised electronic multi-commodity Exchange of India. Some of its key promoters are Central Warehousing Corporation (CWC), National Agricultural Co Operative Marketing Federation of India Limited (NAFED), Gujarat Agro Industries Corporation Limited (GAIC) and Punjab National Bank (PNB).

## Commodity Trading System

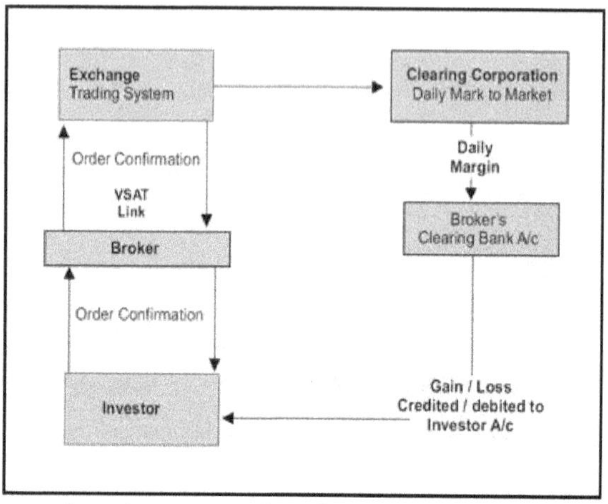


After the process of opening account is done the investor may want to trade in commodity. IT is important to understand the process after the trade is placed.

An investor places a trade order with the broker (at the dealing desk) on phone. The dealer puts the order in exchange trading system. At the initiation of the trade, a price is set and initial margin money is deposited in the account. At the end of the day, a settlement price is determined by the clearing house (Exchange). Depending on if the markets have moved in favor or against the investors' position the funds are either being drawn from or added to the client's account. The amount is the difference in the traded price and the settlement price. On next day, the settlement price is used as the base price. As the spot market prices changes every day, a new settlement price is determined at the end of every day. Again, the account will be adjusted by the difference in the new settlement price and the previous night's price in the appropriate manner.

The commodity trading system functions on a real time basis through online means. Farmers, exporters, importers, and traders are the main participants in this market. The commodity trading system operates through online channels. Trading takes place on a real time basis and is either routed through satellite communication system or the internet.

**Commodity Trading System-Order Matching Mechanism:** Traders place their order through a registered commodity broker of a commodity exchange. The trader's order is entered by the authorized dealer into the online terminal. The order finds its match automatically through the online channel. If it doesn't find a match at that very moment then it gets stored in the online order book until and unless a similar and opposite order matches it. When two similar and opposite orders (that is, one buy and one sell order) match, then a trade is said to be complete.

**Commodity Trading System - Trade Clearing Mechanism:** In a commodity market, trade clearing takes place through a registered clearing house of an exchange. Clearing house helps the system to function smoothly and properly by guaranteeing timely settlement registration of a trade and its consequent follow up delivery of the commodity to the concerned buyer and simultaneous payment to the seller settlement of funds in non-delivery cases

**Commodity Trading System-Clearing and Settlement:** Clearing and settlement of commodities in the commodity trading system commences only after the end of trading hours on the expiration date of the contract. Processing of delivery matching considers the following:

1. Location of the order
2. Available warehouse capacity
3. Total quantity of commodities that have already been deposited and given to dematerialize.

### *After the Completion of the Delivery Matching Process, the following Steps are Followed*

a. Information on the final outcome of the matching process (amount of commodities to be delivered or received and amount of unmatched position) is given to the clearing members of the exchange.
b. Unmatched positions (gains or losses) are cash settled.

### *Commodity Delivery takes Place through the Following Steps*

1. The concerned buyer asks its depository participant to deliver the commodity.
2. The depository participant, in turn, forwards this request to the designated repository.
3. Depository forwards this message to the registrar and then to the transfer agent.
4. Transfer agent, in turn, verifies authenticity of the request.
5. In case of genuine request, transfer agent passes on the details of delivery to the warehouse.
6. Warehouse then arranges delivery of the concerned commodity to the designated buyer (only after thorough identification check).

## Future Growth Opportunities and Challenges to Commodity Market

The union budget for 2015-16 saw the announcement of the merger of the two regulators- Forward Markets Commission (FMC), regulator of commodities market with Securities Exchange Board of India (SEBI), regulator of capital market. The merger process will take place between September 2015 and early 2016.

The merger will generate many opportunities for the commodity market to grow. There will be better market integrity as SEBI has the power to raid, search, impose fine and take action on irregularities. Products like options, exchange traded funds, weather derivatives, freight derivatives will be introduced, which will further accelerate the growth of commodity market. With merger, it is also expected that there will be new participants, who will be entering into commodity market viz; Banks, FPI and Mutual funds. More over there will be penetration of exchanges and intermediaries into each other's market segment.

A lot of challenges also arise with the merger. Finding additional manpower and resources to monitor the commodity market is one thing that SEBI should look into. Aligning the securities and commodities brokers to uniform regulations is also a challenge. Another important area where SEBI should look into is that of physical settlements, as the delivery and settlement process in commodity and stock exchanges differ significantly.

## Gold ETF

Gold Exchange Traded Funds (ETFs) are simple investment products that combine the flexibility of stock investment and the simplicity of gold investments. ETFs trade on the cash market of the National Stock Exchange, like any other company stock, and can be bought and sold continuously at market prices.

Gold ETFs are passive investment instruments that are based on gold prices and invest in gold bullion. Because of its direct gold pricing, there is a complete transparency on the holdings of an ETF. Further due to its unique structure and creation mechanism, the ETFs have much lower expenses as compared to physical gold investments.

| List of Gold ETFs listed on NSE | | | | |
|---|---|---|---|---|
| **Issuer** | **Name** | **Symbol** | **Underlying** | **Launch Date** |
| Axis Mutual Fund | Axis Gold ETF | AXISGOLD | Gold | Nov-10 |
| Birla Sun Life Mutual Fund | Birla Sun Life Gold ETF | BSLGOLDETF | Gold | May-11 |
| CanaraRobeco MF | CanaraRobeco Gold ETF | CANGOLD | Gold | Mar-12 |
| Goldman Sachs Asset Management | Goldman Sachs Gold Exchange Traded Scheme | GOLDBEES | Gold | Mar-07 |
| HDFC Mutual Fund | HDFC Gold Exchange Traded Fund | HDFCMFGETF | Gold | Aug-10 |
| ICICI Prudential Mutual Fund | ICICI Prudential Gold Exchange Traded Fund | IPGETF | Gold | Aug-10 |
| Quantum Mutual Fund | Quantum Gold Fund (an ETF) | QGOLDHALF | Gold | Feb-08 |
| Religare Mutual Fund | Religare Gold Exchange Traded Fund | RELIGAREGO | Gold | Mar-10 |
| SBI Mutual Fund | SBI Gold Exchange Traded Scheme | SBIGETS | Gold | Apr-09 |
| UTI Mutual Fund | UTI GOLD Exchange Traded Fund | GOLDSHARE | Gold | Mar-07 |

### *Features*

- Gold ETFs offers investors an innovative, cost-efficient and secure way to access the gold market.
- It offers investors means of participating in the gold bullion market without taking physical delivery of gold.
- The Scheme offers only Growth Option.

### *Benefits*

- Potentially cheaper to have price exposure to gold price as compared to other available avenues.
- Quick and Convenient Dealing through Demat Account.
- No Storage & Security Issues for investors.
- Transparent Pricing.
- Mutual Fund Taxation.
- Listed and traded just like a stock.
- Ideal for Retail Investor as min lot size is one unit.
- NAV of a Unit will track price of approximately 1 Gram of Gold.

### *How are Gold ETFs Traded?*

General question in mind of common investor is that how to trade in ETFs? It is as simple as trading in any other equity. For trading in Gold ETFs, one has to do similar work as to do in equity trading. You are required to

- Register with a broker having membership of NSE
- Fill up KYC form
- Open a de-mat account
- Post margins and
- Commence trading

For more understanding see figure 1.1 and 1.2

Process Diagram for creation of ETF Units (Figure 1.1)

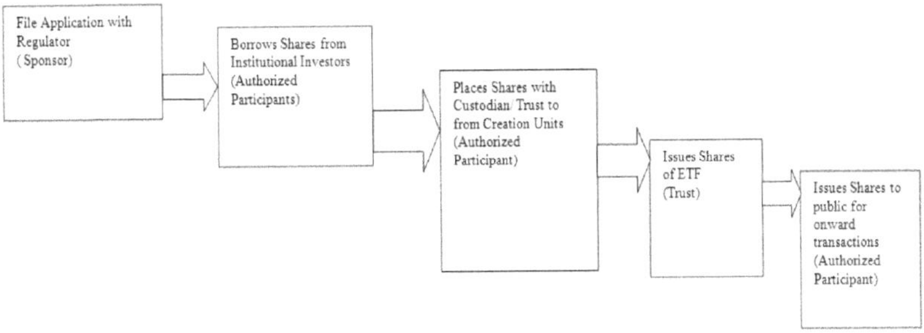


Redemption of ETFs ( Figure1.2)

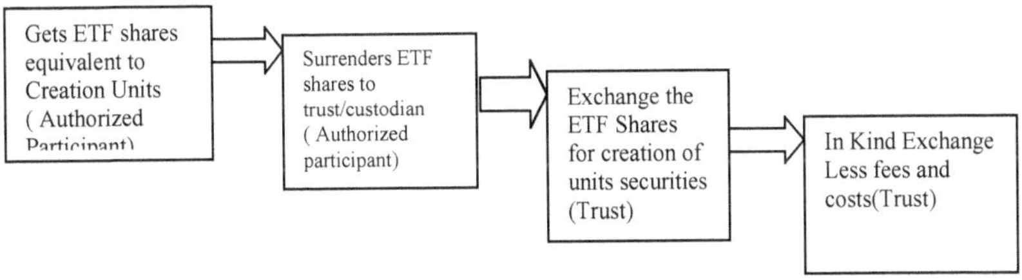


(Source: THE OVERVIEW OF GOLD ETFS AND ITS VARIOUS POSITIVEFEATURES MOHD SALEEM; MATLOOBULLAH KHAN, International Journal of Marketing, Financial Services & Management Research, Vol.2, No. 4, April (2013), ISSN 2277- 3622)

### *Working*

Gold ETFs are exchange traded funds that passively track the performance of Gold Bullion. These funds buy gold with investor's money (on the behalf of investors) and convert it into units.

The reason for buying gold ETFs essentially boils down to convenience. Having to go to a obscure shop, pick an item that the general investor has no real idea about, not getting ripped off in some way, transporting the gold back home safely, and then storing it somewhere secure and always worrying about the safety of your gold in your own home can all be worrying matters. If you decide that you need money, or that you would like sell your gold because of the current price action, then you need to go through the whole troublesome process again. When you buy a gold ETF, you can do so in a matter of several clicks on your computer or a simple call to your broker. For someone who's not totally devoted to gold and just wanting to have some exposure to gold in the short term, it can be the easiest and cheapest ways to go about it.

### *Growth*

The first idea of owning gold indirectly came in 1961 through a closed-end fund called Central Fund of Canada. It allowed ownership of gold and silver bullion but it was a mutual fund in which new investors could not come in and be part of the action unless they bought shares from the current shareholders. The Benchmark Asset Management Company Private Ltd in India were the first to apply for creating a gold ETF in 2002, but at the time didn't receive the regulatory approval necessary.

Instead the first gold ETF was launched in Australia by the name Gold Bullion Securities in 2003. Since then dozens of alternate gold ETFs have appeared globally performing essentially the same function but in different ways.

Gold ETF is the unique product that offers retail investors to invest in gold in dematerialized form through their normal demat accounts. With the simplified features and many other benefits, this asset class proves to be the best product for the retail investors.

Across the world, gold is seen largely as an investment product where the investors, both retail and non-retail, are investing in it for pure economic reasons. In contrast, gold is a majorly consumer product in our country. We Indians buy gold for consumption, typically in the form of jewellery. In India we have a special significance for gold in our culture in a variety of contexts ranging from a form of adornment to a status symbol to an investment for the tough times.

Gold Exchange Traded Funds (Gold ETF) is the unique product offering from the exchange that retail allows investment in gold in dematerialized form through their normal demats accounts. This product is designed to overcome most of the difficulties faced while investing in gold. With Gold ETF there is no risk of losing your precious investment due to theft. Being in the dematform, your investment remains safe from the prying eyes. Another trouble of putting money in physical gold is that a lot of your hard earned money gets spent on making charges (in case of jewellery) or premium pricing (in case of coins or bars from banks). With Gold ETF, the gold is available at the standard international market rates which is available transparently and is devoid of any markups

***TOP GOLD ETFs***

| ***Fund*** | ***Net assets ( In RsCrore)*** |
|---|---|
| Goldman Sachs Gold ETF Fund | 2356.40 |
| R*Shares Gold ETF | 2230.25 |
| SBI Gold Exchange Traded Scheme | 1241.08 |
| Kotak Gold ETF Fund | 784.58 |
| HDFC Gold Exchange traded fund | 744.40 |
| UTI Gold exchange traded fund | 606.48 |
| Axis Gold ETF Fund | 365.77 |
| ICICI Prudential Gold Exchange traded fund | 169.59 |
| CanaraRobeco Gold Exchange Traded fund | 157.66 |
| IDBI Gold Exchange traded fund | 141.84 |
| Birla sunlife gold ETF | 119.74 |
| Reliance Invesco Gold Exchange traded fund | 65.54 |
| MotilalOswal Most shares gold ETF Fund | 55.35 |

Source: Value research Online Complied By: B S Research Bureau

***Problems***

The main disadvantage of gold ETFs surrounds the fact that the gold is not in your possession. Looking at the fine-print in most of the gold ETFs, we can see that the fund does not need to keep a certain amount of gold in its possession, and that its obligation to its stakeholders are not in the form of physical gold but as a financial debtor. So if something goes wrong with the company behind the fund, and they need to declare bankruptcy or be liquidated then you're not assured to get anything. This can prove to be a big problem, especially because gold is most valuable under a cloud of financial chaos in other parts of the economy, financial world, and business in general. So unless one invests their money in an ETF that assures their customers that the gold is in allocated accounts that will be kept untouched even in times of potential default, then one must be aware of the risks involved with gold ETFs.

For more sophisticated investors, or those with investing capital that exceeds a few hundred dollars, there are significant drawbacks to investing in gold-specific ETFs that go beyond the day-to-day fluctuation of gold prices. These problems include tax implications, non-gold-related market risk and additional fees.

### *Taxed as a Collectible*

An investment in an ETF, that tracks gold prices, does not consist of actual gold ownership on the part of the shareholders. An investor cannot make a claim on any of the gold shares and their ownership in the ETF represents an ownership in a "collectible." Despite the fact that the managers of gold ETFs do not make investments in gold for their numismatic value, nor do they seek out collectible coins, the shareholder's investment is treated as a collectible. This makes long-term investing in gold ETFs (for one year or longer) subject to a relatively large capital gains tax (maximum rate of 28%, rather than the 15% rate that is applicable to most other long-term capital gains). In order to avoid this tax implication, investors often exit their positions before a year, which diminishes their ability to profit from any multiyear gains that may occur in gold.

### *Market Risk*

ETFs that track gold are also exposed to a host of company risks that have nothing to do with the actual fluctuation in gold's value. In the SPDR Gold Trust prospectus, for example, the trust can liquidate when the dollars in the trust fall below a certain level, if the net asset value (NAV) drops below a certain level, or by agreement of shareholders owning at least 66.6% of all outstanding shares. These actions can be taken, regardless of whether the gold prices are strong or weak.

### *Fees*

Finally, gold ETFs are inherently diminishing investments. Because the gold itself produces no income and there are still expenses that must be covered, the ETF's management is allowed to sell the gold to cover these expenses. Each sale of gold by the trust is a taxable event to shareholders. That means that a fund's management fee, along with any sponsor or marketing fees, must be paid by liquidating assets. This diminishes the overall underlying assets per share, which, in turn, can leave investors with a representative share value of less than one-tenth of an ounce of gold over time. This can lead to discrepancies in the actual value of the underlying gold asset and the listed value of the ETF.

## References

1. Financial services in India, G Ramesh babu, Neha publishers & Distributors, 2005
2. Financial services, M Y Khan, McGraw hill publishers, Edition 3, 2004
3. Financial Markets and Institutions, S.Gurusamy, tata McGraw hill publishers, Edition 3, 2010
4. Financial Institutions and Markets, Jeff Madura, Cengage learning India pvt ltd, Edition 9,2012
5. Financial Services, ThummuluriSiddaiah, Pearson Education, 2011
6. Financial Markets, Institutions and Services, N.K.Gupta, Monika chopra, Ane books pvt ltd, 2010
7. Financial services in India- Concept and Application, Rajesh Kothari, Sage publications, 2011
8. Merchant Banking and Financial Services, S Gurusamy, McGraw Hill Education (India) Private Limited, Edition 3, 2009
9. The Indian Financial System, Bharati V Pathak, Pearson Publishers, Edition 4, 2014
10. Banking and Financial services, Hemant S ahluwilia, Adhyayan Publishers & Distributors, 2008

11. Financial Markets and Institutions, Frederick S Mishkin, Pearson Education edition 6, 2011
12. Foundations of financial Markets and Institutions, Frank J Fabozzi, Paerson education, Edition 4, 2014
13. Financial Institutions and Markets, Meir Kohn, Oxford University press India Ltd, Edition 2, 2013
14. Financial Markets and Institutions, Frederick S Mishkin and Stanely Eakins, Pearson Prentice Hall, Edition 7, 2011
15. Banking Theory and practices, Shekhar and Shekhar, Vikas Publishing house, New Delhi, 1999
16. Money, banking and Financial markets, Auerbach Robert D, Neha Publishers and Distributors, 2012
17. Central banking for emerging market Economics, Vasudevan. A, Academic Foundation, 2003
18. Capital Market and Securities,CSBhupendra Jain & CS Sneh Bhatia, Fly Stone Publication 2015.
19. Indian Mutual Funds Handbook, SundharSankaran, Vision Books, Edition 4, 2016.
20. Merchant Banking and Financial Services, MadhuVij, Mcgraw Hill Education,2013.
21. SoheliGhosh, "Mutual Funds in India: A Popular Investment Avenue", Notion Press, 2015.
22. Bhole L M, "Financial Institutions and markets", Tata McGraw-Hall, New Delhi, 1999.
23. Dr.M. Selvam, Smart journal of Business Management Studies.Vol.1.No:2, July-December 2005, ISSN 0973-1598.
24. Hull, "Options, Futures and other Derivatives", Pearson India, 2013.
25. Dr R. Shanmugham, "Financial Services", Wiley, 2011
26. ARTICLES JUNCTION BLOG by © SandeepPatil and ManojPatil.
27. WDM Segment: Brochure
28. http://www.ibef.org/industry/financial-services- india.aspx
29. http://mospi.nic.in/Mospi_New/upload/fess_10.html
30. www.nsdl.co.in
31. www.sebi.gov.in
32. www.rbi.org
33. www.nseindia.com
34. NSE fact book 2015.
35. http://kalyan-city.blogspot.in/2011/10/what-is-merchant-banking-meaning.html
36. http://www.investopedia.com/walkthrough/corporate-finance/1/financial-institutions.aspx
37. http://www.investopedia.com/articles/personal-finance/050515/how-swift-system-works.asp
38. http://www.goodreturns.in/classroom/2014/11/what-are-the-various-types-financial-markets-india-324202.html
39. https://www.mutualfundindia.com/
40. http://www.crisil.com/ratings/credit-ratings.html
41. http://www.investopedia.com/terms/c/creditrating.asp
42. http://economictimes.indiatimes.com/definition/venture-capital
43. http://www.investopedia.com/exam-guide/cfa-level-1/alternative-investments/venture-capital-investing-stages.asp
44. https://rbi.org.in/Scripts/BS_SpeechesView.aspx?Id=964
45. http://www.rediff.com/money/2005/jul/06guest.htm
46. http://wrap.warwick.ac.uk/1082/1/WRAP_Floyd_Securitization_theory_and_securitization_studies_WRAP.pdf

# List of Abbreviations

**AMC-**Asset Management Company

**AMFI-**Association of Mutual Funds in India

**BO-**Back Office

**BSE-**Bombay Stock Exchange

**CRISIL-**Credit Rating Information Services of India Limited

**CM-**Capital Market

**CDS-**Currency Derivate Segment

**CM-**Commercial Market

**DEMAT-**Dematerialization

**ETF-**Electronic Traded Fund

**FIMMDA-**Fixed Income Money Market and Derivatives Association of India

**ICICI-**Industrial Credit and Investment Corporation of India

**IFCI-**Industrial Finance Corporation of India

**ICRA-**Investment Information and Credit Rating Agency

**IOU–**I Owe You

**LIBOR-**London Interbank Offered Rate

**MIBOR-**Mumbai Interbank Offered Rate

**MBS-**Mortgage – Backed Security

**NEAT-**National Exchange for Automated Trading

**NABARD-**National Bank for Agriculture and Rural Development

**NCDEX-**National Commodity and Derivative Exchange

**NMCE-**National Multi-Commodity Exchange of India Ltd

**NAV-**Net Asset Value

**NSE-**National Stock Exchange

**NSCCL-**National Securities Clearing Corporation

**PMS-**Portfolio Management Service

**PSU-**Public Sector Undertakings

**PAN-**Primary Account Number

**SCRA-**Securities Contract Regulation Act

**SPV-**Special Purpose Vehicle

**WDM-**Wholesale Debt Market

www.ingramcontent.com/pod-product-compliance
Lightning Source LLC
LaVergne TN
LVHW082346171026
850499LV00040B/1349
* 9 7 8 9 3 8 5 4 7 7 4 8 5 *